English Learners' Access to Postsecondary Education

CRITICAL LANGUAGE AND LITERACY STUDIES

Series Editors: **Professor Alastair Pennycook** (*University of Technology, Sydney, Australia*) and **Professor Brian Morgan** (*Glendon College/York University, Toronto, Canada*) and **Professor Ryuko Kubota** (*University of British Columbia, Vancouver, Canada*)

Critical Language and Literacy Studies is an international series that encourages monographs directly addressing issues of power (its flows, inequities, distributions, trajectories) in a variety of language- and literacy-related realms. The aim with this series is twofold: (1) to cultivate scholarship that openly engages with social, political, and historical dimensions in language and literacy studies, and (2) to widen disciplinary horizons by encouraging new work on topics that have received little focus (see below for partial list of subject areas) and that use innovative theoretical frameworks.

All books in this series are externally peer-reviewed.

Full details of all the books in this series and of all our other publications can be found on http://www.multilingual-matters.com, or by writing to Multilingual Matters, St Nicholas House, 31-34 High Street, Bristol BS1 2AW, UK.

Other books in the series

CRITICAL LANGUAGE AND LITERACY STUDIES: 27

English Learners' Access to Postsecondary Education

Neither College nor Career Ready

Yasuko Kanno

MULTILINGUAL MATTERS
Bristol • Blue Ridge Summit

DOI https://doi.org/10.21832/KANNO3740
Library of Congress Cataloging in Publication Data
A catalog record for this book is available from the Library of Congress.
Names: Kanno, Yasuko, author.
Title: English Learners' Access to Postsecondary Education: Neither College nor
   Career Ready/Yasuko Kanno.
Description: Bristol, UK; Blue Ridge Summit: Multilingual Matters, 2021. | Series:
   Critical Language and Literacy Studies: 27 | Includes bibliographical references
   and index. | Summary: "This book provides an in-depth look into the systemic
   undereducation of high school English learners and the role of high schools in
   limiting ELs' postsecondary options, despite the availability of resources and the
   best of intentions, through a longitudinal ethnographic case study of a diverse
   high school in Pennsylvania"—Provided by publisher.
Identifiers: LCCN 2021027742 | ISBN 9781800413733 (paperback) |
   ISBN 9781800413740 (hardback) | ISBN 9781800413764 (epub) |
   ISBN 9781800413757 (pdf) Subjects: LCSH: English language—Study
   and teaching (Secondary)—Pennsylvania. | Language arts (Secondary)—
   Pennsylvania—Evaluation. | Education, Secondary—Pennsylvania.
Classification: LCC LB1631 .K27 2021 | DDC 428.0071/2—dc23
LC record available at https://lccn.loc.gov/2021027742

British Library Cataloguing in Publication Data
A catalogue entry for this book is available from the British Library.

ISBN-13: 978-1-80041-374-0 (hbk)
ISBN-13: 978-1-80041-373-3 (pbk)

Multilingual Matters
UK: St Nicholas House, 31-34 High Street, Bristol BS1 2AW, UK.
USA: NBN, Blue Ridge Summit, PA, USA.

Website: www.multilingual-matters.com
Twitter: Multi_Ling_Mat
Facebook: https://www.facebook.com/multilingualmatters
Blog: www.channelviewpublications.wordpress.com

The policy of Multilingual Matters/Channel View Publications is to use papers
that are natural, renewable and recyclable products, made from wood grown in
sustainable forests. In the manufacturing process of our books, and to further
support our policy, preference is given to printers that have FSC and PEFC Chain
of Custody certification. The FSC and/or PEFC logos will appear on those books
where full certification has been granted to the printer concerned.

Typeset by Deanta Global Publishing Services, Chennai, India.

Contents

Series Editors' Preface

It is a great pleasure to welcome Yasuko Kanno's new book to the Critical Language and Literacies Studies (CLLS) series. As series editors, the addition of this important work also provides an opportunity to pause and reflect on a series that began in 2009 and now includes 27 publications from around the world, each engaged with particular problems, settings and configurations of language and power, some closely linked to identities and their varied intersectionalities, with others more local and community-based than national and global in perspective. In our own writing, each of us has had recent opportunities to explore what is of central concern for the series – the meanings and purposes of criticality in language studies (e.g. Chun & Morgan, 2019; Kubota & Miller, 2017; Pennycook, 2021). Certainly, definitions and priorities have changed over time, in part, reflecting new understandings of inequity and oppression arising from increased dialogue with those historically excluded from privileged domains of knowledge production. The paradigmatic pendulum for critical work has also swung in insightful directions – in some cases, more structural and deterministic, while in others, more constructivist and agentive. Definitional and functional boundaries around texts and literacy practices have also expanded, integrating more trans-semiotic, multimodal, embodied and affective components in meaning making analyses. Innovative, transdisciplinary thinking arising from engagement with indigeneity, ecology, post-humanism and post/decolonial perspectives have also helped refocus and reinvigorate our understanding of criticality for the 21st century. Looking back, the CLLS series, as a whole, has been at the forefront of these developments.

In a chapter titled 'Regrounding Critical Literacy', Allan Luke (2014) observed that 'unpacking the relationship between discourse representation and reality remains *the* core question of critical literacy as theory and practice' (2014: 146). Kanno's innovative contribution addresses this core question in exemplary fashion. The reality she unpacks is the persistent marginalization of English Learners (ELs) in US high schools, and their systemic exclusion from postsecondary education (PSE) and the improved life chances it could provide at-risk students. The specific discourse representation she implicates in this marginalization is the pervasive deficit orientation underpinning curricula, school-based language policies, and interpersonal relationships between teachers, counselors and ELs at the high school she researched. Bourdieu's concept of *habitus* (1977, 1986; see also Wacquant, 2016), at both the individual and institutional level, is prominent in framing the mediation between structure and agency and the interaction between macro and micro factors involved in Brighton High School (pseudonym). Kanno defines a school's institutional habitus as its 'collective beliefs about what its students are capable of, what is within their reach, and what they deserve. Such institutional habitus in turn guides the school's policies, practices, and expectations for its students'. EL students, within this institutional orbit, come to accept and internalize the low expectations communicated to them. EL students with the academic ability to succeed in four-year degree programs, for example, come to doubt their ability to do so, enrolling in a local two-year community college program, instead. Still, the formation of an individual habitus does not lend itself to causally direct outcomes or easily predictive trajectories, a key strength of Bourdieu's theory and one that is illuminated by Kanno's research methodology, which details the life stories and school experiences of each of her seven EL participants at Brighton.

This book is clearly not a testament to social reproduction or a coordinated grand design for molding obedient and hard-working citizens through education. Indeed, Kanno reveals a litany of mismanagement and haphazard decision-making at Brighton, which is memorably illustrated by way of a quote from Harklau (2016) worth repeating: 'These mistakes have less in common with sociological visions of inexorable institutional social reproduction and more in common with Kafkaesque visions of random bureaucratic dysfunction' (2016: 602). Predictably, this habitus of dysfunction is most harmful for students (i.e. ELs, racialized, ethno-linguistic minorities) lacking the kinds of social and linguistic capital most valued by the school and broader society. Most disappointing is the individual habitus of many teachers and staff, who are quick to blame EL shortcomings (linguistic, familial) for the academic underachievement witnessed. As Kanno shows, these teachers and staff believe they are acting in the best interests of EL students by protecting them from the inevitable disappointment of failure. The effect, however, is the withholding of the kinds of appropriate and challenging academic content that would adequately prepare ELs for either PSE or meaningful career prospects beyond high school.

Kanno's research approach may be strategically effective in another important way. Arguably, by providing intimate portraits of participants (i.e. teachers, counselors and students) and the reasons for the misguided or counter-productive decisions they come to make, readers can potentially identify and empathize with the barriers ELs face in ways that mobilize local stakeholders to action and in ways unmet by abstract theoretical discussions or macro-educational studies. The transformative potential of life stories and narratives align with the attention they give to the idiosyncrasies of power locally experienced by social actors. Such stories add a necessary degree of complexity and caution in response to over-generalized analyses and the simplistic solutions they generate. In the sociology of education, one is reminded of classic school-based ethnographies such as Paul Willis's (1977) *Learning to Labour* or Peter McLaren's (1989) *Life in Schools*, both of which take a more deterministic perspective on social reproduction and the inevitable cooptation of student resistance. Kanno's approach is a more nuanced, bottom-up perspective on macro discourses and processes, which other CLLS authors have productively explored. Beatriz Lorente (2018), for example, effectively utilizes interview data of Filipina domestic workers to illuminate the precarious conditions of transnational domestic labourers and the English scripts of servitude articulated by these vulnerable workers. Bill Johnston's (2017) study of English teaching in an Evangelical school in Poland draws upon the voices of students and teachers to problematize narrow proclamations regarding the ethical and professional parameters of such work. The transformative potential of and through interview data is perhaps most evident in Christian Chun's (2015) study, in which his ongoing conversations with Emilia, the EAP classroom teacher, serve to revise course materials and interactions in ways that challenge dominant neoliberal discourses on economic globalization.

Kanno's study makes other innovative contributions to the CLLS series. For one, it is the first extensive focus on EL students in a high school in the USA, a major migrant receiving country, in which policymakers struggle over the provision of education for voluntary and involuntary newcomers, including those categorized as undocumented and potentially subject to forced repatriation. Situated in the US, Kanno's study exposes ingrained disparities (e.g. inaccessible tuition fees in esteemed private colleges and university) and a system of complicated admissions procedures, SAT tests and timelines that appear inscrutable to ELs who might dream of accessing a four-year college and university degree programs. Kanno also draws attention to stubborn monoglossic language ideologies and policies in the US that favour English and devalue the rich bi/multilingual repertoires of ELs. She has also undertaken one of the most elaborated applications of Bourdieu's theory of habitus in the series, though Inge Kral's (2012) ethnographic study of Ngaanyatjarra literacy practices in contact with the Australian English-medium schools warrants important mention. Bourdieu's work on the various forms of capital (symbolic, social, cultural) also features prominently in Andrea Sterzuk's (2011) study of Indigenized Englishes in Saskatchewan schools. Though not labelled as such, the individual habitus of white settler teachers in Sterzuk's interview data reveals a similar pattern of low expectations and racial/cultural mismatch that are causally implicated in the relative high rate of school failure for Indigenous children.

Of note, Kanno begins her book preface by acknowledging the timing of its publication during COVID-19, pointing out how the pandemic has served to expose and further exacerbate existing inequities in the US education system for vulnerable populations such as English language learners (ELs). For critical researchers and educators, it is worth reflecting on what Kanno's observation reveals about language and power, as well as emergent opportunities for critical work in times of crisis. As Kanno has persuasively argued, labels such as EL arbitrarily attach students to a system of lowered expectations that limit their possibilities for PSE. These labels become self-actualizing, as students begin to internalize and perform the underachievement that these stigmatizing labels assign to them. Despite evidence to the contrary, the institutional habitus of schools in liberal democratic societies leads towards denial of complicity or responsibility. Instead, decision makers give voice to the meritocratic ideals of the nation-state, proclaiming the promise of social mobility and greater equity for ELs, racialized and socioeconomically challenged students through education.

Alternatively, educational discourses stress the importance of the work of individual teachers or counselors, exceptional actors who can make a difference for some students. As Kanno makes clear, however, while the hard work and dedication of such people should be acknowledged, solutions based on individualistic enterprise miss the point that these are systemic and multi-dimensional concerns. The promise of social mobility is unattainable for most, given the systemic barriers involved, though this doesn't seem to deter the misleading optimism of public and school officials. A good example of this public deceit or denial comes from Harklau's (2000) study, in which four high school, Latina ELs are publicly praised as 'an inspiration for everyone' (Harklau, 2000: 46; cited in Kanno, this volume) yet later positioned as the worst kinds of students at the two-year community college they subsequently attended. We are reminded here of the double-edged effects of the racialized invocations of speaking 'good' or even 'perfect' English (Alim & Smitherman, 2020).

In the context of the pandemic, such hollow proclamations of EL inspiration can be seen as closely parallel to those currently received by another highly visible at-risk group, the so-called 'frontline workers', many of whom work in COVID 'hot zones' with inadequate and unregulated safety provisions, some living in overcrowded spaces (e.g. migrant farm workers), and almost all earning low wages that contradict the public gratitude routinely expressed for 'our heroes'. The pandemic has indeed served to expose the racialized, gendered, and class/poverty-based inequities involved. And as Kanno's comprehensive study shows, ELs are a disproportionate part of this vulnerable precariat given their lack of high school preparation for either PSE or technical careers that require advanced training. School participation by ELs during the pandemic dropped more significantly than many other groups, not because English is not their first language (as if this were a problem itself), but because of what this implies in terms of class, race and minority status, the working conditions (or unemployment) of their parents or guardians, the limited access to online resources, or the struggles they face not just within, but also against, the educational system.

Apparently, it takes a crisis like a global pandemic to nudge decision makers and powerful employers into long-overdue action. No doubt, the vulnerability perceived by more affluent and powerful social groups may propel the impetus for immediate change in certain sectors of society, though workers in these sectors are just as likely to be forgotten once the pandemic recedes. Across Canada and Australia, for example, the unsafe conditions for seniors and workers in long-term care homes have focused a sharp lens on government neglect and the crucial need to raise wages for caregivers. We await the outcome. Perhaps we might hope for positive developments with respect to education and the exacerbation of inequities encountered by ELs in the United States. Of note, and close to the publication of this book, the influential TESOL organization (Teachers of English to Speakers of Other Languages) is scheduled to host an advocacy and policy summit in June 2021, bringing together second/additional language experts, administrators from the US Department of Education, and Members of the House of Representatives. Summit discussion topics indicate a focus on improving conditions and PSE opportunities for EL learners including K-12 settings such as Brighton High School. If summit participants are looking for an evidence-based study with effective and principled recommendations for action, they would be hard pressed to find anything more relevant than Yasuko Kanno's *English Learners' Access to Postsecondary Education: Neither College nor Career Ready*. We are thrilled to have this essential text as part of our series.

Brian Morgan, Alastair Pennycook, Ryuko Kubota

References

Alim, H.S. and Smitherman, G. (2020) 'Perfect English' and white supremacy. In J. McIntosh and N. Mendoza-Denton (eds) *Language in the Trump Era: Scandals and Emergencies* (pp. 226–236). Cambridge: Cambridge University Press.

Bourdieu, P. (1977) Cultural reproduction and social reproduction. In J. Karabel and A.H. Halsey (eds) *Power and Ideology in Education* (pp. 487–511). New York: Oxford University Press.

Bourdieu, P. (1986) The forms of capital. In J.G. Richardson (ed.) *Handbook of Theory and Research for the Sociology of Education* (pp. 241–258). Westport, CT: Greenwood Press.

Chun, C. (2015) *Power and Meaning Making in an EAP Classroom: Engaging with the Everyday*. Bristol: Multilingual Matters.

Chun, C. and Morgan, B. (2019) Critical research in English language teaching. In A. Gao (ed.) *Springer Second Handbook of English Language Teaching*. Norwell, MA: Springer Publishers. DOI: 10.1007/978-3-319-58542-0_56-1.

Harklau, L. (2000) From the 'good kids' to the 'worst': Representations of English language learners across educational settings. *TESOL Quarterly* 34 (1), 35–67.

Harklau, L. (2016) Bureaucratic dysfunctions in the education of Latino immigrant youth. *American Journal of Education* 122 (4), 601–627.

Kral, I. (2012) *Talk, Text and Technology: Literacy and Social Practice in a Remote Indigenous Community*. Bristol: Multilingual Matters.

Kubota, R. and Miller, E.R. (2017) Re-examining and re-envisioning criticality in language studies: Theories and praxis. *Critical Inquiry in Language Studies* 14, 129–157.

Johnston, B. (2017) *English Teaching and Evangelical Mission: The Case of Lighthouse School*. Bristol: Multilingual Matters.

Lorente, B.P. (2018) *Scripts of Servitude: Language, Labor Migration and Transnational Domestic Work*. Bristol: Multilingual Matters.

Luke, A. (2014) Regrounding critical literacy: Representation, facts and reality. In M.R. Hawkins (ed.) (2014) *Framing Language and Literacies: Socially Situated Views and Perspectives* (pp. 136–148). New York: Routledge.

McLaren, P. (1989) *Life in Schools: An Introduction to Critical Pedagogy in the Foundations of Education*. New York: Longman.

Pennycook, A. (2021) *Critical Applied Linguistics: A Critical Re-Introduction* (2nd edn). New York: Routledge.

Sterzuk, A. (2011) *The Struggle for Legitimacy: Indigenized Englishes in Settler Schools.* Bristol: Multilingual Matters.

Wacquant, L. (2016) A concise genealogy and anatomy of habitus. *The Sociological Review* 64, 64–72. DOI: 10.1111/1467-954X.12356.

Willis, P. (1977) *Learning to Labour: How Working Class Kids Get Working Class Jobs.* New York: Columbia University Press.

Preface

I am completing this book in the middle of the COVID-19 pandemic. The global spread of this terrifying virus has upended our lives and our education systems on an unprecedented scale. As US public schools have scrambled to switch to remote learning virtually overnight without prior teacher training or adequate infrastructure, serving the needs of already marginalized students remotely in a time of crisis has proven to be a nearly impossible task. Thus, a common refrain is that this pandemic has laid bare the already existing inequities in education in the United States; that vulnerable populations such as English learners (ELs) and students with disabilities have been disproportionately affected by the pandemic. It is true that education in the United States has never been equal at the best of times. If this pandemic has shone a spotlight on the existing inequities, that is at least one positive outcome of these trying times. But glimpsing existing inequities at a time when the whole education system is experiencing a crisis is not the same as understanding the underlying mechanism of these inequities. In my mind, there is nothing inherently more 'vulnerable' about ELs than any other students: it is the education *system* that is making them vulnerable by treating them as 'lesser than', and stripping them of opportunities to learn. I hope that the lasting contribution of this book is that it exposes how even under much more favorable conditions – no pandemic, a booming economy and the first African American president in the history of the nation – ELs were still excluded from arguably the most consequential educational opportunity: access to postsecondary education. This exclusion is systemic and institutional: it is not just a matter of uncaring or incompetent teachers or resource-deprived schools. Even when teachers are caring and well qualified, and schools are reasonably well resourced, ELs are systematically eliminated from rigorous academic preparation and the information necessary to continue further education after high school. This book is my current best articulation of why and how this inequity takes place.

Acknowledgements

This is my third single-authored book, and you would think that by now I would have figured out how to write a book more efficiently. Evidently, I have not as this book took just as long to complete as the first two. During the long process of fits and starts, hiatuses and feverish trances of intensive writing as if there were no tomorrow, many people have helped me, and I am grateful for their kindness, brilliance and generosity.

First of all, I am eternally grateful to the Brighton High School educators and students who participated in the study. In the book, I may come across as highly critical of the school, but I have never lost sight of the fact that without their willingness to open up the school for my investigation, none of what I wrote in this book could have been documented. Brighton educators were remarkably generous in granting me access: I could more or less observe any classes, speak with any faculty and staff members and obtain any documents that I requested. For that I am deeply thankful. Special thanks go to Mr Woznyj, who expressed great enthusiasm when I first approached him about the project. He was the kind of educator who believed that any involvement in a research project is an enrichment experience for his students, and he took the time to understand the goals of my project and helped me recruit student participants and access other educators at the school.

The seven ELs in this study – and an eighth one, Sam, who is not included in this study but was part of the original project – were my joys, wonders and frustrations during the three years of data collection. It was a real privilege to witness this critical phase of their transition to adulthood, and I always marveled at how wise and resilient they were sometimes and how still so young and clueless they were at other times. It would be presumptuous of me to assume that I captured everything there was to know about their access to postsecondary education; I am sure that there were many layers that I did not unpeel. But I am thankful for what they shared with me.

My friends and colleagues at Temple University offered the encouragement and advice I needed to sustain a longitudinal study such as this one. I am particularly grateful to Jim Byrnes for underscoring the importance of intentionally designing a rigorous study from the onset in a way that meets the standards of the highest-level journals in one's field; and to

Michael Smith, for allowing me to pop by his office when I was bursting to share the latest discoveries from my fieldwork. Elvis Wagner and Jill Swavely were (and are) two trusted friends with whom I had numerous hallway conversations about the progress of this study. Christine Woyshner was (and is) always a sympathetic listener who understands the plight of a book writer in a college that prioritizes journal articles. My doctoral students, Mark Emerick, Sarah Grosik and Brooke Hoffman, assisted with various aspects of this project with the fresh energy and enthusiasm of novice researchers.

Colleagues in my field have been generous in giving me listening ears, helping hands and constructive feedback that stretched my thinking. Two colleagues to whom I am particularly indebted are Amanda Kibler and Rebecca Callahan. They read the entire book manuscript and pointed out some of my blind spots. The book is in much better shape because of their thoughtful feedback. Many thanks also to Betsy Rymes for introducing me to Mr Woznyj; to Paul K. Matsuda for the opportunity to present early findings from this study as a plenary speaker at the 2015 American Association for Applied Linguistics Conference; to Bonny Norton, Linda Harklau, Stephanie Vandrick and Christine Casanave for being amazing long-term mentors and showing me different models of how to be strong women and brilliant scholars in the field of applied linguistics. Further thanks to Manka Varghese for starting this line of work with me back at the University of Washington around 2007; to Wayne Wright for encouraging me to submit this book to Multilingual Matters and for late night journal-editor jokes; and to Su Motha for our annual conference breakfast conversations about book writing, qualitative research and lots of gossip to laugh about.

I moved to Boston University in the middle of writing this book, and the relocation from Pennsylvania to Massachusetts has provided insights into how different states approach EL education differently. Chris Leider, Marnie Reed and Mary Hughes, all members of the TESOL program, have helped me get acclimated to Boston, giving me a sense of home. Doctoral student Nick David copy-edited the whole manuscript, eliminating verbiage, suggesting more precise words and gently pointing out places where I was making no sense. I am grateful for his thoughtful edits.

I am 100% certain that this book would not have happened without the support of Sara Kangas, former-doctoral-student-turned-best-writing-buddy-ever. At one point, I was seriously considering washing my hands of this book, focusing on writing a series of journal articles instead. But Sara told me that she enjoyed reading more 'narrative-y' accounts of my EL participants' experiences, whose details tend to get omitted in journal articles because of word limits. I was able to complete this book only because I had an immediate reader in Sara, *and* I had to produce something every two weeks for our meetings. She read every single chapter about five times – she could probably recite the whole book at this point. Thank you, Sara, for your infinite patience and abundant encouragement.

My academic sisters, Sheela Athreya, Jiyeon Kang and Jennifer Granick, cheered and pushed and celebrated mini-progress all summer long, and gave me the energy that I needed to cross the finish line with this book. Thank goodness for their love and complete acceptance of who I am.

My husband, Toby, and my son, Kenji, have patiently put up with my obsession with writing, but then again have always reminded me that there is more to life than writing – like, baking! Toby once opined, 'I can't eat your writing, but I can eat your cookies!' and that just about summarizes the relationship these two men have with my writing. As of publication, Kenji is a senior in high school, and it has been eye-opening to go through college planning with him as a parent (e.g. 'What do you mean you will start prepping for the SAT the night before the test?') while writing about these seven students' college planning. On a number of occasions, I have consulted Kenji about what it is like to be a high school student in the United States, to the point he observed, 'Mom, I'm like a key informant in your study'. I herein gladly acknowledge his contribution.

This book incorporated elements from the following published journal articles:

Kanno, Y. (2018) Non-college-bound English learners as the underserved third: How students graduate from high school neither college- nor career-ready. *Journal of Education for Students Placed at Risk* 23 (4), 336–358. © 2018 Taylor & Francis. Republished with permission.

Kanno, Y. (2018) High-performing English learners' limited access to four-year college. *Teachers College Record* 120 (4), 1–46. © 2018 Teachers College, Columbia University. Republished with permission.

Kanno, Y. and Kangas, S.E.N. (2014) 'I'm not going to be, like, for the AP: English language learners' limited access to advanced college-preparatory courses in high school. *American Educational Research Journal* 51 (5), 848–878. © 2014 Sage. Republished with permission.

1 Introduction

There are two pieces of conflicting information regarding the education of English learners (ELs), multilingual students who are in the process of developing grade-level English language proficiency in US public schools. On the one hand, the laws of this land guarantee ELs' rights to equal educational opportunities (Equal Educational Opportunity Act, 1974; Lau v. Nichols, 1974). As far back as 1974, the seminal Supreme Court case *Lau v Nichols* declared that public schools are responsible for taking 'affirmative steps' to remove language barriers that inhibit ELs from meaningful participation in educational programs. More recently, the US Department of Justice and the US Department of Education (2015) jointly issued a 'Dear Colleague' letter, reiterating states' and school districts' obligations to ensure ELs' equal educational opportunities. In short, states and districts have the legal responsibility to 'ensure EL students have equal opportunities to meaningfully participate in all curricular and extracurricular activities, including the core curriculum, graduation requirements, specialized and advanced courses and programs, sports, and clubs' (US Department of Justice and the US Department of Education, 2015: 8).

On the other hand, there is clear evidence that ELs do not have the same access to postsecondary education (PSE) after high school as students for whom English is their first language (henceforth, English L1 students). One study found that only 19% of those students who were ELs in 10th grade went on to enroll in four-year colleges or universities compared with 45% of English L1 students (Kanno & Cromley, 2015). Nearly half of 10th-grade ELs were found not to be enrolled in any form of PSE (four-year, two-year or trade school) two years after their scheduled high school graduation. Granted, PSE is not part of compulsory education in the United States, and states and school districts have no obligation to send their high school graduates to PSE. Nonetheless, if K-12 public schools fulfilled their obligation to ensure ELs' equal participation, it is hard to imagine there would be such stark disparities.

This book is an attempt to shed some light on this puzzle: What is it that US public schools are doing – or not doing – that falls so spectacularly short in preparing ELs for PSE? I address this question through an ethnographic case study of one public school and seven of its ELs' transitions to PSE. By providing an in-depth look at one school and its participants, I hope to paint a complex and nuanced picture of the interactions among ELs' own aspirations and challenges; educators' good intentions and assumptions about ELs' capabilities; and the social class of the community. The task of preparing students who are still in the process of acquiring society's dominant language for the highest level of education the country has to offer is complex and difficult. I wish to document the challenges and complexities involved in this endeavor, and the lessons that I have learned as I have tried to understand the process.

High School ELs' Access to Postsecondary Education: What We Currently Know

ELs' access to and success in PSE is a surprisingly understudied area of research (Kanno & Harklau, 2012; Nuñez et al., 2016). A large volume of research has been dedicated to exploring the college access and success of other underrepresented groups of students such as racial/ethnic minority, low income and first generation (e.g. Baker et al., 2018; Bowen et al., 2005, 2009; Lopez & Horn, 2020; Pascarella et al., 2004; Perna, 2006; Saunders & Serna, 2004); however, when people talk about 'diversity' in the context of higher education in the United States, they seem to forget linguistic diversity. Consequently, linguistic minority students' – and particularly ELs' – access to college has garnered much less attention.

However, a small but growing body of research on high school ELs' access to and success in PSE has begun to emerge in the last 15 years or so, and this body of research has identified some factors and structural barriers that inhibit ELs' access to PSE. One critical factor that has emerged is ELs' access to advanced college preparatory courses in high school. Once students are identified as ELs, their opportunity to learn rigorous academic content is often greatly compromised – in flagrant contradiction to the spirit of *Lau v. Nichols* (Callahan et al., 2010). There is a deep-seated assumption in US schools that ELs must learn English before they are ready for any serious academic learning:

> Despite the well-supported claim that becoming fluent in English is a transition that could happen concurrently with the overall academic transition to college, it appears that English language acquisition is instead treated as a gatekeeping process for access to college preparatory content. (Rodriguez & Cruz, 2009: 2392)

Thus, as early as middle school,[1] ELs are subject to what Umansky (2016a) calls *leveled tracking* (limited access to advanced-level courses such as accelerated and honors courses) and *exclusionary tracking* (exclusion from required core-subject courses). As academic tracking expands in high school, ELs' leveled tracking is further exacerbated (Callahan, 2005; Callahan & Shifrer, 2016; Callahan *et al.*, 2010; Carlson & Knowles, 2016; Gamoran, 2017; Kanno & Cromley, 2015; Thompson, 2017). Since the rigor of academic preparation in high school is a powerful predictor of not only students' college access but also their degree completion (Adelman, 2006; Cabrera *et al.*, 2005), ELs' restricted access to a rigorous college preparatory curriculum narrows their PSE options.

Another barrier that many ELs encounter on their way to college is financial constraints (e.g. Almon, 2010; Kanno & Grosik, 2012; Kanno & Varghese, 2010; Nuñez *et al.*, 2016). Compared to non-ELs, ELs, on the whole, come from lower-income families (García et al., 2008; Grant-makers for Education, 2013), and their lack of finances limits the range of realistic college options (Kanno & Grosik, 2012; Nuñez *et al.*, 2016). Moreover, ELs and their families often lack knowledge about the different types of financial aid available and may assume that they are financially responsible for the sticker price of a college (Nuñez *et al.*, 2016). As a result, they may not even apply to four-year colleges in the first place, thinking that they would not be able to afford a four-year college education even if admitted (Kanno & Cromley, 2015).

Further, given low teacher expectations and the stigma attached to the *EL* label, many ELs may adjust their aspirations and come to believe that college is beyond their reach (Gándara & Orfield, 2012). The stigma surrounding the EL label is well known (e.g. Dabach, 2014; Gándara & Orfield, 2012; Lillie *et al.*, 2012), especially toward long-term ELs, those who have been classified as ELs for five years or more (e.g. Flores *et al.*, 2015; Kibler *et al.*, 2018; Olsen, 2010; Thompson, 2015; US Department of Education, 2016). Callahan and Humphries (2016: 286) observe that 'placement in ESL [English as a second language] coursework may act as a signaling device, alerting educators and others to project limitations onto EL students' academic potential'. Drawing on Link and colleagues' (Link *et al.*, 1989; Link & Phelan, 2013) *labeling theory*, Thompson (2015) and Umansky (2016b) remind us that any institutional labels such as *ELs* and *students with disabilities* have the intended effect of bringing specific services to a particular population *and* the unintended consequences of stigmatizing the labeled. Thus, 'there are compelling arguments as to why classifying students as ELs might be beneficial for students and there are equally compelling arguments as to why it might be harmful' (Umansky, 2016b: 716). The stigma surrounding ELs and the consistent message from teachers about their lack of capability, then, may lead many ELs to doubt their own potential. It is thus unsurprising that a clear difference in college aspirations appears statistically, too. While 75% of English L1 high school students aspire to earn a bachelor's degree, only 58% of ELs have the same goal (Kanno & Cromley, 2015).

In the emerging body of literature on multilingual students' access to PSE, qualitative studies that followed the same students longitudinally are scarce. However, there are three important exceptions. In a series of studies of Latinx immigrant students' transition from high school to college, Harklau (2000, 2012, 2013) has shown surprising disjunctions in the relationship between students' backgrounds and high school experiences and their access to and success in PSE. In a study of four Latina ELs' transition from high school to a community college, Harklau (2000: 46) found that ELs were praised as 'an inspiration for everyone' in high school whereas at a two-year community college, their academic ability was negatively compared against that of international students, and they were subsequently positioned as the worst kind of student. In her five and a half year study that followed five Latinx immigrant students from 8th grade to PSE, Harklau (2012, 2013) discovered that individual students' college access sometimes took an unexpected turn. A student with strong potential to attend college decided to enter the workforce, so that she could gain financial independence and power within her family (Harklau, 2013). Conversely, another student with clear disadvantages such as learning disabilities and unstable family income was able to reach college on the strengths of resources from her suburban school, support from her religious community and strong self-efficacy (Harklau, 2012).

In another example of a longitudinal study, Kibler (2019) followed five Mexican immigrant-origin youth for eight years beginning in ninth grade to document their bilingual and biliteracy development over time. They were all classified as ELs at the onset of the study. These students' journeys were not easy, and only one student 'succeeded' in the conventional sense, completing a four-year college education. However, in rich portraits of the five bilingual students, Kibler demonstrated that despite multiple setbacks and challenges, these students charted their own postsecondary trajectories while using and developing their bilingualism and biliteracy along the way. Finally, Ruecker (2015) explored the role of academic writing in seven Latinx students' transition from high school to PSE. On the whole, those students who had better academic preparation and better literacy skills in English during high school made a smoother transition, but almost all participants struggled with the discrepancies between the standards and genres of high school writing and the literacy demands of PSE, a theme that echoes in Harklau's (2000) and Kibler's (2019) studies as well.

These qualitative longitudinal studies add rich perspectives to multi-lingual students' transition from high school to PSE, reminding us that the paths from high school to PSE are not straightforward. However, in focusing more on individual students' journeys, especially their literacy development, these studies do not fully explore the role of high schools in shaping multilingual students' transition to PSE nor the impact of EL classification on their individual journeys in high school. Building on these longitudinal studies, then, this book aims to provide an in-depth look at how a group of multilingual students who were classified as ELs in high school navigated their access to PSE and how their high school shaped this process.

College and Career Readiness

One key concept in examining high school ELs' transition to PSE is college and career readiness (CCR), because the extent to which high school students successfully access and transition to PSE hinges on their CCR. In this book, I argue that, despite its considerable resources and its educators' hard work and good intentions, the school I studied failed to make ELs college and career ready, and that the students suffered the consequences. However, in order to document this process, we need a shared understanding of what it means to be college and career ready.

CCR has received broad and bipartisan political support in the United States for more than a decade now, bolstered by the Obama administration's initiative to dramatically increase college graduates by 2020 (Malin *et al.*, 2017). It has been explicitly incorporated into the Common Core State Standards (National Government Association Center for Best Practices & Council of Chief State School Officers, 2010; Porter *et al.*, 2011), a large-scale initiative adopted by 41 states and the

District of Colombia to set common academic standards across the nation. David Conley (2014: 4), an influential proponent of CCR, argues that 'one of the most important goals of the Common Core State Standards is that they provide the knowledge and skills necessary to succeed in college, career, and life'. More recently, the Every Student Succeeds Act of 2015 (ESSA), the most recent reauthorization of the Elementary and Secondary Education Act of 1965, has allocated a number of funds to CCR-related initiatives. Of special note is Title I, which channels funds to low-income districts and schools which can be used for CCR efforts (Malin *et al.*, 2017). In all, then, CCR represents a unifying goal to align all levels of K-12 education – elementary, middle and high school – in such a way to prepare students for college and career by the end of high school (Malin *et al.*, 2017).

College readiness

There is no question that the vast majority of discussions regarding CCR relate to the college-readiness aspect. Conley (2008: 4) defines *college readiness* as 'the level of preparation a student needs in order to enroll and succeed, without remediation, in a credit-bearing general education course at a postsecondary institution that offers a baccalaureate degree or transfer to a baccalaureate program'. He takes a broader conceptualization of college readiness than just academic preparation, and identifies four components: (a) core academic knowledge and skills; (b) key cognitive strategies; (c) self-managing skills; and (d) college knowledge (Conley, 2007, 2008) (Figure 1.1). The first two components are typically what we associate with college readiness and are featured

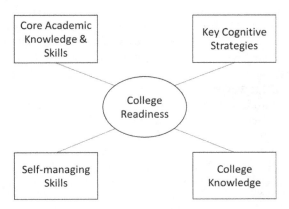

Figure 1.1 Conley's (2007) model of college readiness

prominently in the college admissions process (Roderick *et al.*, 2009). First, core academic knowledge refers to discipline-specific academic knowledge in subjects such as English, mathematics, social studies, science and world languages, while literacy, numeracy and research skills cut across disciplines and allow students to be successful in a range of subjects (Roderick *et al.*, 2009).

Second, key cognitive skills also apply to many disciplines and include the abilities to problem-solve, analyze, synthesize and reason. The ability to effectively employ these cognitive strategies to intellectually rigorous college-level work is what differentiates college-ready students from simply college-eligible students. In many ways, these strategies correspond to the higher echelons of Bloom's Taxonomy of Educational Objectives (*analysis, synthesis* and *evaluation*, as opposed to *knowledge, comprehension* and *application*) (Krathwohl, 2002). As we will see in Chapter 2, advanced cognitive skills are intentionally and frequently cultivated in advanced-level courses in high school while ELs' coursework, concentrated mostly in sheltered EL and remedial-level courses, tends to focus predominantly on lower-level strategies.

Third, although these cognitive skills and foundational academic knowledge are what is typically associated with college readiness, non-cognitive skills such as self-management skills (e.g. time management, long-term planning, help-seeking ability and the ability to form and work with study groups) also contribute to college readiness (Conley, 2007, 2008; Roderick *et al.*, 2009). Many of these behaviors are necessary at the high school level too, but in high school they are heavily scaffolded by the adults around the students such as parents, teachers, guidance counselors and sports coaches. By contrast, in college, many of these self-management responsibilities are transferred onto the students themselves with an expectation of more independence.

Finally, the fourth component of college readiness consists of *college knowledge*, practical knowledge of how to navigate the college planning and application processes, and once admitted, how to persist and succeed in college (Conley, 2007; Vargas, 2004). College knowledge is not distributed equally among students and families of different racial/ethnic backgrounds and socioeconomic status (SES) (Conley, 2007; Roderick *et al.*, 2009; Vargas, 2004). A process taken for granted by middle-class families with college-educated parents may be completely unfamiliar to low-income families with non-college-educated parents. And not knowing is costly. As we will discuss in Chapter 3, 'it takes only one mistake in the entire chain of events for the college application process to derail' (Conley, 2005: 22).

Career readiness

Current trends in research regarding career readiness emphasize its commonalities with college readiness, on the grounds that 'graduates who go directly to work need solid academic skills and those who go to college will also have careers' (Oakes & Saunders, 2008: 5). Mishkind (2014), who reviewed state definitions of CCR, reports that of the 37 states that have an explicit articulation of what they mean by CCR, 33 have adopted single definitions for both college readiness and career readiness that are very similar to Conley's definition of college readiness: that is, the level of academic readiness that allows students to enter college-level courses and succeed without the need for remediation.

Arizona, one of the four states that define the two terms separately, asserts that a career-ready person 'qualifies for a job that provides a family-sustaining wage and pathways to advancement and requires postsecondary training or education' (Mishkind, 2014: 7). The definition is elaborated and includes the qualifications and skills that such a person needs to have:

> [A career-ready job candidate] is a high school graduate and has the English and mathematical knowledge and skills needed to qualify for and succeed in the postsecondary job training and/or education necessary for their chosen career (i.e. technical/vocational program, community college, apprenticeship or significant on-the-job training). (Mishkind, 2014: 7)

Arizona's statement reflects the current thinking about career readiness across the country: that, regardless of the training they received in high school, high school graduates will not be instantly career ready. Rather, students will need either further training at the postsecondary level or significant apprenticeship on the job.

This emphasis on further training at the postsecondary level mirrors the current reality of the US workforce, where the prospects for high school graduates without additional training are extremely limited (Achieve, 2012; Ma *et al.*, 2019). In contrast, middle-skill jobs, those jobs that require some training and education beyond high school but less than a bachelor's degree (e.g. plumbers, firefighters, hairstylists, nurse aides, legal assistants and engineering technicians), provide both a family-supporting wage and chances for promotion. Moreover, middle-skill jobs are currently the only job sector where demand for workers outpaces supply (National Skills Coalition, 2017). These days, when policymakers and educators mention career readiness, many are implicitly or explicitly referencing the kind of high school preparation that leads to further PSE and training, and eventually, middle-skill jobs.

Despite the significant overlap between college and career readiness, at their core, the two are not identical. Clark (2015: 3) defines career readiness as 'the level of "foundational skills" an individual needs for success in a career pathway or career cluster, coupled with the level of "career planning skills" needed to advance within a career path or transition to other career paths'. In Clark's model of career readiness – much like Conley's (2007, 2008) model of college readiness – foundational skills consist of *cognitive* and *non-cognitive skills* (Figure 1.2). The cognitive skills overlap with the core academic knowledge and key cognitive strategies in Conley's college readiness model and include foundations in literacy, math and problem-solving. The non-cognitive skills for career readiness comprise a slightly different set of skills from the non-cognitive skills for college readiness, placing a far larger emphasis on the ability to collaborate with others in the workplace. Examples of this include strong communication skills; the willingness and ability to contribute to team efforts; and the flexibility and discipline to adapt to new practices in a workplace. Further, just as cognitive and non-cognitive skills alone do not make students college ready unless they know how to navigate college planning and application (i.e. college knowledge), the cognitive and non-cognitive skills associated with career readiness cannot be put to good use if students do not know how to explore the career options best suited to them and the education and training necessary to reach those goals. Thus, Clark (2015) includes a third element, *career-planning skills*, as an integral component of career readiness.

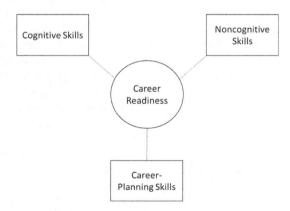

Figure 1.2 Clark's (2015) model of career readiness

In summary, there is a significant overlap between college readiness and career readiness. Both place a strong emphasis on students' solid academic preparation in high school so they can pursue PSE without the need for remediation. Both have a non-cognitive component and a navigational knowledge component to complement academic preparation. However, differences arise between college readiness and career readiness in what is included in the non-cognitive skill and navigational knowledge components, underscoring the fact that career readiness cannot just be subsumed under college readiness. Having described the concepts of college readiness and career readiness, in the next section, I discuss another pair of key theoretical constructs in this book: individual and institutional habitus.

Theoretical Framework: Individual and Institutional Habitus

In this book, I draw on Bourdieu's (1977b, 1984) theory of *individual habitus* and the more recently derived theory of *institutional habitus* as its theoretical framework. Bourdieu proposed the concept of *habitus* as part of his effort to dismantle the dichotomy between social structure and individual agency. Fundamentally, the debate regarding structure and agency centers on how social structures condition human experiences on the one hand, and to what extent individuals can exercise their agency to determine their own fate on the other. Bourdieu explored the relationship between structure and agency and bridged the two through his theory of habitus. Habitus is a set of dispositions formed through individuals' upbringing, especially through their socialization within their family. But one's habitus continues to evolve through subsequent experiences such as school education and work while at the same time continuing to shape one's actions and decisions (Bourdieu & Wacquant, 1992). This way, Bourdieu situates habitus as the mediating factor between structure and agency: habitus transports the existing structure into a person's action while a person's action contributes to the preservation of the structure. This does not mean that we as humans are entirely imprisoned in the way we have been conditioned to think and behave within the existing structure (e.g. Giroux, 1983). As Bourdieu and Wacquant (1992: 133) remind us, 'Habitus is not the fate that some people read into it'. Human beings can resist the initial impulse deriving from their habitus and deliberately choose a different response. Nonetheless, our actions in any situation are imbued with the history of interactions we have had in the past and the social structures in which we have led our lives thus far. We are not entirely free agents.

Habitus is a key concept in Bourdieu's theory of *cultural reproduction* (Bourdieu, 1986; Bourdieu & Passeron, 1990), which delineates the role of school education in the reproduction of societal inequalities. Bourdieu argues that schools privilege the children of the dominant social class by taking their *cultural capital* – their language, literacy practices and cultural dispositions – as the norm and treating all children as if they had access to the same cultural capital: 'By doing away with giving explicitly to everyone what it implicitly demands of everyone, the educational system demands of everyone alike that they have what it does not give' (Bourdieu, 1977a: 494). Thought this way, proficiency in the English language, especially facility with academic language in English, is a quintessential form of cultural capital in US schools. Although US schools are required by federal law to provide sufficient support services to guarantee ELs' equal access to educational programs (Lau v. Nichols, 1974; US Department of Justice & US Department of Education, 2015), in reality, ELs are often thrown into inequitable instructional situations. They are provided with insufficient support or are denied access to challenging coursework because of their English language proficiency, as we saw in the earlier literature review.

Importantly, no form of capital has an absolute value; rather, the value of a particular form of capital is determined in relation to a particular market, or a *field*: 'structured spaces that are organized around specific types of capital or combination of capital' (Swartz, 1997: 117). A form of cultural capital that has high value in a field may be considered totally worthless in another. There is no question that in certain fields such as international business and diplomacy, multilingualism is a highly coveted and marketable form of cultural capital – or rather, *linguistic capital*, which is a very important part of cultural capital. However, in the field of US public K-12 education, multilingualism, especially the multilingualism of immigrant students of color, is a devalued form of linguistic capital (Flores, 2015; Flores & Rosa, 2015). In contrast, and rather counterintuitively, monolingual English proficiency dominates as a legitimate, even desirable, form of linguistic capital.

If we translate this theory into the context of EL education, it would suggest that placed in a field where their multilingualism is consistently devalued, ELs might come to internalize this deficit orientation and 'misrecognize' (Bourdieu & Passeron, 1990) their lack of opportunities as a logical consequence of a meritorious system in which they come out short compared with their English L1 peers. If individual habitus 'involves an unconscious calculation of what is possible, impossible, and probable for individuals *in their specific location in a stratified order*' (Swartz, 1997:

106–107, added emphasis), and ELs' sense of possibility is constrained by their history of experiences with marginalization in school, they may not venture to take on such a risky proposition as applying to a four-year college, because they may assume, 'That's not for the likes of us' (Bourdieu & Passeron, 1990: 157).

Habitus was originally proposed as the dispositions of individuals. When I speak of individual habitus, then, I am referring to this original sense of the term. However, recently in the college choice literature, the role of high schools and their habitus – what is called *organizational* habitus (McDonough, 1997) or *institutional* habitus (Bagdon, 2012; byrd, 2019; Horvat & Antonio, 1999; Reay, 1998; Reay *et al.*, 2005; Smyth & Banks, 2012) – has been explored, specifically in limiting the range of college choices for students and orienting them toward particular postsecondary trajectories. This way, institutional habitus has been conceptualized as a mechanism through which high schools play a key role in social reproduction by putting their students in their place according to their social class, as can be seen in McDonough's (1997: 107) original definition of the term: 'the impact of a cultural group or social class on an individual's behavior through an intermediate organization, the high school'.

Just like individual habitus, a school develops its own institutional habitus through its relationship with its community, the history of educating a particular student demographic, and its own position in the system of prestige and reputations of schools (byrd, 2019; McDonough, 1997; Reay, 1998; Reay *et al.*, 2005). Drawing on the last two decades of scholarship on institutional habitus, in this book, I define school institutional habitus as a school's collective beliefs about what its students are capable of, what is within their reach and what they deserve. Such institutional habitus in turn guides the school's policies, practices and expectations for its students.

Institutional habitus not only guides institutional actions but also provides *discourses* that explain why things are the way they are at and around the school. Here, I am drawing on the Fairclaughian sense of discourse, 'language as a form of social practice' (Fairclough, 2015: 55). But more specifically, in this book, I refer to *institutional discourses* as the collective narratives by which educators at a school make sense of their experiences at the school and rationalize their decisions and actions. For example, one institutional discourse that was pervasive at the high school in this study was 'protecting ELs from failure'. When educators steered ELs away from advanced courses and placed them in less demanding courses, it was explained in terms of protecting ELs from failure, rather than in terms of educators' lack of ability and willingness to scaffold ELs' learning and provide access to advanced course content. In other words, the discourse reflected *and* reinforced the school's existing institutional habitus of what ELs were capable of, while drawing attention away from the school's failure to provide equal access to educational opportunities for ELs.

Of course, not all members of a school community may agree with the institutional discourses; however, to the extent that these discourses reflect the taken-for-granted assumptions of the school and provide ready explanations for experiences that could be interpreted in a number of ways, they function as a powerful inculcating mechanism for its members and serve to reinforce institutional habitus:

> The relationship between discourse and social structures is not the one-way relationship which I have suggested so far. As well as being determined by social structures, discourse has effects upon social structures and contributes to the achievement of social continuity or social change. (Fairclough, 2015: 67)

In other words, institutional discourses not only reflect institutional habitus, but also perpetuate it.

PSE choice, then, is one of the important elements of a high school that is shaped by its institutional habitus. Each high school develops a sense of what PSE options are realistic and appropriate for its own students. Again, in doing so, each school creates institutional discourses that explain why these PSE options make sense for its students. Educators then utilize those discourses to recommend certain choices to students and parents and to discuss individual student's PSE prospects with their colleagues. This way, a high school reduces the literally thousands of potential PSE options to a more concrete and manageable set of choices for its students by 'making some choices virtually unthinkable and yet others routine' (Reay *et al.*, 2005: 47).

In this book, I conceptualize a student's PSE choice[2] as a result of the interaction between their own individual habitus and the institutional habitus of their high school. What the student sees as within the realm of their own possibilities – i.e. their individual habitus – clearly has a direct impact on the PSE options they consider. However, what their school sees as within the realm of possibilities for them – i.e. the institutional habitus – also powerfully shapes the student's individual choices. Here, it is important to note that a school's institutional habitus does not necessarily orient all its students to the same PSE institutions. Within a school, some students may be singled out as 'more capable' than others and therefore are given more resources and support to aim for a higher caliber of college; conversely, other students may be conceived of as less likely to go to college and therefore may receive lower levels of attention and investment from the school.

The Setting and Participants

In the remainder of this chapter, I introduce Brighton High School and seven of its EL students with whom I worked. A more detailed description of the methods appears in the Appendix for those readers who are interested in the technical aspects of the study.

Brighton High School

Brighton High School[3] is technically a suburban public high school in Pennsylvania, but because it is located in a town just outside a metropolitan city, the school has an urban fringe feel to it. The school catchment area is largely working class, although it includes pockets of relatively more affluent areas with tree-lined streets and single-family homes. The high school itself is located in the lower-income, commercial side of town. The area is not particularly scenic: the school sits at the intersection of busy streets with multiple lanes, with a supermarket, strip malls with fast-food chains and gas stations nearby. But the school building is well maintained, and the surrounding area feels safe. During my fieldwork, I never felt concerned walking or driving in the area at night. The atmosphere of no frills but safe and friendly extends to inside the school as well. Security personnel visibly patrol the school; visitors must stop at a security desk just inside the main entrance for an ID check. But whenever I visited, the security people were friendly and greeted me with a ready smile.

One of the first things I noticed about Brighton High was its size. With more than 2500 students, it is one of the largest high schools in the region, and it *feels* very large. The school extends to several wings, and it is quite a sight when the buzzer announces the end of a period and teenagers pour out of the classrooms into the hallways to retrieve different textbooks and binders from their lockers, before rushing to their next classes while catching up with their friends. New teachers and frequent visitors quickly learn alternative routes to avoid walking against the tides of youth.

A large school not only has its benefits, such as the capacity to offer a diverse array of elective classes and many music, arts and athletic clubs, but it also has its challenges, as Mr Woznyj, chair of the EL department noted:

> It's a great school if you're motivated. If you are, like I have a daughter in the district in second grade. And I always say I'll gladly send her here if she's a strong student, a motivated student. If you are middle of the road even a little bit, you have a tendency to daydream, or just not really be driven; it's very easy just to get swept up in this place. (IN 01/06/2012)[4]

He further added that the size of the school was disorienting for many ELs who had just immigrated from another country and were trying to get their bearings in their new country: 'A school this size, it's very over-whelming. And I hear that from every one of the students, like the first day in the cafeteria has to be mind-blowing' (IN 01/06/2012).

Another highly salient characteristic is the cultural and linguistic diversity of the school. At Brighton, one sees students from all racial backgrounds: at the time of my fieldwork, the racial/ethnic composition of the school was 42% White, 42% African American, 13% Asian and 3% Hispanic. This diversity again stems from the location of the school, as school principal Mr Lawrence pointed out at the very beginning of our conversation:

> It is a large, by definition, suburban high school, but I would definitely say that we are very quickly becoming urbanized due to our proximity to [a metropolitan city]. If you look at our enrollment trends when I started here 12 years ago, we were about 60% White, 30% African Amer—, no, maybe 20, 25% African American, 15% other of all the other ethnicities combined. As we sit here today we're 40% White, 40% African American, roughly 20% other. So, in a very short period of time we've become very—, ah, demographically different school. (IN 01/24/2012)

The linguistic diversity of the school is just as pronounced as its racial diversity. Consonants and vowels that do not belong to the English language and different tones and rhythms provide a rich cacophony of music as one walks in the hallways. Taken together, Brighton students speak more than 40 different languages, including many African languages such as Twi and Mandingo. And it is not only ELs who speak another language; many English-proficient students are also children of immigrants and are multilingual speakers.

The EL population of the school reflects the larger racial/ethnic and linguistic diversity of the school. One of the aspects that attracted me to

Brighton High was the diversity of its EL student population. Because this was a study of ELs' access to PSE, not Hispanic ELs' or Chinese ELs' access to PSE, it was important to me that I work with a school that had a very diverse EL population, and Brighton amply met that requirement. During 2011–2012, there were approximately 190 ELs enrolled in the school, from ninth to 12th grade. Ethnically, 42% of ELs were Asian (largely coming from Bangladesh and Vietnam), 40% Black (from West African countries such as Liberia and Sierra Leone), 15% Hispanic and 3% White. The majority of ELs at Brighton were foreign-born immigrant students. Most ELs at the school were low-income students, and their parents/guardians typically did not have a college education.

There is an undeniable and palpable vitality that comes from having youths from such diverse cultural and linguistic backgrounds going through the coming of age together. However, once inside, a visitor quickly learns that the school is also grappling with issues of poverty, students with large gaps in their education and families separated by immigration and other traumas. Principal Lawrence shared, 'We've also become a more Title I eligible school,[5] based on the number of students that qualify for free and reduced lunch and … the experiences that they bring to us have shifted' (IN 01/24/2012). At the time of my fieldwork, 37% of the students were from low-income families, receiving free or reduced-price lunch, but beyond the statistics, the staff could feel the fast pace at which the community was growing poorer, more transient and less educated. Guidance counselor Mrs Salomon was more blunt than Mr Lawrence about the recent changes that she had observed over the past several years:

> I feel like that things have changed. I've been here 16 years. And I feel like there's been um, there definitely, when I started um, I felt like the students that we're getting that were EL students, I felt like had better background knowledge. And I feel like that they had probably more intact family structure. And a work ethic that was strong. I definitely felt that, that probably over the past, I want to say 7 or 8 years, that has sort of changed. We're getting way more students that have had gaps in their educational career…. There's a lot more social work concerns that we're dealing with, which is really difficult, and a lot more students with, that have eventually been identified as learning disabled, too. And that's something that has been newer. So, I do feel like that the types of students that we're seeing have changed. (IN 11/09/2011)

Here, Mrs Salomon is speaking about ELs in particular, but many of the recent trends in the EL population she observed – the general decline in academic standards, single-parent households and students living with relatives, absence of work ethic, learning disabilities – are also mentioned by several teachers and counselors about Brighton students in general and the community from where they came. But ELs, since they are the new-comers in the community and are, on the whole, poorer than non-ELs, in many ways symbolize new challenges that the staff did not face when the township of Brighton was a largely White suburban community.

The EL participants

The fieldwork for this study lasted three years, from May 2010 to June 2013, with the most intensive data collection taking place between January 2011 and June 2012. I chose to work with 11th graders (or *high school juniors* as they are called in the United States) because junior year is when PSE planning goes into high gear, both for the students and for the school, but students' PSE choices are still in flux (Selingo, 2020). I wanted to document the whole process of PSE planning, from the time students began making concrete plans for life after high school through to their final decisions.

In choosing the study participants, I had largely three key selection criteria. First, because the goal of the study was to explore high school ELs' access to PSE, the students had to be those who were ELs when they entered high school. Scholars in the last decade have pointed out the importance of following ELs longitudinally even after they have been reclassified as English proficient because if we focused only on their academic performance and educational outcomes while they are still classified as ELs, we would lose sight of their long-term outcomes (e.g. Kieffer & Thompson, 2018; Saunders & Marcelletti, 2013). In the context of this study then, ELs are defined as multilingual learners who entered high school with EL classification, including those who were later reclassified as English proficient. Second, given that I was going to follow how ELs navigated PSE planning and access, the participants had to be those who were planning to pursue PSE, at least in 11th grade. In other words, those who were not considering PSE at all and instead were planning to enter the workforce or the military were eliminated from the study.

However, given that most ELs at Brighton were planning to pursue PSE in one form or another, these two criteria alone did not narrow the pool of potential participants very much: I had more than 50 juniors from whom to choose. Then, a third selection criterion was academic performance in high school. Past research clearly suggests that academic preparation in high school is the strongest predictor of college access and degree completion, much more so than race/ethnicity, gender and SES (e.g. Adelman, 2006; Cabrera *et al.*, 2005; Kanno & Cromley, 2013). In order to capture how ELs of a wide range of academic performance at Brighton – not just the highest-performing ELs – navigated PSE access, I sought the help of Mr Woznyj, chair of the EL department, to identify high-performing ELs, low-performing ELs and those in the middle. Mr Woznyj understood the importance of this selection criterion and, based on his extensive knowledge of the EL students at the school, personally handpicked a group of 16 students who represented the range of ELs' academic profiles at Brighton for me to meet. Finally, after ensuring that the potential pool of participants met those three main criteria (EL classification at the point of high school entry, PSE aspirations and various academic performances), I endeavored to further diversify the sample in terms of race/ethnicity, gender and SES whenever possible.

The final sample of seven participants[6] consisted of four current ELs who were relative newcomers to the United States, having arrived within the last three years (Erica, Alexandra, Ken and Eddie), one long-term EL (Carlos) and two reclassified students (Josephine and Kadi) (see Table 1.1 for a summary of participant profiles). In terms of academic performance, they included those students whom Mr Woznyj considered high achievers (Erica and Alexandra), those seriously at risk (Eddie and Carlos) and those in the middle (Ken, Josephine and Kadi). Their academic range was also reflected in their cumulative grade point averages (GPAs; i.e. high school grades): from 90.2% (Erica) to 57.1% (Carlos) based on 70% as the minimum passing grade. Ethnically, two students were African, four Hispanic (one from Spain and three from Latin America) and one Asian. Four females and three males were included in the sample. In terms of SES, they were all low-income students receiving free or reduced-price lunch, except for Erica.

The Structure of the Remainder of the Book

The book consists of six chapters with an appendix that provides technical details concerning the ethnographic methods of the study. Prefacing each chapter are stories from one or more of the seven ELs in the study. Each narrative is placed before the chapter that has thematic content most relevant to the student's experiences, and their narratives are further explored in the subsequent chapter. In the paragraphs that follow, I summarize each narrative and chapter of the book in order.

Table 1.1 Summary of students' profiles, ranked in order of high school GPAs from highest to lowest

Students	Gender	Language status	Native country	L1	Age of arrival	Length of residence	ACCESS[a]	GPA (%)	PSSA reading[b]	PSSA math	Postsecondary destinations
Erica	F	Current EL	Spain	Spanish	16	2	4.9	90.2	Below Basic	Proficient	LCC[c]
Alexandra	F	Current EL	Dominican Republic	Spanish	15	3	4.8	89.5	Basic	Below Basic	LCC
Ken	M	Current EL	Philippines	Tagalog	15	2	5.2	89.2	Basic	Below Basic	Widener U.
Josephine	F	Reclassified	Ghana	Twi	14	3	4.8	86.2	Basic	Basic	LCC
Kadi[d]	F	Reclassified	Guinea	Mandingo	12	6	N/A	82.3	Basic	Below Basic	LCC
Eddie	M	Current EL	Mexico	Spanish	14	3	3.1	72.3	Below Basic	Below Basic	No PSE
Carlos[e]	M	Current EL	Ecuador	Spanish	10	7	5.1	57.1	–	–	No PSE

Note: The participants are listed in order of high to low cumulative high school GPAs.
[a] ACCESS: Assessing Comprehension and Communication in English State-to-State for English Language Learners, the English proficiency assessment administered to ELs every year in Pennsylvania
[b] PSSA: Pennsylvania System of School Assessment, the state assessment in Pennsylvania, state academic standardized tests.
[c] LCC: Local community college (pseudonym).
[d] Kadi was an EL at her previous high school in Minnesota but had already been reclassified as English proficient by the time she arrived at Brighton in Grade 10. She did not have to take the ACCESS test.
[e] Carlos's PSSA scores are not available because he missed taking the exams in the 11th grade.

Ken's story

Ken, a Tagalog L1 speaker from the Philippines, had clear career aspirations to become a registered nurse and applied to several nursing programs at regional public universities. However, given his low-level coursework at Brighton and less than competitive SAT[7] scores, he was not admitted to any of his first-choice schools. While he was admitted and enrolled in Widener University, a non-selective university, a condition of his college acceptance was that he attend a summer bridge program for academically underprepared students.

Chapter 2: Limited Access to Rigorous Academic Curriculum

One major factor inhibiting ELs' access to PSE is their limited access to advanced college preparatory coursework. At Brighton, once ELs completed EL sheltered courses, they were almost always placed in remedial-level courses in general education (i.e. non-EL courses). Brighton's educators wanted to 'protect ELs' from being overwhelmed in high-track courses and erred on the side of placing students in low-track courses. ELs, on their part, either did not know they had a say in course selection or lacked the confidence to demand more challenging courses. The low-level coursework in their high school transcripts and low SAT scores severely limited these students' chances for four-year college admission.

Alexandra's story

Alexandra, a Spanish L1 speaker from the Dominican Republic, wanted to go to Pennsylvania State University (a top state university) and eventually become an immigration lawyer. But as the first child in a low-income, immigrant family to go to college, she had no idea how to apply to four-year colleges. She missed the deadline to take the SAT and thus was ineligible to apply to the four-year colleges she was considering. Ultimately, she decided to attend a local community college (LCC), hoping to transfer to Pennsylvania State University at a later date.

Josephine's story

As a daughter of a single-parent family, Josephine, a Twi L1 speaker from Ghana, knew that paying for college was going to be a major challenge. And yet, having received no consistent college guidance, she only applied to private four-year colleges, thinking that they would provide the kind of small and intimate learning environment that suited her temperament. Because of her lack of academic competitiveness, she was rejected by all four-year colleges but one, which she realized she could not afford, so she decided to attend LCC instead.

Chapter 3: Underdeveloped College Knowledge

This chapter discusses how ELs' limited college knowledge (Conley, 2005; Vargas, 2004) hampered their PSE access. Although the parents of the study participants wanted their sons and daughters to go to college, most were not in a position to provide concrete guidance because they had not attended college themselves. Students were reluctant to approach teachers and counselors for information unless they had already developed trusting relationships with them. The school, on the other hand, took the *clearinghouse* approach to college guidance (Hill, 2008), wherein college information was made available to everyone; however, the school failed to make the information accessible to ELs.

Erica's story

Erica, a Spanish L1 speaker from Spain, was the highest achiever and the only middle-class student among the focal students, and yet she had the weakest four-year college orientation of the top five students. She felt intensely insecure about her English, preferring the company of Spanish-speaking peers, and believed that she was not ready for the academic demands of a four-year college. Although she secretly dreamed of going to a four-year college, when nudged by her father to attend LCC to save money, she readily consented.

Kadi's story

Kadi, a Mandingo L1 speaker from Guinea, was the only student in the study to enroll in Brighton's career and technical education (CTE) program. During her senior year, she spent half of the school day at a nearby county CTE institute, where she trained to obtain a nurse aide certificate. At the institute, she met a mentor who encouraged her to attend LCC while working as a nurse aide to save money, and then to transfer to a nursing program at a four-year college. Kadi followed her mentor's advice and planned to enroll in LCC after graduation.

Chapter 4: Different Reasons to Choose a Community College

This chapter explores different reasons why four of the EL participants chose to attend a community college. Erica and Alexandra opted for

LCC because they felt that, linguistically, they were not ready to cope with four-year college coursework. Josephine decided that she could not afford a four-year college, and Kadi viewed LCC as a stepping-stone to becoming a registered nurse. All four students' decision to attend LCC was influenced by the institutional discourse that their teachers and counselors adopted: 'You can always transfer to a four-year college later'. In making this recommendation, Brighton educators seemed to genuinely believe that it was entirely possible – in fact likely – for LCC students to transfer to a four-year college later. But statistics suggest that transferring from a community college, including LCC, to a four-year college is anything but automatic for ELs.

Eddie's story

Eddie, a Spanish L1 speaker who was born in the United States but grew up in Mexico, had a baby in 11th grade with his girlfriend, a fellow Brighton student. Parenting responsibilities and his own illness led to chronic absenteeism and multiple failed courses. Eddie wanted to become a car mechanic but did not know how to do so in the United States. In the end, he graduated from high school after taking extra summer school classes, but having received no guidance on how to pursue a career in automotive technology, he subsequently took up construction work.

Carlos's story

The only long-term EL in the study, Carlos, a Spanish L1 speaker from Ecuador, was considered seriously at risk. He skipped the whole fall semester of 12th grade and was widely expected to drop out. Knowing that his high school graduation mattered to his parents, however, Carlos came back in the spring of 12th grade, and eventually graduated after repeating his senior year. Regrettably, he received no career guidance in the process and started working as a busboy at a local restaurant after high school graduation.

Chapter 5: Not Career Ready

This chapter examines how Brighton failed to make non-college-bound ELs such as Carlos and Eddie career ready. While underachieving and chronically absent, these two ELs had viable talents and interests, which, if recognized and integrated into their school curricula, could have led them to productive careers. As a large comprehensive high school, Brighton in fact had CTE programs that matched these students' interests.

However, educators saw the problems that Carlos and Eddie faced as resulting from their or their parents' poor choices or deficiencies. Consequently, these educators failed to recognize Carlos and Eddie's potential or the institutional practices which marginalized the students, and concentrated their energy on just getting them to graduate. Carlos and Eddie thus obtained a high school diploma but without becoming career ready in the process.

Chapter 6: ELs' Access to Postsecondary Education

This final chapter revisits the main themes from the previous chapters and provides a theoretical exploration of how, together, these themes reduce ELs' access to PSE. I argue that Brighton consistently applied lower expectations to ELs, such that even the highest-performing EL students were neither expected nor supported to apply to a four-year college. Instead, LCC was deemed an appropriate choice for them given that their English language proficiency was still under development. ELs, on their part, internalized some of the deficit orientation directed at them and did not demand more learning opportunities or better college guidance from the school. Meanwhile, lower-performing students such as Carlos and Eddie were even worse off. In a high school that held markedly lower expectations for ELs and yet simultaneously espoused a strong 'college-for-all' orientation, they were given little guidance on how to plan for a life after high school that did not include college. In other words, they were left to fall into the 'underserved third' (Deil-Amen & DeLuca, 2010), a disenfranchised group of students who leave high school neither college nor career ready. Based on these findings, at the end of the chapter, I offer several recommendations that could begin to address the systemic inequities that reduce ELs' access to PSE.

Notes

(1) Typically, middle school in the United States encompasses Grades 6–8 and high school Grades 9–12, although there are some regional differences.
(2) Throughout this book, PSE includes four-year colleges and universities, two-year community colleges and trade/vocational schools, while college refers specifically to four-year colleges and community colleges.
(3) The names of the school, the districts and the participants in this study are pseudonyms. I kept the real names of the four-year colleges and universities to which the students applied in order to provide a sense of the types of schools they thought were within their reach. Unlike the community college nearby, which I call Local Community College (LCC), in which many of the study participants eventually enrolled, the universities and four-year colleges they applied to were not particularly close to the

location of their high school and therefore pose low risk to the confidentiality of the participants and the school.

(4) Because this is a longitudinal study, I mark the dates of interviews or field notes cited. Interviews are identified as IN followed by month/date/year; field notes are marked as FN.

(5) Title I, as noted previously, is the largest federal education grant program, which provides supplementary funding to public schools with high concentrations of low-income students. The funds can be used to provide additional support to help academically struggling students to meet the state standards in core subjects (US Department of Education, 2018a).

(6) I actually worked with eight students for the larger project. However, in this book, I decided to focus on seven of the students, leaving out the eighth participant, Sam. See the appendix for more details.

(7) The SAT and the ACT are two standardized tests that are widely used for college admissions in the United States. Many four-year colleges require applicants to submit either SAT or ACT scores.

Ken's Story

Ken came to the United States from Taguig, the Philippines, at age 15 and entered 10th grade at Brighton. He was the youngest of the study participants – still 16 when I first met him – and indeed he appeared quite young. While the other male students had already reached their full height and had developed a hardness about them, Ken was still a 'boy' – still in the process of growing in height and had a disarmingly affectionate smile.

Ken immigrated to the United States with his parents and two sisters and settled in the Brighton area because relatives already lived there. Ken did not seem to know the exact reasons for his parents' decision to immigrate; he described their motivation generically as getting a better life and better jobs. His father's job was to look after lab animals that would be used in experiments at a nearby large hospital. His mother worked at the cafeteria of another hospital. Neither parent was college-educated but had strong expectations for all their children to obtain a college degree because, in Ken's words, 'they don't want us to get the things [i.e. hardships] that they've been through' (IN 05/26/2011).

Spring Junior Year

Ken wanted to become a nurse. This decision was clearly influenced by his mother, who was pursuing a nursing degree at LCC during this study, and also by his older sister, who was in the pharmacy program at the same college. Ken never actually expressed any intrinsic interest in nursing itself, such as wanting to help others or become involved in the medical field. Rather, the primary attraction seemed to be the stability of a nursing career and wide employment opportunities. He noted that his parents had told him that 'there's a lot of money if you became a nurse' (IN 05/19/2011). Similarly, there was a strong utilitarian orientation toward going to college as well: going to college was first and foremost a means to getting a good job. Setting his mind on becoming a nurse, Ken had a clear goal of getting into a nursing program at a university.

Ken was generally known as a hard-working student who earned good grades in his classes. Indeed, except for a pair of large stud earrings that he took to wearing, his demeanor and appearance gave him the air of a 'model minority' (Lee, 1996) student. He noted, however, that this hard-working self was a new identity for him: ''cause back in my country, I was like, I don't study. I don't care about school' (IN 05/19/2011). He started studying much harder once he arrived in the United States because, as he put it, 'I'm scared' (IN 05/19/2011) – scared of the new country, the large school in which he had been placed and the people who spoke a language he did not really understand. All the fear of the unknown and unfamiliar drove him to study hard because he did not know what would happen if he failed in his academic work. He had studied English as a subject matter from first grade in the Philippines but spoke very little of it when he first arrived. However, by the time I met him in the spring of his junior year, he had reached 5.2 on the Assessing Comprehension and Communication in English State-to-State (ACCESS) test, and 1081 on the Scholastic Reading Inventory (SRI).[1]

Neither parent was college educated back in the Philippines, but his mother and a sister had started attending a community college. Having family members who were currently attending a community college gave Ken a certain amount of hands-on college knowledge (Conley, 2005; Vargas, 2004). He took the PSAT in 10th grade – the only participant in the study to do so – and he visited LCC with his mother in the 11th grade. He also took the SAT for the first time in May of his junior year. Thus, in the spring of his junior year, there was every indication that Ken was on track with his college planning.

Fall Senior Year

During the fall semester of his senior year, however, something unexpected happened: Ken started slacking off. He skipped some study hall periods by going straight to lunch, and for that he received a few detentions. His grades began to drop too – not dramatically, but enough for his teachers and counselor to notice. It was Mrs Anderson, his EL teacher and the teacher of his study hall period, who alerted me that Ken was skipping some classes. Later, his guidance counselor, Mrs Salomon, confirmed that other teachers had noticed too. After talking about another participant, Eddie, 'fall[ing] into the wrong crowd', she noted that she was concerned that Ken was 'going the same route'. Mrs Salomon continued, 'I think teachers that had him last year are saying the same thing. Their concern is that they feel like he's off-track. Yeah. Like he's more on the social part and probably not [with] some good friends' (IN 11/09/2011). At first, Ken denied that his attitude had changed, claiming that he skipped a few study hall periods ''cause it's so boring' (IN 11/14/2011). However, later he admitted that he was indeed off track:

Yasuko: Mrs. Anderson, she said that she thought you know, you were very hard working and studious in the 11th [grade], but going into the 12th, she felt that you were kind of starting to slack off and then you, maybe you started hanging out with 'wrong' friends. ... Do you think that's true?

Ken: Yeah, that's true [laughs]. (IN 06/8/2012)

With his academic motivation sagging, Ken's college planning slowed down as well. I interviewed him in September of his senior year, and I was surprised by his lack of progress *and* lack of concern. When I asked Ken what progress he had made during the summer, he gave an unenthusiastic 'Nothing' (IN 09/19/2011). Nonetheless, when pressed further, he named Drexel, Temple, Penn State and Neumann Universities – all in-state universities – as the schools where he was considering applying: the first time that he named particular colleges. He was planning to apply to the nursing programs at these universities, with Drexel University's nursing program being his top choice.

Admittance into a university's nursing program is often more challenging than being admitted to other programs at the same university because nursing programs usually have specific admissions requirements. For example, Drexel University's nursing program had the following admission requirements:

- Four years of high school English,
- Three years of high school mathematics, including algebra 1, algebra 2 and geometry,
- Two years of high school science, including biology, chemistry or physics, and
- Two years of high school social studies

An analysis of Ken's high school transcript showed that he did meet all the course requirements, but all his courses were low-level courses.

At Brighton, core academic courses were leveled, and they ran (from low to high): remedial, regular (i.e. on-grade level), advanced, honors and advanced placement (AP). Educators referred to remedial and regular courses as 'low-track' courses and advanced, honors and AP courses as 'high-track' courses. EL sheltered courses were not part of this leveling; however, as I describe in Chapter 2, students completing sheltered courses usually transitioned to remedial courses. In mathematics, then, Ken took geometry and algebra 1 at the remedial level, and algebra 2 and another college-level algebra course at the regular level. In science, his biology course was at the remedial level, while his chemistry course was at the regular level. All his English courses had an EL designation (Table S1). Altogether, his high school GPA was 89.2%. To a sympathetic admissions officer familiar with EL education, Ken's transcript would represent an EL who, since his arrival barely two years prior, had made good strides in the US education system. But to an average admissions officer, his transcript would indicate substandard academic preparation in high school.

Also, Drexel University held an orientation session for those students who were interested in applying to the nursing program in November. Many nursing programs hold such meetings (both at four-year and community colleges) and interested candidates are strongly encouraged to attend. Although Ken had mentioned he was planning to attend the orientation

Table S1   Ken's mathematics, science and English courses

Subject	Grade	Course	Level
Mathematics	10	EL Prealgebra	Sheltered
	11	Geometry	Remedial
	11	Algebra 1	Remedial
	12	Algebra 2	Regular
	12	College-Level Algebra 2	Regular
Science	10	EL Physical Science	Sheltered
	11	Biology	Remedial
	12	Chemistry	Regular
	12	Earth Science	Elective
English	10	EL Language Development (×2)	ELD
	11	EL Reading	ELD
	11/12	EL Language Arts (×2)	ELD

Note: English language development (ELD) courses focus specifically on ELs' English language proficiency development.

at Drexel, in the end he never did. Similarly, he never visited any of the universities to which he was planning to apply. All his preferences and aspirations, therefore, were based on the information he gathered on the Internet and college fairs at Brighton as well as word-of-mouth reputations he heard from people around him. At times, such word-of-mouth information was less than accurate. For example, the main reason why Ken preferred Drexel was that his father told him that because of its quarter system, students could graduate from its nursing program in less than four years. However, the university's website clearly stated that its nursing program was either four or five years.

Although his mother and sister were attending LCC and could give some concrete guidance on Ken's college planning, applying to a four-year school was new territory for the family, and Ken had many questions as he prepared his college applications. For instance, he was not sure whether it was better to submit his applications online or to send hard copies by mail (Brighton strongly encouraged students to apply online whenever it was an option). However, he expressed a strong aversion to seeking the guidance of his assigned counselor, Mrs Salomon. Mrs Salomon was a dedicated and experienced counselor with expertise in college applications; she could have clarified many of the questions that Ken had about applying to college in a matter of minutes. However, when I asked Ken why he had not consulted Mrs Salomon about his applications, he responded, 'I don't know her!' (IN 11/14/2011). Also, because of the recent detentions he had received, in Ken's mind, going to see a guidance counselor was probably strongly associated with getting into trouble. He was, comparatively speaking, more comfortable approaching Mrs Anderson, his EL and study hall teacher. However, the problem was that Mrs Anderson had limited knowledge about college planning herself, having just moved from an elementary school the previous year.

Spring Senior Year

In the February of his senior year, four months before his graduation, Ken's parents suddenly decided to relocate to New Jersey. For quite some time, his parents had been planning to buy a house in New Jersey where there was a large Filipino community. Ken was aware of their plans but did not anticipate they would leave until after his graduation. However, in February, his parents decided to move. Ken was completely caught off guard, and he was shocked when his parents arrived at the school in the middle of a school day and told him to gather his things because they were leaving immediately. The precise reason for his parents' sudden move is not clear to me because Ken himself was unclear. He told me later that his parents had some disputes with their landlord, which prompted their sudden departure.[2]

This untimely relocation was hard on Ken. When other seniors were finishing up their last semester of high school and looking forward to celebrating graduation with classmates, Ken had to start all over again at a new school for the remaining four months. He regretted having no time to let his friends know that he was leaving: 'I [was] always pretty upset when I moved 'cause I didn't get to say, like, you know, good-byes to my, good-byes to my friends and stuff. I just like moved without saying anything' (IN 02/27/2012).

As the relocation happened in February, it had little impact on Ken's college application itself – apart from applying to Rutgers University, now that it was within commuting distance from his new home. Although Ken himself found the move traumatic, there may have been some benefits. Mrs Anderson, who was fond of Ken and was concerned about his socializing with the 'wrong crowd', pointed out that his relocation physically removed him from those bad influences. Indeed, after the move, Ken seemed to refocus on finishing high school and getting ready to go to college.

In the end, Ken applied to Drexel, Penn State, Rutgers and Widener Universities, all to their nursing programs. He also applied to LCC as a backup. The only university that accepted him was Widener University, a medium-size suburban private university in Chester, PA. He was admitted, not to its nursing program, but to 'exploratory studies' (i.e. undeclared major). Moreover, his admission came with the condition of successfully completing the summer bridge program called Project Prepare. According to Widener's website:

> Widener University's program, known as Project Prepare, offers academic coaching throughout the academic year for *academically disadvantaged students* who enter Widener University through the Project Prepare summer bridge program. ... These students must successfully complete this program *in order to gain admission into Widener University's Exploratory Studies program.* (Emphasis added)

Although Widener is a much less selective university than the other three, these conditions of acceptance suggest that even by Widener's standards, Ken was considered 'academically disadvantaged'.

Intent on going to a four-year college, Ken decided to attend Widener University in the fall and was determined to eventually enroll in its nursing program. About his conditional acceptance, however, Ken was ambivalent at best. He said, 'I'm pretty happy about it, I mean [pause], if I [pause] I don't know [pause] maybe not [pause] I'm not satisfied. I'm not satisfied about it' (IN 06/8/2012). In particular, through his experiences of the college application process and its outcome, Ken realized that he had not received sufficiently rigorous academic preparation since his arrival in the United States. Interestingly, his move to a new school added to that realization. His new school was smaller and more academically oriented than Brighton. Talking to the guidance counselors there about the process of transferring course credits from Brighton and finishing his college applications, Ken realized the kinds of courses he should have been taking to qualify for his intended major. Reflecting on his experiences at Brighton, he said, 'I feel like I took classes that haven't reached my expectations 'cause I didn't really need the–, some of my classes', and he concluded, 'I just wish that [I had had] the opportunity to be more ready, you know' (IN 06/08/2012).

Notes

(1) An ACCESS score of 5.2 is well above the threshold level of 4.8 that was considered fluent English proficient in Pennsylvania at the time of this study, while a score of 1,081 on the SRI put Ken at the lower end of grade-level reading skills for 11th-grade students. In other words, as far as his English language proficiency was concerned, Ken reached the reclassification threshold within two years of arrival, which suggests that his English language proficiency at the time of arrival was higher than he himself claimed. However, because he scored Below Basic in the state standardized mathematics test (see Table S1) – a reclassification requirement was a score of basic at the minimum – he was retained as an EL in 12th grade.

(2) Ken's family's financial situation had been stable. For his parents to pick him up at the school unannounced and tell him to gather his things for an immediate and permanent departure is a highly unusual situation and indicates a crisis of some sorts – possibly an eviction. Unfortunately, I was never able to find out the exact nature of the family's sudden relocation.

2 Limited Access to Rigorous Academic Curriculum

We saw in Ken's story how limited access to advanced coursework on the one hand, and his lack of awareness of the importance of such coursework for college admission on the other, prevented him from being admitted to any of the nursing programs to which he applied. The limited access to advanced college preparatory courses was not unique to Ken, but a common theme across the participants. This chapter examines why and how this low tracking of EL students happened at Brighton and the consequences of this low tracking for their PSE choices, especially four-year college admission.

ELs' Concentration in Low-Track Courses

As I noted in Ken's story, Brighton's core academic courses (English, mathematics, social studies and science) were divided into five levels: remedial, regular, advanced, honors and advanced placement (AP). Remedial and regular levels were considered low tracks, while advanced, honors and AP levels were considered high tracks. As Table 2.1 shows, with the exception of Erica and Alexandra, who were Spanish first language (L1) speakers and took AP Spanish, none of the ELs took high-track courses. Instead, there is a strong representation of remedial-level courses on their transcripts.

Upon closer inspection, the students' transcripts reveal some connection between the students' level of achievement and their coursework. High-achieving ELs took relatively higher-level courses than low-achieving students. For example, although there were four Spanish L1 students among the participants (Erica, Alexandra, Eddie and Carlos), only Erica and Alexandra enrolled in AP Spanish. This indicates that not all Spanish L1 students had automatic access to advanced-level Spanish; rather, being recommended to take AP Spanish was a mark of institutional recognition of high performance. Some variations also appeared in their

Table 2.1 Participants' course-taking patterns

| Students | GPA (%) | EL | | Low-track | | High-track | | |
		ELD[a]	Sheltered[b]	Remedial	Regular	Advanced	Honors	AP[c]
Erica	90.2	4	2	5	7	0	0	1
Alexandra	89.5	5	2	5	3	0	0	1
Ken	89.2	7	3	7	2	0	0	0
Josephine	86.2	5	3	14	2	0	0	0
Kadi	82.3	1	0	8	0	0	0	0
Eddie	72.3	10	10	9	1	0	0	0
Carlos	57.1	5	0	23	1	0	0	0

Note: Only core courses (English, social studies, mathematics and science) and world language courses are included in the table. The number of courses each student took is not uniform for the following reasons: (a) some students enrolled at Brighton in the middle of high school or left before graduation, and only the courses that they took at this school are included in the table; and (b) some students failed some courses, and repeated courses are counted twice.
[a] English language development (ELD) courses include EL English, EL Reading and EL Language Arts.
[b] EL sheltered courses include EL Physical Science, EL Biology, EL US History and EL Global Studies.
[c] The AP course that Erica and Alexandra took was AP Spanish.

mathematics courses. Knowledge of mathematics, above all other subjects, serves as a gatekeeper to accessing higher education regardless of whether or not students are science, technology, engineering and mathematics (STEM) majors (Battey, 2013; Martin, 2009). More specifically, recent research suggests that taking algebra 2 is a strong indicator of a student's chances of graduating from high school (Kanno & Cromley, 2015), and taking one mathematics course beyond algebra 2 is a key indicator of a student's viability in a four-year college (Adelman, 2006). Algebra 2 was a graduation requirement at Brighton. Four of the seven students took one course beyond algebra 2 while the remaining three stopped at algebra 2. The higher-achieving students Erica and Ken took college algebra (below pre-calculus, but one course above algebra 2, and the highest regular-level mathematics course that students could take in 12th grade). Josephine and Kadi also took one course above algebra 2, but it was Remedial Probability and Statistics.[1] Nonetheless, these are fine-grained variations within the narrow range of the lower-track course at Brighton. The fact remains that with the exception of Erica and Alexandra's enrollment in AP Spanish, the participants had no access to high-track courses during their tenure at Brighton.

Initially, it was not clear whether this pattern was happenstance – did the study participants happen to be concentrated in low-track courses? – or was this, in fact, a reflection of ELs' overall course-taking patterns at Brighton? In order to answer this question, I requested from the school a list of 12th-grade ELs and recently reclassified students (those who had exited the EL program but were still monitored on their progress), and the AP course rosters, and I cross-referenced them. AP rosters for 12th grade students constitute the best indicator of students' tracking at Brighton since in order to reach AP courses in 12th grade, a student must have taken high-track courses beforehand (see Figures 2.1 and 2.2).

The result was clear: the low-level course-taking pattern that I identified among the participants was a reflection of ELs' course-taking patterns at Brighton at large. Of all 12th graders at Brighton in 2011–2012, 15.2% took at least one AP course. Some students took multiple AP courses: for example, nearly all students who were enrolled in AP Physics in 12th grade were also enrolled in AP Calculus at the same time. Twenty four students took three AP courses, 11 students took four courses, and four students took five courses. In contrast, none of the 46 EL seniors took AP courses, except for two Spanish L1 speakers and two French L1 speakers who took AP Spanish and AP French, respectively. Reclassified students did not fare much better: among the 15 reclassified

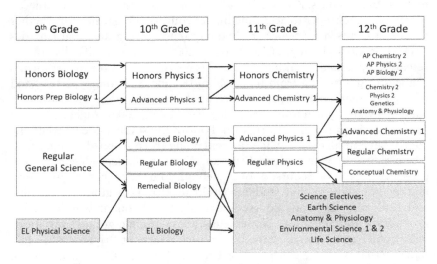

Figure 2.1 Science course sequence from ninth grade to 12th grade. *Note*: Arrows represent possible course pathways. The shaded areas represent the most common course selections for ELs. Science electives were not leveled and could technically be taken by any students; however, in practice, they were taken predominantly by low-track students who did not qualify for higher-level, lab-based science courses such as Chemistry and Physics.

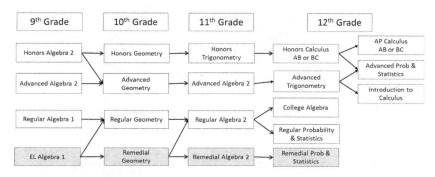

Figure 2.2 Mathematics course sequence from ninth grade to 12th grade. *Note:* Arrows represent possible course pathways. The shaded areas represent the most common course selections for ELs. *Note:* In ninth grade, Erica and Alexandra had not yet enrolled in Brighton. They arrived in 10th grade. The percentages indicate students' course grades.

seniors, only one student took an AP course (AP Computer Science). Clearly, ELs at Brighton had limited access to high-track courses.

From EL Sheltered to Remedial Courses

How did ELs' uniform low tracking happen? In order to answer this question, I need to first explain how course sequencing and course leveling worked at Brighton High School.

Brighton had established course sequences for each core subject area (see Figure 2.1 for a chart of the science course sequences and Figure 2.2 for a chart of the mathematics course sequences). Teachers usually referred to these sequences in recommending students' courses for the next year unless there was a particularly compelling reason to change a student's course level. Similarly, guidance counselors generally honored teachers' recommendations unless they knew the particular circumstances of a student's academic or personal life that warranted a different course choice. In other words, although these sequences were not entirely rigid and there was some flexibility in making individual accommodations, they represent the default academic trajectories for the majority of students from year to year.

One of the most striking patterns that I found in the study participants' academic course trajectories was that once they completed their EL sheltered courses, regardless of how they performed in those classes, they were nearly always placed in remedial sections of the next subject course in the sequence. For example, once an EL completed EL Algebra 1 in ninth grade,

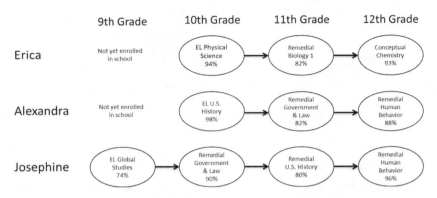

Figure 2.3 Three participants' course pathways from EL sheltered courses

they were most likely to be placed in remedial geometry, rather than in regular, advanced or honors geometry (Figure 2.2). Figure 2.3 shows three examples of the course-taking patterns of EL students who started out with EL sheltered courses. As the figure clearly shows, Erica took EL Physical Science in 10th grade and earned 94% in course grade, but she was nonetheless placed in Remedial Biology 1 in 11th grade. Interestingly, although she did not do as well in Remedial Biology 1 (82% final grade), she was nonetheless moved to Conceptual Chemistry, a regular-level chemistry course, in 12th grade, instead of one of the elective science courses that most ELs take in their senior year. I believe that this reflects the school's recognition of Erica's overall academic achievement (at least among ELs). Similarly, Alexandra took EL US History in 10th grade, earning 98% at the end, but was nonetheless placed in Remedial Government and Law in 11th grade and stayed at the remedial level for social studies through 12th grade. Josephine's course-taking pattern is probably the most telling of the three, since she spent all four of her high school years at Brighton, starting mostly with EL courses in Grade 9. In other words, Josephine's transcript reflects the typical course-taking pattern of those students who entered Brighton in the ninth grade as ELs. As Figure 2.3 shows, Josephine started out her social studies sequence with EL Global Studies in ninth grade (and did not do very well), exited into Remedial Government and Law in 10th grade, and earned 90% in that course. Nevertheless, she was placed in Remedial US History in 11th grade, where she received a grade of 80%. She concluded her social studies sequence with Remedial Human Behavior in 12th grade and ended the course with 96%. All these three cases show two patterns: (a) the movement from EL sheltered courses into remedial courses was near-automatic; and (b) once placed in a remedial-level course, students' chances of ever climbing out of remedial-level courses were extremely low. It did not matter whether the student did well or not in the previous course, the next course was almost always another remedial course.

Trapped in the Remedial Track

This second pattern, ELs' entrapment in the remedial track, raises the question of why that was the case. In principle, ELs should have been able to progress from an EL sheltered course to an AP course by their senior year by ascending one level each year. However, as we have just seen, this rarely happened. The guidance counselors I consulted about this matter told me that although there were some exceptional students who managed to defy the odds, it was so rare that they could count such students on one hand. Close examination of remedial classes gives us some insights into why this ascendance was so rare: it concerns both the demotivating atmosphere and the low-level instruction in remedial courses.

First, with regard to the demoralizing atmosphere of the remedial classes, Mr Woznyj, EL Department Chair, lamented that many ELs who were once bright-eyed and highly motivated in his classes would rapidly lose their drive and become acclimated into the culture of the remedial classes. Taking Josephine as an example, he said,

> [Josephine] struck me as a smart, kind of sharp.... And I said, 'This is a girl who could succeed working the right way.' And she had the work ethic. But, when you put her in, even a regular-level class in this building where just behavior and attitude towards education is so different than even EL [classes], I see the students change. You know, I see them more—My joke is that they're Americanized now or Brighton-ized. (IN 01/06/2012)

Indeed, observing Josephine in one of her classes brought home to me how disruptive the environment was and how extraordinarily difficult it would be to sustain one's motivation in such a milieu. In Ms Morris's US history class, a substantial amount of class time was spent on controlling student banter and side conversations. In the following segment, students were supposed to work individually on a worksheet on Nixon's presidency, but as far as I could see, Josephine was the only student who was actually working on the worksheet:

> (1:41 pm) Josephine takes out a lip balm and swipes it across her lips. She seems to have finished the task. She is the only one who has finished so

far – no wonder since she was the one who concentrated on the task the most. (1:45 pm) The noise level goes up again. One student shouts, 'Ba, ba, ba, boom!' to which another student responds, 'Just shut up.' Mrs. Morris stands in front of a student who is making a noise and tells him, 'Knock it off.'

Josephine is looking through her notebook. The noisy boy raises his hand. Morris takes about 10 seconds before she responds. The boy makes a whole speech about how he suffers the whole day in hell but when he comes to her room, his day brightens up. Another student says, 'You're a liar,' to which the first boy says, 'I speak from my heart, man.' Mrs. Morris doesn't react one way or other and just pretty much ignores him. Josephine is reading another book, maybe a novel from another class (FN 05/26/2011)

What was striking about this scene was first, how disruptive the supposedly individual seat work was, and second, how Josephine was totally uninvolved in any of the student banter – a pattern that I witnessed repeatedly with the EL participants in their remedial classes.

Remedial classes were marked with frequent interruptions, sudden loud noises and nearly constant chatter. Teachers who routinely taught remedial-level (or even regular-level) classes seemed to deliberately adopt a tough persona in front of students. Even teachers who were soft-spoken in front of other adults suddenly sounded tough and blunt in their remedial-level classes, emanating the 'Don't mess with me' aura. For instance, when one student in Regular Geometry complained about the grading system, Ms King, a young math teacher, gave him the cold shoulder: 'The world does not revolve around you, sorry' (FN 05/19/2011). A teacher's harsh reprimand was usually prompted by a student's rude or inappropriate remark. These exchanges were so commonplace that they were an integral part of the normal pedagogical discourses of the remedial classes. The teachers usually looked unfazed by this level of disruption in class,[2] but nonetheless often responded with a biting comeback to prevent the disruption from escalating or simply to express their displeasure.

Another major characteristic of remedial classes was low-level instruction. Much of what happened in those classes was busywork, designed to keep students in their seats and keep them quiet rather than promoting higher-order thinking. In my analysis, I have coded as many as 51 instances of low-level instruction in remedial- and regular-level classes (Table A1 in the Appendix), which included (a) asking known-information questions that can be answered with a word or phrase, (b) materials that were of dubious academic value and (c) content that was clearly below grade level. For example, in one Life Science class, the teacher, Mrs Baker, showed Al Gore's 'An Inconvenient Truth'. Because of the controversial nature of the film, it could have served as a basis for a lively and thought-provoking conversation. Watching the film, I also felt that although Al Gore's overall message was powerful, there were some places in the film where the data were manipulated to support his claims. In other words, the film presented good material for a critical discussion of both climate change and what constitutes evidence. My hopes went up momentarily: finally, a teacher who was willing to engage students in a critical discussion! However, what ensued was a series of comprehension-check questions based on a worksheet. There were 38 questions on the worksheet, of which the following is a subset with every fifth question taken:

Q5. What year did Al Gore go to Kyoto, Japan?
Q10. What happened on April 3, 1989, that shook Al Gore's world?
Q15. How many cities in the West were hit with all-time temperature records in that same year [2003]?
Q20. How soon could the Arctic sea ice be gone in summer?
Q25. How fast is the current extinction rate compared to normal levels?
Q.30 How long will a frog stay in a pot of water that is gradually getting hotter and hotter?
Q35 Who said, 'It is difficult to get a man to understand something when his salary depends on his not understanding it'?

In other words, Mrs Baker was simply checking students' comprehension of the film, making sure to keep them awake in the darkened classroom during an after-lunch period. For the entire 45 minutes, Mrs Baker paused the film every so often to ask a few of these questions, all squarely at the levels of knowledge and comprehension on Bloom's Taxonomy (Krathwohl, 2002). Not once did she ask her students what they thought of the film or the arguments that Gore presented.

In sum, given that remedial-level classes were marked with frequent disruptions and clashes between teachers and students, they did not provide the kind of learning environment that increased student motivation. Moreover, even the rare students who managed to sustain their motivation would not have been able to move up the track given the low-level content taught in these courses. By the end of one semester, there would be a clear difference in the content knowledge of students placed in a remedial-level course and those placed in the same subject-matter course at a higher level, thus reducing the chances of ever climbing out of the remedial track.

Teachers Did Not Recommend and Students Did Not Ask

Another factor in ELs' low tracking was the interaction between the school's institutional habitus and the students' individual habitus. More concretely, educators wanted to 'protect ELs' from the potential failure of being placed in too advanced courses for their capacity while ELs did not advocate for themselves. I saw no evidence of educators recommending high-track courses to any of the seven participants in this study, nor did I see evidence that any of the study participants requested higher-level courses than were recommended.

Teachers and guidance counselors generally seemed much more concerned about overwhelming ELs with the high demands of reading and writing involved in high-track courses than underchallenging them by placing them in low-track courses. Thus, 'protecting ELs' was a prevalent institutional discourse that reflected Brighton's institutional habitus concerning ELs' capabilities. This discourse was referenced by educators in different departments to explain ELs' low tracking. For example, when I asked Mrs Hernandez, one of the counselors, why ELs ended up in low-track courses, she acknowledged that it was a balancing act with which she often struggled. Nonetheless, she preferred to err on the side of caution:

> If they take an advanced class, you know, and maybe with this professor or that professor, the workload might be such [that], I want, I'd rather that they be in an environment where they can really ingest all the information and really own it and really understand it, rather than be constantly running after whatever it is. (IN 11/02/2011)

Even Mr Woznyj, EL Department Chair, who vehemently complained about the chaotic and demoralizing environment in remedial classes, hesitated to place ELs in advanced classes because of the potential high reading and writing demands in those courses:

> I've taught honors to remedial. And I know, like we are reading *The Scarlet Letter* and you're reading 50 pages a night and then you're writing, not five-paragraph essays; you're writing kind of more sophisticated essays. ... The jump from a room that's so diverse where really [as a teacher] you'd have to keep it at kind of a middle level to what they're going to face in an AP, it's so large that it can't be a direct jump. It's very hard to go from an EL class to an AP class. (IN 01/06/2012)

Mr Woznyj is accurate in stating that it is not reasonable to send a student from an EL class directly to an AP class; such a trajectory is simply too unrealistic. However, he is less than accurate in suggesting that an EL student can gradually move their way up by climbing the ladder one step at a time every year. As we have seen, such a progression rarely happened: students were semi-automatically placed in remedial classes once they completed EL sheltered courses regardless of their performance. Once they were placed in the remedial tracks, they tended to stay there.

On their part, EL students did not request higher-level courses than they were recommended. It is important to note that at Brighton, course recommendations were not absolute; they were *recommendations*. In other words, if a student or their parents felt that a recommended course was not appropriate, they could request to take a different course – a higher-level or lower-level course – and the school would oblige.[3] Mr Burke, Director of Guidance, noted, 'If the student wants to argue for a higher level or lower level, they could make their case with the teacher. Discuss it with the teacher ... they can convince the teacher to do that' (IN 10/03/2011). As an educator who valued students who took the initiative in charting their own paths, Mr Burke in fact appreciated those students who advocated for themselves to take the courses they wanted, and some students did make such requests.

However, as Mr Woznyj attested, EL students rarely contested the school's course recommendations. As Harklau (1994: 352) observed, in order for students to challenge the school's tracking decisions, 'students had to realize that there were indeed systematic differences between classes and that there was something to be negotiated', of which, I found, most of the study participants were unaware. First, they had a nebulous understanding of all the course leveling that went on in the school and exactly where in the level they were located. I would often ask them what levels of courses they were taking, and they would say they did not know. Second, so accustomed to always being told what to do – as opposed to being consulted about their preferences – ELs simply assumed that the coursework decisions that the school made for them were non-negotiable. However, there are subtle but important differences in their acquiescence, and it is worth discussing those differences in some detail, especially among Erica, Alexandra and Ken, who were the three highest-performing students in this study and therefore were in a better position to negotiate for higher courses. Ken categorically declared, 'Only electives, you can only pick electives' (IN 05/26/2011), suggesting that he was not even aware that students had a say in choosing their core courses. Alexandra, unlike Ken, did not say that students could not choose; rather, she went along with her guidance counselor's recommendation. She said, '[My counselor] say[s] that these classes are good to take for me right now' (IN 09/28/2011), which implies that it did not occur to her to question the recommendation. Finally, Erica, being the daughter of a college-educated father who was closely involved in her school education and also having taken some relatively higher-level courses herself, had some awareness of course leveling. Nonetheless, she too assumed that if her guidance counselor did not recommend high-track courses for her, that meant that she just was not qualified:

Yasuko: Would you have been able to do that [i.e. take AP courses] if you had asked?

Erica: Mm, maybe, but I wasn't sure because they used to like, they normally give you the schedule, so I thought I was not able to take AP classes. So that's why I didn't ask. (IN 05/22/2012)

Also, as I will discuss in her narrative, Erica had an intense linguistic insecurity about her English proficiency, which also added to her self-assessment that she was not the kind of student who could take AP courses. In fact, the only instance in which she exerted agency and asked for a course change was to be moved down from a regular (i.e. non-EL) English class to an EL English class even when, according to Mr Woznyj, she was not doing poorly in the regular class. In other words, she requested to be moved down to an easier class, but never asked to be moved up.

If we consider how ELs were positioned within the overall institutional habitus of the school, these students' responses make sense. It is abundantly clear that at Brighton, ELs were constantly subject to lower educator expectations and were assumed to need hands-on support, a slower instructional pace and generally less challenging academic content. If individual habitus 'represents an individual's internalization of possibility' (Horvat, 2000: 209), and if ELs have a prolonged institutional history of being placed at the lowest rung of the academic hierarchy, it is a logical response on the part of the students not to expect any special attention or be asked for their preferences and instead to acquiesce to the roster of courses that are handed down to them. This way, educators did not recommend high-track courses for any of these seven students, and the students never asked for them.

A Different World: Honors and Advanced Placement Courses

Just as the EL participants were confined to low-track courses throughout high school, another group of students inhabited the world of high-track courses and never knew anything other than honors and AP classes. Observing these high-track classes was like stepping into a different world. Students in these courses were exposed to different discourse patterns and had much more intimate and trusting relationships with their teachers. In honors and AP classes, teachers treated their students as colleagues in inquiry, rather than a group of unruly teenagers who needed to be controlled. They asked challenging questions and, in turn, gave their students room to express their ideas. Often, there was a sense of humor and laughter in the classroom, a sign that they enjoyed each other's company. In this sense, these high-track classes resembled college classes more than remedial classes and served as a preview of what was to come in college. In other words, in some parts of the school – the parts that did not involve ELs – Brighton's institutional habitus of expecting students to go to four-year colleges and preparing them for college was highly visible.

For example, in Mr Garnier's AP Physics class, students' motivation to learn and the rapport between teacher and students were evident. In the particular class that I observed, students were working on past AP exam problems. Mr Garnier turned the task into a game by announcing that the worksheet was for credit and that the number of points they gained depended on how fast they could solve the questions correctly. Students worked in pairs, and as soon as they solved one question, they rushed to Mr Garnier's desk to have him check their answers. One question read:

> A platform executes simple harmonic oscillations along a vertical line. An object with a mass of 1.0 kg rests on the platform. The amplitude of the oscillations is 0.5 m. What is the least period of these oscillations if the object is not to be separated from the platform? (FN 12/13/2011)

Within two minutes of seat work, one student walked over to Mr Garnier's desk and aced the above question. The student celebrated the victory by high-fiving with his partner, proclaiming, 'Knocked that one right!' (FN 12/13/2011). Within three minutes, three other students had answered the same question correctly. However, not all questions were answered correctly the first time. Mr Garnier had a mocking way of responding to these errors, but in the context of established rapport between him and his students, the students did not seem to mind:

> [Garnier says,] 'Why do you people insist on multiplying by G?' One student asks him, 'Wait, do I get one extra point?' to which Mr. Garnier answers without missing a beat, 'No!' Most kids seem used to Mr.

> Garnier's light sarcasm and laugh it off rather than be mortified. They seem to take it as a game rather than a judgment of their ability. ... To the tall White female student pairing with an African American male student, Mr. Garnier says, 'No, you didn't fix that one. It's just ridiculously, simply, a minor mistake.' The female student repeats, 'Ridiculously simple mistake,' and mulls over the problem standing up. Her partner chimes in, and they go back and start working again. (FN 12/13/2011)

The whole mode of instruction in that class was students as independent learners and Mr Garnier serving as a motivator and facilitator of their learning.

In this and the other high-track classes I observed, the teachers' individual instructional styles differed. However, the courses were all marked by advanced-level content (Conley's [2007] core academic knowledge and skills for college readiness), the promotion of problem-solving and analytical skills (key cognitive strategies) and the teachers tapping into students' intrinsic motivation to learn. It is easy to imagine students who are placed in classes such as these in high school making a smooth transition to college classes. They are already used to their teachers treating them with respect and intellectually challenging them. Students in the high-track classes would find undergraduate classes comfortable and familiar milieus. In contrast, for students who were not exposed to high-track courses such as these, the gulf between high school and college classes would be much wider; it would be an entirely new way of relating to instructors and learning.

Limited Guidance on Cultural Capital Accrual

Thus, the seven ELs' coursework clearly indicates that they were given little opportunity to be exposed to the kind of academic preparation that would make them college ready. However, in other ways too, the ELs were not given enough guidance on how to accrue cultural capital effectively. Given increasingly competitive college admissions, it is important for all students to earn academic credentials and awards whenever they can. Yet, even when opportunities presented themselves, the ELs did not take advantage of them as much as they could have, while teachers and guidance counselors did not facilitate such capital accrual.

For example, Erica was on the honor roll (grade point average [GPA] of 85% or above with no single grade below 80%) in 10th grade and on the distinguished honor roll (GPA of 90% or above with no single grade below 85%) in 12th grade; Alexandra was on the distinguished honor roll in 10th grade. Erica had the possibility of being inducted into the National Honor Society but was advised against it by her counselor. She was told, 'It's not a good deal' (IN 05/22/2012) because it would cost $80 to become a member and yet the membership did not confer much value. However, distinctions such as being on the honor roll and being a member of the National Honor Society are, in fact, important forms of cultural capital that can signal a student's accomplishments during high school.

Within Brighton, these honors and accomplishments were used as a basis for awarding the school's own scholarships. At the end of their senior year, many students were celebrated for their various accomplishments at the Award Night. This is one of the happy events to which the families of the awardees are invited.[4] At the Award Night, members of the National Honor Society were recognized, with their names listed prominently on the evening's program – but clearly Erica's name was not on the list. Also, students who accomplished being on the distinguished honor roll for all four years were formally recognized and commended; had Erica enrolled in Brighton from ninth grade, she might have accomplished this feat. However, since she only enrolled in Brighton from 10th grade, this was not an award for which she was eligible.

Likewise, Alexandra achieved an exceptionally high score on the National Spanish Examination she took in 12th grade and was consequently inducted into the Sociedad Honoraria Hispánica (the National Spanish Honor Society), the very first student at Brighton to achieve this honor. For this accomplishment, Alexandra was given recognition at the Award Night – the only one among the seven students in this study who was invited to attend the event. However, apart from being given the recognition at the Award Night, no teacher or guidance counselor suggested that this was a major honor that Alexandra should highlight in her college application, or even that with an honor such as this she should definitely consider applying to a four-year college. As a result, although Alexandra was personally very proud of this accomplishment, she did not recognize it as a form of cultural capital that she could use to her advantage for her college applications.

These are two salient examples of the interaction between a school's institutional habitus and ELs' individual habitus. Even when ELs were distinguishing themselves by measures that were institutionally visible (e.g. honor roll, National Honor Society), the school did not invest in promoting these students' competitiveness for four-year college admission because they were ELs. The ELs, in turn, because of a combination of their own linguistic insecurity, their historical positioning in US schools and a lack of college knowledge, came to regard such absence of institutional support as nothing out of the ordinary. They did not demand better recognition of their achievements or better guidance on how to convert these achievements into viable cultural capital for four-year college admission. Unfortunately, this lack of self-advocacy on the part of ELs became part of the feedback loop perpetuating the school's institutional habitus. ELs' quiet acquiescence, in fact, further reinforced educators' assumption that even high-performing ELs like Erica and Alexandra were after all better off going to LCC because they lacked maturity and independence to chart their own four-year college trajectory. Even Mr Woznyj, who knew Brighton's EL students better than anyone else, criticized these two students for their passiveness:

> Those two girls would never approach me for help ever. Even if they're completely clueless. ... So, I could see them just getting or having questions, but just sitting back saying, 'Well, this isn't gonna just happen, you know. So, I guess it doesn't happen'. (IN 01/06/2012)

In other words, because ELs did not demand better recognition of their achievements, there was nothing disrupting the school's institutional habitus, and their lack of self-advocacy was taken as one more reason to steer ELs toward a community college pathway.

Consequences of Low Tracking for College Application

The limited access to high-track courses affected ELs who had aspirations to attend a four-year college. First, a transcript consisting of mostly EL and remedial courses resulted in a less than competitive college application. In the admissions process, US colleges and universities carefully examine applicants' high school transcripts with an eye toward whether or not the student took the most rigorous curriculum possible in their high school (National Research Council, 2002; Selingo, 2020). In other words, if a school does not offer AP Calculus, the highest AP mathematics course available, it is not within individual students' power at that school to take the course, and therefore it is not counted against them that they did not take AP Calculus. However, if a school offers a number of honors and AP courses, college admissions officers will certainly scrutinize individual applicants' high school transcripts from that school to examine the extent to which they availed themselves of these opportunities. Since Brighton offered a number of honors and

AP courses, not having taken *any* of those courses could be interpreted as students' lack of willingness to challenge themselves academically.

The negative consequences of the absence of high-track courses on one's high school transcript can be observed most clearly in Ken's college application, as we have seen in his story. From the beginning, Ken had a very clear career goal of becoming a nurse and aimed to enroll in a nursing program at a four-year university. In the end, however, he was rejected by all the nursing programs to which he applied, and I believe that this was in part due to his not having taken mathematics and science courses at an advanced level at Brighton. His sole acceptance letter came from a non-selective university as an undeclared major on the condition that he enroll in the university's summer remedial education.

Another negative consequence of low tracking is low performance on the college entrance exams, such as the SAT and the ACT. It is well known that standardized tests are not accurate measures of ELs' academic abilities because, in testing ELs in English, they inevitably confound their emerging English language proficiency with their academic knowledge (e.g. Abedi, 2004; Lane & Leventhal, 2015; Solórzano, 2008). That said, it is also likely the case that my participants' lack of opportunities to learn rigorous academic content in high school contributed to their low SAT scores. The top three students in this study, Erica, Alexandra and Ken, achieved cumulative GPAs of 89%–90%, which means that they were successful within the context of the courses given to them; however, their SAT scores were low (Table 2.2). Alexandra did not take the SAT for reasons that I will describe in later chapters; however, Ken and Erica took the exam. Ken scored 330 in critical reading, 480 in math and 390 in writing (for a total score of 1,200), whereas Erica scored 300 in reading, 390 in math and 230 in

Table 2.2 EL participants' GPAs and SAT scores

Student	GPA	SAT reading	SAT math	SAT writing	Total
Erica	90.2	300	390	230	920
Alexandra	89.5	–	–	–	–
Ken	89.2	330	480	390	1200
Josephine	86.2	430	370	401	1201
Kadi	82.3	470	410	380	1260
Eddie	72.3	–	–	–	–
Carlos	57.1	–	–	–	–

Note: Alexandra, Eddie and Carlos did not take the SAT.

writing (for a total score of 920). These scores are considerably lower than the mean scores of Brighton students: 440 in critical reading, 464 in math and 428 in writing (for a total score of 1,332). Moreover, Ken's scores were nowhere near the scores that average Drexel University students achieve, which were 540–640 in critical reading, 570–670 in math and 520–630 in writing in 2012. His low SAT scores, together with his non-competitive high school transcript, I believe, contributed to his being rejected by all nursing programs to which he applied.

Only after the participants had gone through college applications, and only after all the postsecondary decision had been made, did an awareness that they should have pursued higher-level courses more aggressively seem to arise. In the end, Erica decided to attend LCC without applying to any four-year college. But when I asked her what she would have done differently in her college preparation, she stated without skipping a beat, 'I would talk with my counselor about AP classes' (IN 05/22/2012), suggesting that she regretted not taking more advanced courses. Similarly, having been rejected by all the nursing programs, Ken lamented, 'I feel like I took classes that haven't reached my expectations 'cause I didn't really need some of my classes'. In Ken's case, his transfer to another, more academically rigorous school in the last semester of his senior year – disruptive though the move was – also gave him a basis for a comparison of the kind of academic preparation he could have received. Seeing that his peers at the new school had progressed further in math and science courses, Ken felt that he should have pursued calculus and physics while in high school. On the basis of his college application experience and his experience at his new high school, he had the following advice to ELs still in high school: 'I would tell them to take the classes that they—, that's related to the classes they're going to take in college and they're going to major in, so it won't be so hard to—' (IN 06/08/2012). He did not complete his last sentence, but one would assume that he meant to say that 'it won't be so hard to' be admitted to the program of their choice.

Summary

This chapter described how ELs were systematically excluded from accessing advanced college preparatory courses in high school, and how, as a result, such lack of cultural capital negatively impacted their college application. It was found that regardless of students' academic performance in EL sheltered classes, they were more or less automatically sent to remedial-level courses in the mainstream curriculum. On the basis of an analysis of ELS:2002, Callahan *et al.* (2010: 106) conclude that 'once schools place a student in ESL, access to college preparatory resources is reduced or, at the very least, not enhanced', and we see this exact pattern playing out at a micro-level at Brighton. The problem with this setup is that placement in low-track courses leads to further differentiation of academic knowledge from peers in high-track courses, turning their initial placement in remedial tracks to a permanent placement (Oakes, 2005). It is important to note that at Brighton, such institutional barriers to upward mobility were not a result of the staff's intentional exclusion of ELs from high-track courses or their judgment that ELs were undeserving. Rather, mostly it stemmed from educators' desire to 'protect ELs' from potential failure. Nonetheless, such overprotection was a reflection of the school's institutional habitus, which assumed ELs had lower abilities. As a result, ELs went through four years of high school without sufficient academic preparation to make them college ready. EL students, on their part, had underdeveloped knowledge of their say in the course selection process, and even when they were somewhat aware that students had some say in the matter, their individual habitus, their sense of what was within their reach, propelled them to acquiesce to the limited educational opportunities they were given.

Notes

(1) One aberration to this pattern was Alexandra, who only went up to algebra 2. By her own admission, mathematics was her weak subject.
(2) However, one teacher looked embarrassed about the chaos in his classroom when I observed his class and apologized afterwards for his students' rowdy behavior.
(3) One caveat, however, is that if a student insisted on taking a different course than recommended, there was no going back to the original course. Regardless of how well they were doing in the new course, they would have to remain in that course for the duration of the semester.
(4) Incidentally, this is one event that is extremely well attended by families, underscoring the fact that families do make time to attend school events when their children's accomplishments are formally recognized.

Alexandra's Story

Alexandra arrived from the Dominican Republic to the United States when she was 16. Her family first settled in New York, near close relatives, and Alexandra attended a transitional bilingual education program. However, after one year, the family moved to the Brighton area because her father found a job there. Alexandra was the second youngest of six children, ranging in age from 31 to 14. Because of immigration age restrictions, the three older siblings could not immigrate to the United States and remained in the Dominican Republic, so Alexandra lived with her parents and two other brothers. Her parents were not college-educated and did not speak English. At the time of this study, her father worked for a building maintenance company along with Alexandra's older brother, and her mother stayed at home.

Although none of her older siblings had gone to college, Alexandra and her parents clearly envisioned her attending a four-year college. She had always been an academically talented student, and her strong academic history translated into the family expectation of her going to college. Even at Brighton, where she was still in the process of learning English, Alexandra told me in her junior year that her current GPA was 93% and that she was on the honor roll. But Alexandra also characterized her college going as a matter of opportunity. Her older siblings wanted to go to college too, she said, but they simply did not have the opportunity she had:

> 'Cause they don't [have] the benefits that I can have now, 'cause in my country you need to have a lot of money to go to college, start to have, be a professional person. Well, I have dreams and things that I have to, uh, I need to be a professional person, to help my family. (IN 04/20/2011)

Alexandra was still young enough and had a few years to settle into the US education system before applying to college, and the whole family saw this as the first opportunity to send a child to college.

Spring Junior Year

Alexandra also had a focused career goal: she wanted to become a lawyer, perhaps an immigration lawyer. She explained that since she was an immigrant herself, she understood the plight of many immigrants in the United States and perceived the US government to be unfair to immigrants, especially undocumented immigrants:

> I think the government is unjust [to them] 'cause they came here to work hard, to have a better life, future, whatever for their, for them and their families. And the government sometimes don't, don't give them the uh, the— [Yasuko: Fair treatment?] Yeah. They don't treat them well like, like treat a lot of people from here as well. (IN 09/28/2011)[1]

She was also very clear about her priorities: 'I'm gonna be professional first, and then having a family. For me it's more important than having a family' (IN 04/20/2011).

Given this career goal, Alexandra's college plan was to advance straight to a university and perhaps major in psychology, another area of interest to her. In the spring of her junior year, she mentioned that she needed to take the SAT soon, although she had not registered for the exam. At the same time, she had little concrete knowledge of the steps that she needed to take to become a lawyer. She knew she needed to obtain a bachelor's degree, but beyond that she had little idea. She was even unfamiliar with the concept of law school:

Yasuko: Do you know what kinds of qualifications you need to do—you need to get in order to become a lawyer? What do you have to do to become a lawyer?

Alexandra: No, not really. I don't find that information yet. (IN 04/20/2011)

Fall Senior Year

The first in the family to go to college, Alexandra could not rely on family members for college knowledge and acknowledged that her parents could not provide any college guidance. When I asked whether her parents provided any information on college, she said flatly: 'I bring it 'cause they don't know anything' (IN 11/21/2011). However, she was also reluctant to seek help from her teachers and guidance counselors at Brighton. She said, 'I hate when I need to ask people for something' (IN 05/16/2012). Unsurprisingly, then, her college knowledge was underdeveloped. For example, although she vaguely named Pennsylvania State University and Temple University as her possible college choices at the end of September of her senior year, her knowledge and choice of these universities was based largely on hearsay. She, in fact, knew very little about either of these universities: she did not know that Temple University was in Philadelphia and had a hard time distinguishing Pennsylvania State University (Penn State, a flagship state university in Pennsylvania) and the University of Pennsylvania (UPenn, a private Ivy League university). Further, she was concerned about financing her college education, knowing that without substantial financial help, her family could not afford to send her to college. As of September of her senior year, she had virtually no knowledge of the Free Application for Federal Student Aid (FAFSA – the financial aid form that students have to fill out in order to receive financial aid from the federal government, such as grants, work study and student loans).[2]

However, what truly derailed her plan to go to a four-year college was her failure to take the SAT on time. She was aware of the need to take the SAT; she talked about it as early as March of her junior year. However, despite the fact that the SAT was offered every month at the school (and low-income students were waived the application fee), Alexandra put off taking the exam. It was not until the second week of September, when she finally spoke to her guidance counselor about her college application – a minimal conversation, focusing largely on the procedure rather than any meaningful discussion of college choice – that the need to take the SAT, and to take it immediately, seemed to dawn on her. By then, it was too late to apply for the October exam.[3] Normally, the October exam was the last test students could take and still include their scores in their four-year college applications. The fact that Alexandra had missed the October exam already would have delayed her application. However, Brighton had a special arrangement with Penn State, and students could take the November SAT and still have their scores considered for main campus applications. Since Penn State had always been – however vaguely – her top choice, if Alexandra took the November SAT, she could still apply to the university. However, totally out of character, she also missed the deadline for the November exam, and therefore simply had no SAT scores to submit to colleges.

Why she missed the November deadline remains a mystery to me, especially because she was the most organized of the seven students with whom I worked. She was the kind of student who, when we made an appointment to meet for the next interview, would immediately note it down in her calendar. When I asked her whether she purposely missed the deadline because, perhaps, she did not want to take the exam or was afraid of getting low scores, she flatly rejected this, insisting that she simply forgot. She said, 'When people told me, [I thought] oh my God' (IN 11/21/2011). There may be some truth to this claim. Alexandra was rather stressed about multiple projects due in several of her classes in November, and she seemed much more concerned about these tasks than moving her college application forward.

Nonetheless, what strikes me as a more plausible explanation is that, at least partially, Alexandra allowed herself to skip the November SAT to give herself more time to prepare for it. In November of her senior year, she said, '[I] want to take it [the SAT], but I think I'm not prepared. Maybe I am, but I need practice. [Pause] 'Cause I don't know what's on the SAT' (IN 11/21/2011). Although she missed the November deadline, she did not necessarily think that she was off the hook with the SAT. She believed that she still needed to take the exam at some point.

By November of her senior year, Alexandra did appear to realize that not having any SAT scores precluded the possibility of applying to four-year colleges. At this point, she readily changed her narrative and said that she now wanted to go to LCC and transfer after one year: 'For like a year and then transcript [i.e. transfer] over to university when I take the SAT there. Maybe that's what I want to do' (IN 11/21/2011). She added that friends told her that LCC was a good school and that if she did not like it there, she could always move to another college.

Her decision to change her college plans and attend LCC came from an underinformed vantage point. She did not know that by going to LCC and taking enough college credits, she could potentially transfer to a university without taking the SAT. She was also not aware that at least some of the credits she earned at LCC could be transferred over to a university. Put another way, she believed that she would still have to take the SAT if she wanted to attend a university and also that she would have to put in another four years at the university even if she transferred from LCC. Thus, by choosing LCC, Alexandra was intending to give herself more time to prepare for a four-year college.

Spring Senior Year

By February of her senior year, she had a clear, revised plan: she wanted to spend one or two years at LCC and then transfer to Penn State to study psychology. I asked if she regretted not having taken the SAT in time. To that she said, quite matter-of-factly, 'Yeah, I should have. But I didn't, so now I don't have choice' (IN 02/29/2012).

Ironically, she finished high school with an impressive academic record. Her cumulative GPA was 88%. Moreover, as part of her taking advanced placement (AP) Spanish, she had taken the National Spanish Exam and earned a bronze medal. As discussed in Chapter 2, she was entered into the Sociedad Honoraria Hispánica (Spanish National Honors Society). She was the first person to achieve this honor at Brighton, and for this reason she was invited to participate in the Senior Awards Night in late May. It is quite an honor to attend the event because only students receiving at least one award or a scholarship are invited. Approximately 200 Brighton students were sent invitations to the award ceremony, and among the seven English learners (ELs) in this study, Alexandra was the only student who was invited and given an award.

Given her academic accomplishments, I believe that with better college planning and more support from knowledgeable adults, Alexandra could have been admitted to one of the four-year colleges she was interested in. Part of the problem, she later revealed to me, was that she had moved to Brighton in the 10th grade and had spent the first year getting used to her new school. Her New York school was a much smaller school, and when she moved to Brighton High School, she was overwhelmed by its enormity. Thus, the first year at Brighton was spent adjusting, and it was not until the 11th grade, she said, that she started thinking about college. Alexandra's story, then, illustrates one common problem in newcomer ELs' college planning: they do not have enough time before college application for adequate planning and preparation.

At the same time, Alexandra was quite critical of the lack of support from the school. She pointed out that many ELs lack college knowledge and need more support:

> 'Cause it's not just me. I know a lot of my friends, they don't know like, what to do and they don't know that information. They want that information but they don't know like-, who to ask for the information and where to look at it. (IN 05/16/2012)

She was particularly critical of the new counselor, Mr Olin, who replaced her old counselor in October of her senior year.[4] She felt that he was unresponsive to students' requests to meet with him:

> My counselor, I don't know him. He's new and I never been there. I never talk to him. And I was like, the other day, after school, I was there and I want to talk to him and he was on the phone like, 'Give me five minutes, you need to wait 'cause I'm talking.' I just get mad; I left. (IN 05/16/2012)

It is entirely possible that Mr Olin was simply busy at that time rather than uncaring. However, given the lack of support Alexandra had experienced thus far, she took this interaction as one more sign that Brighton simply did not care about her college planning: 'They don't care. Well, I do care. So I need to look at it by myself' (IN 05/16/2012). True to her words, she filled out the application form for an associate's degree program at LCC by herself, submitted it and was later admitted to the program.

Notes

(1) It is important to remind readers that this comment was made in the context of the Obama administration, not after Donald Trump took office and began a massive crackdown of undocumented immigrants. Even during Obama's presidency, between 2008 and 2012, close to one million undocumented immigrants, more than three-quarters of them without any criminal record, were detained by US Immigration and Customs Enforcement (ICE) (Ewing *et al.*, 2015).

(2) Each year, over 13 million students file the FAFSA and receive more than $120 billion in financial aid (College Board, 2019). The FAFSA is also used by individual colleges to determine the financial aid packages to offer to applicants. In other words, most high school seniors applying to colleges file the FAFSA, regardless of whether they are attending a four-year or a two-year college.

(3) The deadline for the SAT application is usually a month before the exam date.

(4) Her original counselor resigned to take a new position at another school.

Josephine's Story

Quiet and physically small, Josephine, a 17-year-old Ghanaian student, was the kind of student who could easily escape the notice of teachers in a large school like Brighton. Indeed, Mrs Hernandez, her guidance counselor, commented that it was easy to underestimate Josephine because she was so quiet and never caused trouble, unlike some of the other participants. However, around friends and people with whom she felt comfortable, she was much more expressive, reflecting on what kind of college would suit her, making realistic decisions and envisioning a concrete future career – all within the context of limited guidance and financial resources.

Josephine came to the United States three years prior from Kumasi, Ghana, and entered Brighton in ninth grade. Her parents divorced when she was young, and her mother had been living in the United States since Josephine was five. Josephine had grown up with her grandmother. At age 14, she came to the United States with her older brother, Johnson, to be reunited with her mother.

Although Josephine's first language (L1) was Twi, one of the major languages in Ghana, she had been educated in English, and was fluent when she arrived. Nonetheless, she was placed in the English learner (EL) program for two years, but by the time I met her, she had already been reclassified. Because of her longer enrollment in Brighton and also because of her facility with English, especially in social interactions, Josephine was more at home and better integrated into the community of Brighton than more recent arrivals like Erica and Alexandra. She was a member of the knitting club and also attended the EL homework club almost every day after school, along with Kadi.

Additionally, Josephine had one important advantage in her college planning: her older brother, Johnson, was completing an associate's degree at LCC during Josephine's senior year; he was planning to transfer to a university in order to become a doctor. Therefore, Josephine had a family member to whom she could turn for concrete guidance and strategies. Johnson's transfer plan also demonstrated to her how a student could first attend a community college and then transfer to a four-year institution to pursue a professional career. At the same time, there was a considerable financial constraint on her college planning. Her mother was a single parent working two jobs, one in a factory and the other as a caregiver to people with disabilities. Although they owned their home, the family struggled financially, and financing a college education became a constant theme in Josephine's college planning.

Spring Junior Year

Josephine had a strong interest in a career in science, although at the beginning of her college planning she was unsure about which specific field in science. She had a vague interest in meteorology, but at this point she was still searching for what she really wanted to study: 'I like science. I'm willing to study the science field, but, apart from the medical field anything in the science field is OK for me' (IN 04/04/2011). She wanted to go to a four-year college because she did not want too many transitions; however, 'If I'm not ready for that, then I'm going to a community college first' (IN 04/04/2011). In March of her junior year, she named the University of the Sciences in Philadelphia, Drexel University and DeVry University – all private colleges – as the schools on her current list of colleges. Her choices were largely dictated by her exposure to these colleges: she had met representatives from these schools either at a college fair or in one of her classes. Also, she was attracted to private colleges because she believed that they were, on the whole, smaller and offered smaller classes: 'I really learn a lot in smaller classes than big classes, so I was thinking about private universities but it costs a lot, but the public universities have a lot bigger classes' (IN 03/08/2011). Although she knew that paying for college was likely to be a major issue, she had not yet made a real connection between finances and the kinds of colleges she was considering.

Summer before Senior Year

Although Josephine was willing to consider a community college, there was no doubt in her mind that she was going to apply to four-year colleges. As a result, she took her first SAT in June of her senior year. The results were disappointing: 400 in critical reading, 370 in math and

410 in writing for a total score of 1,180. These scores fell below what typical applicants to the University of the Sciences or Drexel University earned. For instance, 50% of the students enrolled in the University of Sciences scored 520–600 in critical reading, 560–660 in math and 520–630 in writing.[1] She knew her scores were low, and seemed particularly bothered by the low math score since she planned on majoring in sciences. On the other hand, she had no concrete sense of the kinds of scores she needed to stand a realistic chance of being admitted to the universities she had in mind. She only said, 'I want to get about 1,700 [in total]' (IN 09/19/2011).

Josephine also looked for a summer job, hoping to earn some money for college tuition, but she was unable to find any employment. She had also been saying that she was planning to visit some of the universities on her list, but did not visit any of them during the summer.

Fall Senior Year

By September of her senior year, the lineup on Josephine's list of colleges had changed somewhat: Drexel University and the University of the Sciences were still on her list, but DeVry University had been dropped while Albright University and Cedar Crest College had been added. Again, her choice was largely influenced by exposure: she listed colleges she came across at college fairs and those that sent her email and information packages. However, at this point, she began analyzing college information more closely to find a good match for her personality and dispositions. For instance, Cedar Crest College, a women's college in Allentown, PA, rose near the top of her chart because it was a small college that offered flexibility to create one's own major:

> I think it's mostly because they keep sending me emails saying—, uh, when I went to the college fair, I looked at it, for the tuition is a little bit higher but I was hoping to apply for scholarships and financial aid to help with it. And, I think I'll really like it because it said, I went to a meeting with the admission office[r] or something like that and [Yasuko: Here, or?] Yeah, she came here. And she said they have a program that you can choose your own subjects to make your own major. (IN 10/31/2011)

Her comments suggest that she had begun carrying out more in-depth research about the programs and tuition of each college in which she was interested.

Josephine was also attracted to Drexel University because of the 'VIP' status that the university offered her. She had met representatives from the university at the college fair she attended in the spring, and at the beginning of her senior year, they sent her an email offering VIP status, which involved an offer of no application fee, no long personal statement and automatic scholarship consideration. According to Mr Burke, Director of Guidance, these VIP statuses that many universities offer are nothing more than a 'marketing gimmick' (IN 10/03/2011). However, for a 17-year-old hopeful who was navigating her college planning mostly on her own, it was easy to interpret a message such as, 'I'm always looking to connect with bright students who show potential for success at Drexel'[2] as a sign that the university had a strong interest in her.

Meanwhile, Josephine became somewhat more focused on what she wanted to study in college. She was taking Life Science in the fall of her senior year, and topics from the course, such as epidemics and immunization, interested her. Her teacher also talked about careers in microbiology, adding that these jobs paid well. Josephine was attracted to fields that both interested her and provided solid job prospects and she started to believe that her future career might be in microbiology.

Josephine said that she was comfortable approaching all her teachers for help, especially Mr Woznyj, the EL Department Chair. However, there was no evidence that she had consulted any of her teachers about her college planning. Her relationship with Mrs Hernandez, her assigned counselor, was purely transactional. Josephine readily went to Mrs Hernandez to ask her to send her transcripts and letters of recommendation to the colleges she was applying to and acknowledged that Mrs Hernandez was very helpful in that way: 'I went to her about [pause] recommendation letters and a pink form for them to release my transcripts, and she was talking about envelopes and the sums that we need. I got the envelopes, but I have to give it to her, and I have to print something from Cedar Crest, and I have to edit and give it to her' (IN 10/31/2011). But she never consulted Mrs Hernandez about her college choices or actual applications. Also, her mother had changed her job to caring for elderly people in their homes, which meant that she often had to leave Josephine and Johnson weeks at a time to take care of her clients. This left Johnson as the only source of guidance for Josephine in her college applications. He did help her with her applications and gave his opinions on which universities were likely to be within their price range. However, he was busy with his own college transfer applications, and did not provide the time or attention Josephine wished. She complained: 'I'm trying to do it with my brother. He's helping with the application. Most of the time, he's busy, so

I'm looking for a time that he's free that then we can do it together'
(IN 09/19/2011). In short, Josephine was largely on her own, trying to
process a massive amount of information in order to make a decision
that could have a profound impact on the rest of her life.

She retook the SAT in November of her senior year, but the scores
were again disappointing: 430 in critical reading, 280 in math and 320
in writing. In fact, although her score in critical reading improved by 30
points, the other two scores were lower, bringing her total score to 1,030,
down from 1,180 back in June.

By the end of the fall semester of her senior year, Josephine had
applied to Cedar Crest College, Drexel University and Virginia Union
University, a historically Black university in Virginia. This last university
was an afterthought: Josephine applied mostly because the school had
sent her a packet indicating that they had waived her application fee and
offered scholarship opportunities. But she knew that her mother did not
want her to live away from home, and it was highly unlikely that she
would attend Virginia Union.

While she was applying to these four-year institutions, the realistic
side of her was increasingly steering her toward a community college for
financial reasons. As early as September of her senior year, Josephine
said, 'I was trying to find a job last summer, but me and my friends were
walking around trying to find a job. But we couldn't find one. And, um,
I might go to LCC first. Then work towards my tuition' (IN 09/19/2011).
In other words, reality was starting to set in that her financial constraints
were likely to limit her choice to a community college, even as she earnestly sent out her applications to four-year colleges.

Spring Senior Year

In the end, Josephine applied to Drexel University, the University of
the Sciences, Cedar Crest College, Virginia Union University and LCC.
Although she had frequently mentioned her plans to visit these colleges
throughout the year, she had never visited any of them. She also applied
for several of the many scholarships Brighton offered to its graduating
class but received none.

Of the four-year colleges she applied to, she was rejected by three,
and was only admitted to Virginia Union University, which offered her a
scholarship. However, she declined the offer because it was too far away
from home. She thus decided to attend LCC in the fall: 'I'm thinking
about going LCC, but I'm thinking about going for like two years ... then
transferring to another college for my bachelor's degree' (IN 04/10/2012).

Given how earnestly she had applied to all these colleges, I assumed that the news that there was no viable four-year college option had to be terribly disappointing. However, Josephine was surprisingly upbeat. There seemed to be two reasons for this. First, applying to these institutions finally brought home to her that even with the financial aid she could expect to receive, her family could not afford the cost of a private college education:

Yasuko: So, were you disappointed when you didn't get accepted to Drexel and stuff like that?

Josephine: A little bit, but I was not really that disappointed because I didn't go in first place because I'm going to LCC. And the tuition is really high too, so. (IN 04/10/2012)

Second, by then she had decided that she wanted to become a pharmacist, and this clearer career focus gave her a sense of direction and with it, greater self-efficacy. Her mother had told her that there were more positions available in pharmacy than in microbiology. As far as Josephine was concerned, microbiology and pharmacology were closely related fields, and she saw the shift from one to the other as a minor adjustment: even as a pharmacist, she imagined herself working for a pharmaceutical company, working in a lab, rather than filling prescription orders at a pharmacy:

> I was thinking about, like, maybe it also depends on where you work in the pharmacy field. But, I'm not really sure because what I really wanted to do is, like, be part of those through—, I don't know how to explain like [pause] control um, something like, take care of the medicine. Or like, something like, see the side effects or something like that. Like that's why I wanted to be a microbiologist because it deals with epidemics and other stuff. (IN 04/12/2012)

Her brother, who was filing his transfer applications at that time, also decided to major in pharmacy, and this no doubt influenced Josephine's decision as well. Because she saw her brother, her closest ally in college planning, complete a community college program and begin moving onto a four-year college to pursue a science career, she knew that successfully transferring from a community college to a four-year college and majoring in science was a viable option. Because she was convinced that that was the pathway she was going to take, she was not devastated by the redirection she had to make.

At the same time, she did harbor some regrets and seemed to blame herself for the way her college planning had turned out:

Josephine: I could have tried harder, though.
Yasuko: Can you talk more about that?
Josephine: I mean, I could have applied to a lot more colleges and other stuff and visited some colleges. (IN 05/31/2012)

From my vantage point, however, Josephine's own efforts were not what was lacking in her college planning. Considering her lack of resources, she did everything that was asked of her: she researched colleges, took the SAT and filed college applications in a timely manner. Rather, what was conspicuously lacking in her college planning was access to rigorous academic preparation and guidance from educators. Although she was friendly with all her teachers and her guidance counselor, and at least some of them recognized her quiet intelligence and resolve, none of them sat down with her to give her concrete guidance on what postsecondary options would be viable for her. This left Josephine with only two college-planning mentors at home: her brother, barely two years older and busy with his own college transfer, and her mother, who had to be away from home for long stretches of time to support her family. Also, given Josephine's willingness to work hard, better academic preparation in terms of access to a more challenging set of courses and a SAT preparation program[3] might have gone a long way to increasing her chances of being admitted to a four-year college. Guidance on college costs earlier on and encouragement to consider public universities rather than private ones also might have made a four-year college affordable for her. In short, Josephine's story illustrates how the efforts of a hard-working EL from a low-income family, when they are not accompanied by institutional support, can only go so far in gaining access to a four-year college.

Notes

(1) The maximum score for each exam is 800. The College Board, the testing agency that offers the SAT, has since eliminated the writing exam from the SAT.

(2) This was part of the email she received from the assistant vice president of recruitment at Drexel University, offering her VIP status.

(3) As I later found out, Brighton, in fact, offered a free SAT preparation course to any low-income students, but none of the study participants seemed aware of this opportunity.

3 Underdeveloped College Knowledge

Chapter 2 discussed the ways in which English learners (ELs) were largely confined to low-track courses and how limited course access negatively affected their postsecondary prospects. In this chapter, I discuss another, similarly important factor to their limited college access: underdeveloped college knowledge. As Vargas (2004: 6) reminds us, 'Above and beyond whether students possess the academic qualifications or desire to attend college, when the time comes to apply, access to "college knowledge" may determine whether or not they ultimately go'. College knowledge is particularly critical for those who want to advance to a four-year college directly from high school because four-year college admission requires elaborate advance planning. Even if students have accumulated valuable academic credentials in high school, if they cannot convert these credentials into viable academic capital through the college application process, their college access will be seriously hampered.

The EL participants in this study possessed plenty of strengths, such as their bilingual proficiency, their desire to contribute to the welfare of their family and community and their optimism for their future (Kao & Tienda, 1995; Yosso, 2005). However, their college knowledge was extremely underdeveloped. Mrs Anderson, one of the EL teachers, observed how her ELs lacked the college knowledge even to know what questions to ask: 'I don't think they know the right questions to ask to even get started, or where to find information, you know, like they might have questions but where do I go to get those questions answered?' (IN 06/02/2011). Indeed, it is unsurprising that EL students were lacking in college knowledge as going to college in the United States is extraordinarily complicated. An entire service industry is built around assisting students and families navigate college admissions. How can we expect youths to arrive from another country and not only learn a new language and a new education system, but also navigate the labyrinthine US college admissions system – all within a few years of their arrival?

Erica, Alexandra, Josephine, Kadi and Ken originally aspired to go to a four-year college, whereas Eddie and Carlos wanted to attend CTE programs at a community college; none of them had sufficient knowledge to effectively connect the dots between their aspirations and actual enrollment. These students' underdeveloped college knowledge either derailed or seriously complicated their college planning in three areas: (a) no campus visits; (b) uninformed college choice list; and (c) failure to assemble college application materials on time. In this chapter, I will first describe these three problems and then go on to discuss why the participants' college knowledge was so underdeveloped.

Lack of College Knowledge and Its Consequences

No campus visits

The participants in this study were unaware of the importance of campus visits in deciding where to apply. College is, after all, where they are going to spend the next four or more years, and the atmosphere of a college in person may be quite different from the image that the college presents on its website and in its glossy brochures. This point is emphasized on the College Board website:

> A campus visit is your opportunity to get a firsthand view of a college. A college catalog, brochure or website can only show you so much. To really get a feel for the college, you need to walk around the quad, sit in on a class and visit the dorms. (College Board, n.d.-b)

However, none of the participants visited the colleges they were considering other than those colleges that either a family member or a friend attended. As I noted in his story, Ken had a set list of universities he wanted to apply to, but he never visited any of them, nor attended the orientation session for future applicants to the nursing program at Drexel University. The only college he ever visited during his junior and senior year was LCC, where his mother was pursuing a nursing degree – even though he did not plan to attend a community college. Josephine and Kadi, who were good friends, had intended to go on campus tours together several times during their junior and senior years, but they never did. Despite having the best chances of all seven EL participants of being admitted to four-year institutions, Erica and Alexandra remained vague about their college choice and never mentioned plans to visit colleges.

I should point out that for these students, visiting a college was not an easy task. Most high school students have their parents take them on college visit tours during the summer or drive them to individual colleges. But the participants' parents/guardians were busy working during the day and were not in a position to take time off to chauffer their children to college visits. None of the students had a car at their disposal. This left public transportation as the only option: in the Brighton area, this meant stringing together multiple buses, or a bus and a subway or a train. Thus, it is not entirely surprising why, even though most of the students talked about visiting campuses, few actually did.

The main consequence of not visiting colleges in person was that the concept of *college* remained abstract to them, not a concrete reality with physical buildings and quads, faculty and students, energy, sounds and activities. Therefore, their lack of urgency to complete their college applications in a timely manner in their senior year is understandable. Applying to four-year colleges and universities is a labor-intensive project, competing with family and social commitments, maintaining grades and participating in sports and other extramural activities. Middle-class and upper-middle-class students and their parents engage in this project with an uncommon degree of fervor (Hamilton *et al.*, 2018; Lareau & Weininger, 2008). Their aspirations are further fueled by college visits during the summer between junior and senior year, which simultaneously sharpen their focus to a few favorite schools. In contrast, none of the participants visited any four-year institutions, so going to a four-year college – though a hoped-for goal – remained nebulous. In some cases, finishing up assignments and projects for their courses appeared more immediately consequential. Alexandra, despite her previous plans to only apply to four-year colleges, had by November of her senior year not even taken the SAT. When I discovered this and asked her why she had not done anything about her college application, she responded that she had been too busy with her class assignments:

Yasuko: OK. Have you started the process yet?
Alexandra: No.
Yasuko: No. And why not? This is getting a bit late.
Alexandra: Cause I don't have time.
Yasuko: OK. So, what have you been up to? What, what are you doing?
Alexandra: Projects, essays. (IN 11/21/2011)

Without having physically stepped onto any college campus, the prospect of earning low grades on assignments presented more of an imminent threat to Alexandra than the prospect of not applying to college on time.

Uninformed college choice list

A second way in which the ELs' underdeveloped college knowledge affected their college planning was their actual choice of colleges. Some students, such as Erica and Alexandra, did not develop a list of colleges at all, instead vaguely intimating that they were interested in Temple University and/or Penn State, two default choices of public universities for high school students in that area. But even for those ELs who did develop a college choice list, their selection was less than well informed. For example, in March of her junior year, Josephine named the University of the Sciences, Drexel University and DeVry University as the schools on her current college list. The choice was dictated largely by name recognition and her perception that private colleges would be smaller and quieter. On the one hand, I was happy about the thought that Josephine had already put into her college choices; on the other, I was concerned that she was expressing her preference for private colleges on the erroneous assumption that private colleges were always smaller and offered smaller class sizes than public institutions. Drexel University, for instance, is a large, bustling urban university in the middle of a metropolitan city, quite different from the small and intimate liberal arts college atmosphere Josephine was seeking. Conversely, a public institution such as Millersville University, a medium-size residential university located in a small rural town in Pennsylvania, might have better fit her image. Another major issue with Josephine's college choice was cost. She came from a single-parent household where her older brother was already in the process of transferring to a four-year college; there would soon be two children in college, supported by one immigrant mother who herself had only completed a high school education. Objectively speaking, for Josephine to put only private institutions – including DeVry University, one of the largest for-profit college chains[1] – on her college list struck me as incongruent with her family's financial situation.[2] Josephine knew that family finances were tight, and she was under considerable pressure from her mother and brother to earn a scholarship to finance her college education. '[My mom] always tell me to study hard so I can get a scholarship so that the tuition will be, not be very hard on her', she said (IN 04/04/2011). But at this point she did not seem to make the connection between the colleges to which she aspired and the reality of her family finances.

One counterexample amid many examples of lack of college knowledge, however, is Kadi's college choice list. Kadi enrolled in a CTE program in her senior year, and her affiliation with the CTE program led to other resources that informed her about college planning in a way that distinguishes her from the other participants. One of her CTE instructors recommended that Kadi attend a local College Access Center, and she started attending the center once a week during the fall of her senior year. With the assistance of a counselor at the College Access Center, she then developed a list of colleges to which she might apply. At this point, Kadi was considering both universities and community colleges, and therefore her list included both. She listed not only the names of the colleges but also information about the application and financial aid as instructed by her counselor at the center. For instance, under LCC, she wrote:

Application fee: $25 application fee, can be waived for financial need.
Deadlines: Financial aid application: July 1.
Application to apply goes online in late October.

In addition to LCC, the list included Eastern University, Thomas Jefferson University, the Urban Community College (pseudonym) and a few colleges with nursing programs in Minnesota because her stepmother wanted Kadi to attend college close to her. Although the selection of colleges that Kadi thought about applying to changed frequently, this initial list was by far the most detailed and realistic list that any of the participants in this study drew in their senior year. Kadi's counterexample therefore underscores the fact that their lack of college knowledge is not due to their or their parents' lack of motivation, ignorance or organizational skills. Rather, it is the result of inadequate institutional support in situations when students' parents are not able to facilitate their children's college planning the way middle-class parents are privileged to do.

Failure to assemble strong college application materials on time

Third, the participants lacked the skill to assemble strong college applications in a timely manner. The students were able to fill out most of the college application forms online without an issue. The submission of transcripts was also largely unproblematic because it was handled by their guidance counselors. However, completing and assembling the other application components – letters of recommendation, the college essay and the SAT – in a timely manner was a struggle for the four-year college–aspiring students in this study. Witnessing their missteps in their college applications reminded me of Vargas's (2004: 8) observation that 'the processes involved in applying to college—taking the SAT or the ACT, for instance—may seem to be common knowledge, but they are not obvious to underrepresented students and their families'. For example, at Brighton, letters of recommendation were typically written by students' assigned guidance counselors. But as I will detail later in this chapter, the EL students largely distanced themselves from their counselors. Each of the guidance counselors at the school had 300 students in their caseloads, and at least two-thirds of their charges were planning to apply to four-year colleges and therefore needed letters of recommendation from them. It is thus likely that the letters that they would write for my participants would be standard letters that would not stand out to college admission officers.

The college essay was another application component that the participants struggled to write – if they attempted to write one at all. Any number of college application guides tell prospective students that the college essay is critical and needs to be carefully crafted and edited. The College Board (n.d.-a), for instance, describes the function of the college essay in the following way: 'Your essay reveals something important about you that your grades and test scores can't—your personality. It can give admission officers a sense of who you are, as well as showcasing your writing skills'.

In stark contrast to some middle-class students and their families who go to great lengths to produce a standout college essay, the ELs in this study did not fully grasp the importance of this step. Josephine was one of the few participants who actually wrote her college essay – most participants did not even reach this step. Some of the colleges she applied to suggested that she could submit one of the academic essays she wrote for school. For example, the requirement for the college essay for Cedar Crest College was 'to submit a one-page essay or graded paper (topic of your choice)'. Figure 3.1 is the essay Josephine submitted to Cedar Crest.

There are several strengths to this essay. First of all, instead of writing a typical college essay that narrates the student's own life and their accomplishments, Josephine chose to discuss a macro-social issue but managed to articulate how it affected her and her family. At the same time, she also demonstrated her awareness of the impact of a bad economy, not just on her own family, but also on various aspects of society. Structurally, the essay clearly demonstrates her grasp of the five-paragraph essay: one introductory paragraph, followed by three paragraphs highlighting different facets of the topic and, finally, one concluding paragraph. However, the essay also suffers from grammatical and lexical errors (e.g. *likeable to do drugs*; *loose* instead of *lose*), and relies on high-frequency,

An issue of personal, local, national, and international concern and is important to me is the economy or bad economy to be exact. This is not only important to me but to everyone around the world. Around the world, people try and struggle to make money and improve the economy. This makes most people do unexpected things and unthinkable things. Most of these things lead to life in prison or turning to drugs as an escape from miseries in their lives. If the economy was better everyone's life will be much better and simpler.

Personally, the economy is important to me because with bad economy, most families will fall apart. This also means my young family members will not have a very good education as my generation of the generations before mine. It's also important to me because the economy right now is not that great. This has led my mother to find a job in another state. My brother also has to go to school and work. This has made my family and I a little distance. If the economy was good, that would bring my family much closer because my mother could find a job close by and my brother will not have to work long hours. We will get spend lots of time together as a family and life would be much better for all of us and also much simpler.

Locally and internationally, bad economy is ruining many people lives. Many people work for many years then due to bad economy, they get fired. Most of these people will struggle and struggle to get back into the working field. Some never do and turn to a life of crime. Some of these people end up in prison and leave behind a family who might loose their home and precious memories. This means the kids in the family are also prone to turning to a life of crime. They are also likeable to do drugs because they will think that is a way to escape life troubles and misery. This also means the economy is far from been better because finding a job would not be the number one priority for many people because they will give up before they begin to look for a job.

Internationally, bad economy can cause as much trouble as it does locally and nationally. If the situation is not taken care of it could lead to things like the great depression which happened when the stock market crushed. Bad economy can make it impossible to recover from situations like natural disasters. In some cases, it can lead to war. It can make nations turn on nations and people on each other. In this world, some people will do anything for money. This contributes to the reason crime rates are so high.

In conclusion, bad economy makes everyone life tougher than it should be and can ruin many people lives. It can make people loose their jobs which ruin innocent lives and also tear families apart and make people turn to a life of crime. It can destroy young lives because these young people might turn to drugs as an escape from life. It can make people turn against each other and also cause war among nations. Crime rates are high because of bad economy.

Figure 3.1 Josephine's college essay (verbatim)

basic vocabulary such as *thing* and *bad economy* (instead of *recession*), and colloquial expressions (*not that great*). Content-wise, the thesis is rather simplistic: a tough economy increases crime while a good economy makes everyone's life better. Most importantly, however, the essay fails to highlight her assets, which would have made Josephine a highly attractive candidate: an immigrant student of color who, despite her family's modest financial means and a relatively short history in the United States, was aspiring to become a scientist. For many four-year institutions, a Black female student from a low-income household who wants to major in science, technology, engineering and mathematics (STEM) would make an attractive applicant. A more college knowledge–savvy applicant would have accentuated these traits, but Josephine's essay is silent on all of these characteristics apart from her economic status.

Finally, taking the SAT presented a real challenge for the participants. The expectation at Brighton was that four-year college-bound students take the preliminary SAT (PSAT)[3] in 10th grade, then the SAT one or more times in 11th grade, and if students are still not happy with their scores, perhaps take the SAT again early in 12th grade. The PSAT was offered once in the fall for 10th and 11th graders, while the SAT was offered multiple times throughout the school year. Both tests were administered at the school, and for low-income students the testing fee was waived. However, among the participants, Ken was the only person who took the PSAT; most others had no knowledge of the PSAT. As for the SAT, Ken, Josephine and Erica first took the exam in the spring semester of their junior year. All three reported that they were disappointed with their scores. Erica was too devastated to try again and decided to attend LCC instead, while Josephine and Ken waited until November of their senior year to retake the exam – without substantially improving their scores. Alexandra only considered applying to four-year colleges, but she kept postponing the SAT, claiming that she was not ready.[4] Unfortunately, the SAT deadline for applications came and went, and by missing this last possible opportunity to take the exam, Alexandra forfeited her chance to apply to Penn State, her first choice.

At Brighton, the staff repeatedly emphasized that seniors must submit their college applications by the end of November and the FAFSA by the middle of February: 'Turkeys and Valentines' was the mantra they devised to help students remember the two deadlines. However, for the participants, there was approximately a six-month lag between what they should have been doing and what they were doing.

From Brighton's perspective, having students submit their college applications by Thanksgiving was important for several reasons. First, by meeting the Thanksgiving deadline, many students could apply during early action or early decision cycles[5] securing a place in their target college early. Second, applying early increased students' chances of being eligible for the various scholarships that colleges offered. Third, applying early allowed time to catch possible errors and correct them.

If, for instance, a letter of recommendation was missing, a student had enough time to secure that letter and submit it in time for the deadline. Fourth, and probably most importantly, having students apply early meant they could then give the time and attention needed to complete the FAFSA application before the deadline. Meeting this second deadline was essential because the vast majority of Brighton students – and certainly all the ELs in this study – needed financial aid to attend the college of their first choice.

However, because of their lack of college knowledge, the participants did not share the guidance counselors' sense of urgency. Even Ken, who had identified a set of universities to apply to and was therefore ahead of the game, was in no rush to complete his applications. Ten days before Thanksgiving, we had the following conversation:

Yasuko: So, when do you think you're gonna send in the applications?
Ken: Maybe next month.
Yasuko: Next month. [Pause] Do you know that the counselor, the counselors are talking about, you should apply by Thanksgiving?
Ken: Yeah, Thanksgiving.
Yasuko: Yeah? Why aren't you doing that by then?
Ken: Why? Like why by Thanksgiving? (IN 11/14/2011)

It was clear from this conversation that although Ken was vaguely aware of the 'Turkeys and Valentines' mantra, he did not understand the reasoning behind it. In fact, the approach Ken and other ELs took to college applications seemed to be the other way around. Instead of thinking of Thanksgiving as the hard deadline for submitting applications, and then planning backwards to assemble the supporting documents, they seemed to believe that they could not start their college applications because they were missing a crucial document (e.g. the SAT), so they deferred preparing other aspects of the application. At the end of September, when I asked Alexandra if she had started on her college essay, she said, 'I didn't do it. I didn't get started on it 'cause I think I needed to have the SAT score' (IN 09/28/2011). Similarly, Ken, who waited until November of his senior year to retake the SAT, claimed that he could not submit his application until his new scores arrived. At this point in their educational career in the United States, they did not have sufficient college knowledge to assemble all the components of their college application in a timely and effective manner.

Reasons for Students' Lack of College Knowledge

So far, I have described the participants' lack of college knowledge and how it negatively impacted their college planning. The obvious question to ask is: Why was their college knowledge so underdeveloped? In this section, I argue that it resulted from a combination of three factors: (a) lack of guidance from their parents/guardians; (b) lack of guidance from the school and the educators' deficit orientation; and (c) students' reluctance to seek help.

Lack of parental guidance

First, all of the EL participants, with the exception of Erica, lacked the concrete and consistent college guidance and support that middle-class American students can expect from their parents. All the EL participants, without exception, reported that their parents or guardians were very supportive of their pursuit of PSE. For example, one day in spring 2012, I called Ken at home and his mother answered the phone. When she realized who I was, she pleaded, 'Dr. Kanno, can you please help Ken get into Temple [University]?'[6] At that point, Ken had been rejected by all the nursing programs to which he had applied, and not many choices were left. There was desperation in her voice: this was a mother who was distressed that her son might not be able to enroll in a four-year college in the fall. Even Eddie, who was living with an uncle and his family, reported that his uncle was encouraging him to go to college. This moral support proved unchanging. In his junior year, Eddie and his girlfriend had a baby, and being a parent is a major challenge to pursuing PSE (Cabrera *et al.*, 2005). While the unexpected pregnancy and the arrival of the baby understandably caused a major upheaval, both families in the end rallied around the young couple and encouraged Eddie to pursue further education. There was a consensus that it would be beneficial to the baby in the long run. Eddie shared:

> Well, I think that's why I want to go to college, so can get a better job and actually my girlfriend's parents, they don't mind if I go to college. They actually want me to go to college. [Yasuko: Is that right?] Yeah. (IN 09/26/2011)

Parental support, however, is not the same as parental *guidance*. With the exception of Erica's parents who were both college educated and had professional occupations, none of the other ELs in this study had college-educated parents – Ken's mother was still enrolled in a nursing program at LCC at the time of this study. Several of the participants reported that while their parents were supportive of their college going, they were not able to provide concrete guidance because they lacked college knowledge in general and US college knowledge in particular. Sometimes, parents named colleges they thought that their children should consider, but the reasons for their recommendations were often vague or even based on misinformation – such as Ken's father's belief that Ken could graduate from Drexel University's nursing program in less than four years because of its quarter system.

Also, although Brighton offered many opportunities for parents to be informed about college planning through free evening information sessions or workshops, parental participation – not just the parents of ELs, but also Brighton parents in general – in those events was quite low. For example, the school held a college planning night in October for the parents of seniors, providing a detailed outline of the college application process, but only about 60 attended, and the financial aid night in January, which included information on how to apply for Brighton's internal scholarships, had only about 70 attendees. Given that Brighton had more than 700 seniors that year, these numbers amounted to fewer than 10% of the parents. Erica's father attended those events regularly, and that is how I had opportunities to speak with him. But none of the other parents came to these events.

Administrators and counselors I spoke to pointed out that EL and non-EL parents stayed away from school for different reasons. Working-class, English-speaking parents stayed away because of their own negative experiences with schooling. 'So, parent engagement is tough', Mr Burke, Director of Guidance, commented,

> I think there's sometimes a lack of trust in the school with parent or parents, you know, a lot of times, a lot of, their engagement with the school is often informed by their own school experience. So, if they had a bad school experience or if they're not well educated and they're embarrassed about that, they don't-, they don't want to put themselves out there. (IN 05/12/2011)

In contrast, educators noted, EL parents were reluctant to get involved because of the language barrier and their unfamiliarity with schooling in the United States. Principal Lawrence was aware of the school's culpability in alienating EL parents:

> There's these unspoken messages of 'We really don't want you here. We really don't want to talk to you.' And when you have a language barrier

on top of that, how many parents just don't feel they engage because we can't speak your language. Or that you just, just from, you know, I speak me—, you know, 'I speak Spanish, you speak English. We're not going to be able to communicate. So, I'm not going to bother.' It's just another barrier. (IN 01/24/2012)

Knowing that EL parents were unlikely to participate in school-wide parent events, the guidance department in cooperation with the EL department started offering some EL parent-specific events, such as a general school orientation in September and a FAFSA workshop for the parents of ELs in February. The EL department informed me that interpreters were available at the orientation session; however, no interpreters were available at the FAFSA workshop. Although EL teachers reported some success with the orientation, the FAFSA workshop was poorly attended despite being heavily advertised and EL teachers strongly encouraging ELs to bring their parents. Nevertheless, only 14 people, including students, showed up. My field notes from that day noted, 'Mrs. Meyers [College and Career Counselor] was dismayed that a lot of people who signed up did not show up. It's true that fewer than half of the computers were filled' (FN 02/15/2012). Although all the participants expressed concerns about how to finance their college education and had limited knowledge of the FAFSA, only Erica and her father attended the meeting and completed the FAFSA by the end of the workshop.

In addition to the language barrier and unfamiliarity, different cultural expectations may have contributed to what was perceived by the school staff as EL parents' lack of involvement in their children's schooling. It is now commonplace for middle-class parents to heavily involve themselves in their children's school education in the United States (Horvat et al., 2003; Lareau, 2000; Sattin-Bajaj, 2014). Attendance at back to school nights and parent–teacher conferences is expected, but so is their participation in various committees, fundraising and field trips. Middle-class parents tend to utilize such opportunities to monitor their children's progress and to glean information that can enhance their children's education and opportunities (Horvat et al., 2003). But such practices are not universal, not even within the United States, and certainly not around the world. In many parts of the world, school education is considered to be the prerogative of the school personnel; to meddle with school business is inappropriate and disrespectful (Arias & Morillo-Campbell, 2008; Han & Love, 2015; US Department of Education Office of English Language Acquisition, 2016). Additionally, in many countries, parents are contacted individually by their child's school only if the child is in trouble; no news is therefore good news. Some of the participants' parents may have been operating on this principle. Indeed, the school contacted the parents/guardians of Eddie, Carlos and Ken for their assorted problems and infractions. Given that the school reached out to these parents individually only when their sons were in trouble, this behavior might have reinforced the parents' cultural expectation that the school would only contact them if their child was in trouble. That parents should be in reasonably regular contact with their children's teachers and guidance counselors and even monitor the decisions made around their children's schooling is a cultural practice that, without explicit guidance from the school, may have remained foreign to many EL parents.

One clear exception to this trend was Erica's father. Mr Lopez was college educated in Spain and was a program director at a K-8 public school in a neighboring school district, and as such, he clearly possessed ample knowledge on how to negotiate with school personnel. For someone who was a single parent holding a demanding full-time position, Mr Lopez was a remarkably hands-on father. Mrs Hernandez, Erica's guidance counselor, noted how Mr Lopez was in regular contact with her, and since Mrs Hernandez was Spanish speaking, she was able to provide more in-depth guidance:

> With Erica, I communicate with her father pretty regularly either by email or by phone. And when Erica and I speak, we're able to have a much more meaningful conversation because I can go back and forth between English [and Spanish] without worrying that she's not understanding what I'm saying. (IN 11/02/2011)

Mr Lopez also actively sought opportunities that might enhance his daughter's education. For example, as noted above, he and Erica attended the financial aid workshop for ELs in February. Earlier that day, the school held an assembly with all senior students about Brighton college scholarships and distributed application forms. By the time Mr Lopez arrived at the parent workshop in the evening, he had already read through the booklet and marked the scholarships for which his daughter would be eligible. In particular, there was one scholarship awarded for '[class] rank, love of foreign language and travel with no penalty to applicants who have been at Brighton for a limited number of years', and Mr Lopez commented that his daughter might be a strong fit for this scholarship. In the end, however, Erica was not awarded that scholarship.

Lack of institutional guidance on PSE

A second contributing factor to ELs' underdeveloped college knowledge was the lack of institutional guidance specifically for ELs. In my observation, such lack of guidance stemmed from two factors: (a) educators' deficit orientation toward ELs and, relatedly, (b) their institutional habitus.

Deficit orientation

Although Brighton proactively promoted students' college planning and offered them a wealth of information and resources, it also took a *clearinghouse* (Hill, 2008) approach to disseminating college-related information. Hill (2008) categorized high schools' organizational norms and practices into three types: (a) *traditional*, (b) *clearinghouse* and (c) *brokering*. Traditional schools aim to send many of their graduates directly into the workforce. Clearinghouse schools, the most common type of high school, have many resources for college guidance but leave it up to the students and parents to navigate those resources. A possible consequence of this approach is that it creates discrepancies in access between students and parents who know how to navigate the high school system and those who do not. Finally, brokering schools are characterized by substantial resources *and* an institutional commitment to actively channel those resources equitably to students and families. By this categorization, Brighton fell squarely into the clearinghouse model, making resources and information on college planning broadly available, but also leaving it up to individual students and families to avail themselves of those resources.

Brighton educators did not necessarily perceive their orientation as clearinghouse, however; in fact, had I asked them, they likely would have identified their approach as much closer to brokering. The overwhelming sense, especially among the guidance counselors, was that they were doing *so* much to reach out to individual students and families while the uptake was frustratingly meager. Mr Burke, Director of Guidance, shared:

> We'll give them very specific guidelines on how to apply for college, and what they need to do, and what they should be doing in junior year and you know, step by step. And we tell them all. And it's all, we write it down, we say it to them, and we give them opportunities to ask questions and all that. We do college chats. I mean, we try to do small group things.

We try to do individual things. We do large group things. And we give a lot of print material out, but they're going, they're the ones that have to really make that a priority in their life. (IN 10/03/2011)

Likewise, Mrs Meyers, Career and College Counselor, was clearly frustrated:

They all get the same information; they all have the same access to the same information. We are extremely proactive here in getting the information out. ... And [yet], you know, if I remind them, they'll look at me like, 'I've never heard of that before.' But they've sat in the assembly, you know. ... basically, they're clueless, and there will be seniors that are coming to me tomorrow [i.e. early May] and will be saying, 'what do I have to do to apply to college?' (IN 05/06/2011)

These quotes suggest that Brighton educators assumed that providing the same information to everyone meant everyone had the same access to the information – a quintessential assumption behind the clearinghouse approach. And because the educators perceived themselves as making every effort to reach out to students and families, when students and families did not adequately respond, deficit thinking crept in. As a result, they tended to attribute the lack of uptake to the students and families' dearth of attention, proactiveness and motivation. However, the assumption that providing the same information to everyone results in everyone having the same access is clearly false. Even if students are paying attention and motivated, if they do not have enough English proficiency to process the information and, equally important, do not have sufficient background information about how the US college system works, much of the information would be lost on them. Mr Woznyj, someone who worked closely with ELs, was well aware that much of the college information that ELs were exposed to was confusing to them, especially to ELs with lower English proficiency:

I think that idea of fluency or just having a comfortability with English, it's definitely there like, 'cause I get a lot of my seniors brining me in just brochures that are sent to them in the mail, saying, Does this mean I—, not even got in, but they don't get that it's an advertisement. Or they say, 'What does this mean? What is this saying?' 'Does this mean I should go here?' [And I tell them,] 'No, you're going to get a bunch of these. Oh, you took the SAT? Oh, somebody has your address now, and you're gonna get a lot.' (IN 01/06/2012)

As his comments suggest, something as mundane as receiving college brochures in the mail can be confusing to students who are unaware that many high school students in their junior and senior years receive a number of such brochures.

Likewise, the information sessions that the school hosted for parents, as useful as they were, could be overwhelming for those who were less than fully proficient in English and who were unfamiliar with the US college system. For example, Brighton hosted a College Awareness Night for the parents of ninth- and 10th-grade students. As the event's name suggests, this was the very first in a series of college planning orientation meetings for parents. Yet, during the 1 hour and 45 minute meeting, a remarkably wide range of topics was introduced and discussed (Table 3.1 summarizes the topics covered during that meeting). I, a current full-time faculty member at a four-year university, came out of the meeting feeling information overload. The most important take-away from that meeting, however, was that although this was ostensibly the very first introduction to college planning, an enormous amount of background information was already assumed on the part of the audience. For example, within the first 15 minutes, the PSAT, college visits and the ACT were discussed, but there was no explanation of what they were: the parents were already supposed to know, and the questions were not about what they were or what their purposes were, but were technicalities of the timing of taking the exams, how to register for them and when to make college visits.

Table 3.1 Topics discussed during the college awareness night in the order discussed

Taking the PSAT
College visits
Registration for the ACT
College planning during junior year: what students should be doing when
Fee waiver for the SAT
How advanced placement (AP) grades count for GPA
College athletic meeting
NCAA Divisions 1, 2 and 3 schools
Developing an athletic resume
Free online SAT prep course
PLAN (Pre-ACT 10th graders)
County College Access Center
Developing an activity resume
Summer enrichment programs
Volunteerisms
Financial aid workshop
FAFSA application
PHEAA (Pennsylvania state financial aid)
College total cost
Grants, scholarships, work study, loans
Brighton scholarships
Be careful what you post on Facebook

Thus, unless parents were already well versed in these US-specific events and components of college planning, much of the information would have been lost on them. It was *not* a matter of being motivated or paying attention.

Institutional habitus about ELs

Another structural reason for ELs' lack of college knowledge concerned Brighton's institutional habitus, more specifically, what educators assumed were the appropriate postsecondary options for ELs. Although Brighton was proactive about providing college guidance to all students from ninth grade on, the school did not consider ELs as a group to be four-year college bound and therefore offered no extra support for ELs planning to attend four-year institutions.

One consistent characteristic of Brighton's institutional habitus was the wide agreement that while some kind of PSE was critical, not everyone had to go to a four-year college. This belief was articulated by Principal Lawrence:

> I'll tell you very honestly, you know, as an educated individual who went to a four-year school, I think your gut reaction is to say, 'Well, everyone should go to a four-year school. We should have everyone prepared for a four-year school.' To me, that's not the society we live in right now. ... Because the community college is starting to prove itself with the number of agreements, our local community college, with the number of credit transfer agreements that they're obtaining, to go there and have something a little more financially affordable for a year, a year and a half, two years, and then go on to a traditional four-year school, finish and obtain a degree, I think is becoming a much more financially realistic path for all students. ... [On the other hand,] if I look at an overall number that we have roughly 80-some percent going on to postsecondary, I'm not happy with that number. I think that number should be literally as close to 100% as we get it. (IN 01/24/2012)

Brighton made substantial efforts to ensure that all graduates had fruitful venues for continuing their education after graduation. One good example of this was the 'Act Now!' event which was held every May. Some 30 senior students who, one month before graduation, had not decided what they were going to do after graduation, were required to attend this meeting. They were given a pep talk about the importance of taking concrete action for the next phase of their lives: 'You've got to step up and do something!' intoned Mr Burke (FN 05/12/2011). They were then sent to a college and career fair to meet with representatives from trade schools, community colleges and even some four-year colleges. In other words, up until the last possible moment, Brighton educators tried to help their graduating students formulate their postsecondary plans.

Also, because of its size, Brighton had an unusually large and rich selection of courses and a large staff. Thus, the school could marshal those resources to enrich the education of a small group of elite students and send them off to highly selective universities. Every year, a few students were admitted to Ivy League schools, such as the University of Pennsylvania and Cornell University, a point of pride for a school that largely serves working-class students. The school also sent a sizable number of students to solid regional universities such as Penn State, Temple and Drexel Universities.

However, ELs were largely excluded from such four-year college pathways. There was a tacit assumption among educators at Brighton that for most ELs, except for the *exceptionally* bright ones, community college was the most realistic postsecondary option. The existence of LCC, which enjoyed a reputation as a solid, academically oriented community college, made it easier for the Brighton staff to recommend LCC to mid-range students. Ms Meyers noted, 'Now, one thing that's very much in our favor is that we have a very good community college in the area' (IN 05/06/2011), suggesting that the presence of this particular community college nearby factored into Brighton's institutional habitus (byrd, 2019).

As Principal Lawrence noted, Brighton educators genuinely believed and advocated that attending LCC for the first two years of college was a sound and financially smart way to eventually achieve a bachelor's degree. In this schema, ELs were the primary candidates for community college education because they were deemed as needing more time to catch up linguistically and academically with their English-proficient peers. There was a strong sense among the faculty that with their still developing English language proficiency, many ELs could not successfully pursue college-level work right away. Thus, they viewed LCC as a perfect solution for those ELs who wanted to go to college but still needed more time to develop their English language proficiency. Furthermore, applying to a community college is a simple process: all one needs to do is fill out an application form and submit one's high school transcript.[7] Because community colleges only required this straightforward application process, no additional support in college planning and application was provided to ELs.

ELs' reluctance to seek help

If Brighton as an institution did not provide extra support to ELs, ELs, with their individual habitus, did not ask for extra help. None of the participants had any close relationships with their teachers or guidance counselors – with the possible exception of Kadi.[8] Their relationship with their assigned counselors was particularly anemic: they went to their counselors only when they needed their signature on a form or when they received a detention. When I suggested to Ken that he should visit his guidance counselor, Mrs Salomon, to get answers to some simple questions about college applications, he flat-out refused. As far as he was concerned, that was not an option. Alexandra went a step further and expressed her strong distrust of her assigned guidance counselor as well as her aversion to receiving help: ''Cause I hate when I need to ask people for something or for, whatever. And they don't pay attention to me' (IN 05/16/2012). Clearly, teachers and guidance counselors could have been of great help when important college information was not forthcoming from their families, or when students did not fully comprehend much of the information that the school provided. By refusing to seek their assistance, the ELs were renouncing this important form of social capital.

However, if we consider students' individual habitus, and how it was reinforced by the school's institutional habitus, why ELs stubbornly refused to seek the help they needed begins to make more sense. Bourdieu (1977a) reminds us that the self-elimination of underserved students from educational opportunities derives from an *anticipation* of real elimination:

> The negative predispositions towards the school which result in the self-elimination of most children from the most culturally unfavoured classes … must be understood as an *anticipation*, based upon the conscious estimation of the objective probabilities of success possessed by the whole category, of the sanctions objectively reserved by the school for those classes or sections of a class deprived of cultural capital. (Bourdieu, 1977: 495, emphasis added)

In other words, underserved students self-eliminate because their individual habitus tells them that even if they reached out to opportunities, based on past experiences, their chances of success would be low. Since no one likes outright rejections, these students then eliminate themselves before their 'out of place' ambitions get dashed by those in power.

Indeed, many of the EL participants assumed that even when resources and opportunities were present at the school, they were, as Bourdieu and Passeron (1990: 157) put it, 'not for the likes of us'. Mr Woznyj observed this aspect of their individual habitus with regard to the scholarships:

> I think [ELs] also sometimes feel like certain things are not available to them, being new to the country, where there's certain things they can't do. I get a lot of questions 'cause I have seniors [who ask] now about, 'Can I get this?' or 'Can I get that?' in terms of the scholarship meeting they just had. (IN 01/06/2012)

Brighton offered a number of scholarships to its graduating students. But ELs' approach to the scholarship application – as well as many other opportunities – was that they were most likely not eligible or qualified. It was not an entirely irrational response on their part. Objectively speaking, many resources and opportunities, even if they were present and available at the school, were inaccessible to ELs. As mentioned earlier, ELs were excluded from high-track courses regardless of their academic performance. Assistance in creating a thoughtful and personalized combination of electives to enhance their core courses was never offered to them. The opportunity to socialize with four-year college-bound students was limited. Subtle and not so subtle institutional discourses that ELs would be better off going to a community college were communicated to them. Above all, these students were never defined as highly competent multilingual speakers with facility with several different cultures; rather, they were defined in terms of their *lack* of English proficiency. In other words, on a daily basis, they were receiving repeated discourses that reinforced their constricted habitus.

If we consider ELs' positioning in school and their vantage points, we begin to recognize Ken and Alexandra's refusal to consult their guidance counselors, not as a flippant refusal to heed adult advice, but as a form of misrecognition (Bourdieu & Passeron, 1990), and consequently self-elimination. In other words, these ELs were positioned in deficit terms, and in the process, students such as Alexandra and Ken might have internalized their marginalized positions as a consequence of their low status in a meritorious system. With their diminished sense of habitus, the ELs in this study might have simply been resigned to the lack of institutional support and concluded, 'Like, they don't care', rather than insisting that they be given the attention and guidance that they deserved.

Summary

College knowledge is critical to students' access to college, especially to four-year colleges. In this chapter, I explored the areas in which the EL participants' college knowledge was particularly underdeveloped and how it negatively impacted their college planning and application. I then investigated the factors that led to their lack of college knowledge.

The students' lack of college knowledge was particularly noticeable in three areas: (a) completing campus visits; (b) compiling college choice lists; and (c) assembling strong college application material in a timely manner. However, since Brighton educators believed that they were extremely proactive in providing students with ample resources and support, they attributed students' lack of college knowledge to their lack of motivation and commitment to going to college. But my investigation revealed that there were structural barriers to ELs' development of college knowledge. Since most of the participants' parents were not college educated, concrete college guidance had to be provided by the school. However, Brighton, with its institutional habitus, assumed that ELs, if they went to college at all, would most likely be going to LCC. Thus, the school did not differentiate college guidance such that ELs would be fully informed of the four-year college application process. Finally, even when ELs recognized that they lacked the information they needed to plan for college, their individual habitus disinclined them from seeking help. Even when ELs were aware of the opportunities and resources that existed within Brighton, more often than not they assumed that they were not really meant for them. In short, the school did not provide ELs with sufficient assistance for four-year college planning and application, and the ELs did not ask for help.

Notes

(1) In recent years, the predatory practices of for-profit colleges have come under increasing scrutiny in the United States: wooing low-income and minority students with heavy recruitment and unrealistic promises of job prospects upon graduation and saddling them with more loans than they will ever be able to repay (Cao & Habash, 2017; Deming *et al.*, 2013). An investigation by the Century Foundation has found that Adtalem Global Education, the parent company of DeVry University, is one of the top five for-profit college institutions whose students are most likely to file claims for the Borrower Defense to Repayment, a student loan forgiveness program for students who have been misled by their schools (Cao & Habash, 2017).

(2) To provide a sense of the cost differentials, tuition and fees for 2019–2020 incoming freshmen students were $54,516 at Drexel University (private), $25,000 at the University of the Sciences (private) and $12,250 at Millersville University (public). Thus, in the United States, there is tremendous variation in the price tag of a four-year college education; the difference between public and private institutions is particularly stark.

(3) The PSAT serves as a practice run for 10th and 11th graders for the real SAT test. It also serves as the qualifying test for the National Merit Scholarships.

(4) Guidance counselor Ms Hernandez pointed out that deferring taking the SAT was quite common among students in general, not just among ELs.

(5) In the United States, many four-year colleges offer early action and early decision plans in addition to the regular application cycle for those students who know which college they are seriously interested in. Early action is not binding; students simply learn the college's decision early. Early decision, in contrast, is binding, and students must commit, at the time of applying, to enroll in that college if accepted.

(6) At the time of the fieldwork, I was a faculty member at Temple University.

(7) Applicants also need to submit proof of their state residency if they want to apply for in-state tuition, and also later apply for the FAFSA.

(8) As noted earlier, Kadi did approach her guidance counselor to discuss pursuing a CTE program during her senior year. In that sense, unlike the other participants, she did not hesitate to approach her counselor to strategize her postsecondary plans. Nonetheless, she did not appear to consult her guidance counselor further about her college plans in her senior year. She relied far more on her CTE teachers and the College Access Center staff for her college planning. The fact that she preferred to take a 40-minute bus ride to seek college guidance at the College Access Center suggests that she felt she had limited access to the guidance that she needed at Brighton.

Erica's Story

Erica was the highest academic achiever of the seven students in this study. Her cumulative GPA at the end of high school was 90.2 (A minus), and she was on the distinguished honor roll. Several teachers and her counselor noted that she was an academically strong student. When I asked Mr Woznyj to help me select participants for this study, Erica was the first student he named as an example of a high-performing English learner (EL).

Erica immigrated to the United States from Madrid, Spain, when she was 16, but she had been coming to the United States every summer to visit her father and aunt for several years. Her parents divorced when she was little, and her father had subsequently moved to the United States. The daughter of a university professor (her mother) and a school administrator (her father), Erica attended private schools and received high-level education in Spain.

Erica's move to the United States stemmed largely from her own desire to live there. She visited her father every summer, but, she said, 'I used to feel really, really, really sad when I had to leave so ... my mom, she said, "Oh, if you want to study there, just stay there and finish"' (IN 05/22/2012). Certainly, the fact that her father was already in the United States and led an established middle-class life as a local school program coordinator helped facilitate her immigration. Also, both her parents, who had kept in close contact as regards their children, believed that the United States offered more opportunities for Erica.

Erica enrolled in Brighton at the beginning of 10th grade. Because of her frequent summer visits to the United States and summer camp experiences, her English comprehension was good, but she had difficulty expressing herself. In the early interviews, which started about two years after her arrival, she sometimes struggled to find the right words to say in English: for instance, she had difficulty explaining her father's occupation. However, in each subsequent interview, her English was noticeably better, so that by the end of high school, she seemed much more comfortable and capable of expressing herself in English.

Spring Junior Year

Given her academic performance and that both her parents were college educated, I had assumed that Erica was planning to attend a four-year college as a matter of course. However, she seemed to waver between going to LCC and advancing directly to a university. She was definite about eventually obtaining a bachelor's degree. For the daughter of college-educated parents with an older sister in Spain who had graduated from university, stopping at an associate's degree was not an option. However, she seemed to believe that in order to attend a four-year college, students had to know what they wanted to study: 'I think I'm gonna do, like, one year in LCC. And then after that I wanna go to another university, but I'm going to LCC because I don't know really what I want to study' (IN 05/06/2011). She had some interest in marketing but was worried that she might be too shy to go into the marketing field. 'The problem is like, I'm a shy person, so to do marketing, you have to make other people to buy the product, to show them. I don't know how to work with that', she said (IN 02/29/2012).

Erica's father, Mr Lopez, was closely involved in her education. Mrs Hernandez, Erica's guidance counselor, informed me that Mr Lopez was in regular contact with her through email and phone calls. By the end of Erica's junior year, Mr Lopez had visited Mrs Hernandez twice in person to discuss Erica's college planning. In general, Mr Lopez pushed his daughter to challenge herself academically, discussing with Mrs Hernandez particular courses that he wanted her to take. Interestingly, however, when it came to college choice, Mr Lopez seemed to prefer that Erica go to a community college first. He was the one who told Erica that those who advance directly to a four-year college first should know what they want to study. Based on this information, Erica reasoned that she would be better off going to a community college since she did not yet know what she wanted to choose as a major.

Summer before Senior Year

During the summer, Erica visited LCC with her father, and was told that she could spend one or two years at LCC and then transfer to a four-year institution:

I talk with my dad because he's the one who is like, looking for all colleges. So, we [went] to LCC to visit. They explain to us how we can do two years at LCC and then we can move to another university. So, um my dad he was thinking, like go to a university is really expensive. So, he thinks maybe I should do one year or two years at college. (IN 09/26/2011)

LCC was the only college that she visited that summer (and ultimately during the entire college planning period), and the trip made LCC more real to her than any other potential choices. Also, around this time, it became clear to me that Mr Lopez was the one driving Erica's college planning, with Erica mostly following along. Throughout the study, when I asked her about her college planning, Erica would often start with, 'My dad wants me to', and 'My dad is thinking', prompting me to rephrase my question: 'Well, what would *you* like to do?'

Although Erica initially framed her potential choice of LCC in terms of her not knowing what to major in, by the summer before her senior year, the main reason had shifted to cost saving. Her father told her that going to LCC was much less expensive than going to a four-year college, and by spending the first one or two years at LCC, she could save a considerable amount of money. At the same time and somewhat confusingly, Mr Lopez was also advising her to study for the SAT, when she would only need these scores if she were to apply to a four-year college: 'But ... he's like really, like, he all the time tell me to study for the SATs because it's really important' (IN 09/26/2011). Given that Mr Lopez received his college education in Spain and the school he worked for did not have a high-school component, it is quite possible that he was not aware of exactly who needed to take the SAT.

Fall Senior Year

At the beginning of the fall of her senior year, Erica was wavering between going to LCC and going to a four-year college. By this point, her father had made it clear that he wanted her to attend LCC, citing the cost difference as the main reason, whereas Erica, on her part, had identified one university she wanted to apply to: Florida Atlantic University: 'I want to go to Florida Atlantic University because my aunt, she lives there' (IN 09/26/2011). This was the first time that Erica named a university she was interested in, and since her father's main objection to a university education was the cost, she reasoned that if she earned a scholarship, her father would not object to her going:

Erica: My plan, like, my plan for right now is like, try to get good
            grades, so they can give me uh, how you say—
Yasuko: A scholarship?
Erica: A scholarship. Yeah. So, I am really focused this year.
            (IN 09/26/2011)

In the end, however, there was no evidence that she seriously followed
up on her scholarship search, nor did she persist in applying to Florida
Atlantic University after her father vetoed the idea: 'I was telling him,
"You can let me go", and he said, "No"' (IN 09/26/2011).

Erica's own hesitation about going straight to a four-year college
at this point largely stemmed from her lack of confidence in English.
She acknowledged that her insecurity about her English language
proficiency sometimes caused her to avoid speaking with her English
L1 peers, staying in the comfort of her Spanish-speaking social circles
instead:

> Because I don't speak a lot of, of English, like people who speak English.
> I speak, but I speak more with my Spanish. So, I know that is my fault.
> Because my dad, he like, 'Oh, you try to, you need to speak more with
> American people'. (IN 11/21/2011)

Mr Woznyj observed that Erica had had a series of Latino boyfriends,
which might have influenced how much time she spent speaking Spanish
as well.

Not just socially, but also in the classroom, where both the opportunity
and need to use English were the greatest, Erica rarely spoke up.
Mr Smith, her 11th-grade American Literature teacher, commented that
although Erica was a good student, she was so quiet that he sometimes
could not tell whether she was truly understanding the content or 'just
nodding her head to be polite' (FN 05/24/2011). Furthermore, when Erica
took the SAT in May of her junior year, the low scores she received – 300
in Critical Reading, 390 in Math and 230 in Writing for a total score of
920 – might have reinforced her belief that she needed to improve her
English proficiency before she could face the rigor of four-year college
work. Regarding the low SAT scores, she said, 'I just remember that my
dad, he told me that I get like 3-something-hundred. 300-something. So,
he thinks [inaudible] really do bad score. I was like, "Oh." But, it was my
fault because I really don't study very good for the SAT' (IN 09/26/2011).
She was worried and asked me, 'What happen like, if you don't get a good
score?' (IN 09/26/2011). I pointed out that the SAT scores are only one

component of the college applications that admissions officers consider and that four-year colleges usually have an English as a second language program for non-native speakers, too. However, even as she talked about applying to four-year colleges, she seemed increasingly convinced that she needed to study English at a community college first. She said, 'I was thinking like, if go to LCC I can study English very good. So, I can go to university, and I won't have like a lot of problems' (IN 09/26/2011).

Erica, then, applied to LCC in early November, and by the time I spoke to her later that month, she had made up her mind about going there:

> Well, I decide go to LCC because first my dad, he was saying that you can, it's gonna be better for me because go to a university, fours-year college is going to cost you more. I wanna learn better my English, um, reading and writing. So, I don't know, I just, I don't think—, It's not a bad school. [Yasuko: No, it's a good school.] I was, yeah, because I was talking with Mr. Woznyj and he say it's was a good idea. (IN 11/21/2011)

She looked relieved about having finally made up her mind and knowing where she was going after Brighton.

Spring Senior Year

By mid-February, Erica had received her letter of acceptance from LCC. Also, she and her father attended the FAFSA workshop that the school held specifically for EL students and their parents in February. Typical of their relationship, as soon as Erica was accepted to LCC, her father contacted the college to inquire about what courses she should be taking the following year. However, Erica herself appeared ambivalent about LCC. Whereas back in November, she appeared relieved that her postsecondary destination had been settled, she now expressed envy for peers who had been admitted to universities: 'I was like, I don't know [laughs]. Like, because I hear, like, a lot of people talking, they're going to Penn State or Drexel, so I feel like, I want to go there, too' (IN 02/29/2012). Perhaps, as she heard the news of her peers' admission to various universities, Erica felt a tinge of regret that she had not at least tried to apply.

Her regrets about not going to a four-year college seemed to lead to regrets about not having taken higher-level courses at Brighton, too. Erica and Alexandra were the only two students in the study who took an AP course (AP Spanish). However, in her mind, taking AP Spanish was not the same as taking other AP courses in English, and she had not viewed herself as AP material. As she put it, 'I'm not going to be like for the AP' (IN 09/26/2011). Yet, at the end of her senior year, her own experience of college planning and those of her friends now made her wonder whether, perhaps, she should have been more aggressive about requesting more advanced coursework: 'What I saw is like people that have AP classes, like they get ... being accepted like in college [pause]. Um, they get like scholarships [pause]. So I will go back and do that, like take AP' (IN 05/22/2012).

Kadi's Story

Kadi, originally from Guinea, had by far the most complicated family history of the seven students. Her mother passed away when she was three – Kadi said in a war, but she was not entirely sure. Then her father, who was an imam, a spiritual leader and teacher of the Islamic faith, immigrated to the United States without her. In his absence, Kadi grew up with her grandmother. She moved to Minnesota to be reunited with her father when she was 12. By then, her father had remarried, and by association, Kadi acquired four stepbrothers and three stepsisters. When she turned 16, however, her father passed away after a long illness, and just prior to starting her 11th grade, Kadi moved to the Brighton area to live with an uncle and his family.

When Kadi moved to Minnesota, it was one of her stepsisters, Debbie, who took her under her wing and helped her make the transition to an American school. Kadi, a Maninka L1 speaker, said that she spoke a little English when she arrived in the United States, but that her English was nowhere near sufficient to understand her classes. However, the more serious challenge was that Kadi had never attended school in Guinea: she had no literacy skills in any language, and her first day of school in Minnesota was her first day of formal education. The school district initially wanted to place her in eighth grade according to her chronological age, but Debbie intervened and insisted that Kadi be held back and placed in fifth grade. As a result of their negotiation, they compromised that Kadi start in sixth grade.

By the time I met Kadi, there were no signs of academic struggle: she was passing all her classes and in some of them doing quite well. Given her current academic performance, I was surprised to learn about her lack of formal education. Kadi attributed her fast catching-up to Debbie's mentoring. She said that every day after school, her sister tutored her for about four hours:

> Because after school me and her, when I come from school, eat, and then she finally tell me go upstairs and study and she, she would go with me and give me some spelling and spell it out and help me with my homework. (IN 04/04/2011)

In addition to her own tutoring, Debbie enlisted the help of a neighbor in teaching Kadi how to speak English:

> We speak different language [i.e. Maninka] at home. My sister, she used to get mad when anybody speak that language to me. She used to get mad, yelling. And she would kick me out of the house. She say, 'Go to your friend house and learn to speak English'. (IN 10/14/2011)

In middle school, Kadi also received extensive EL support. She spent practically all of her sixth-grade year in an EL class because she did not know how to read:

> Then my EL teacher, her name was Miss Ryan, something like that, she, you know, I used to have her class like *every* day. No class, no schedule, only her class. So, every time, every time I go to my other classes, they always be like, 'Read'. And which is, I don't even know how to read. So, they just keep me with her for the whole day. (IN 10/14/2011, original emphasis)

After spending all of middle school as an EL, she was reclassified as English proficient at the end of ninth grade. When she arrived at Brighton in 10th grade, therefore, she did not receive any EL services. It is clear that she was fortunate enough to receive substantial support both at home and in the school. However, Kadi's own tenacity and ability to seek help also contributed significantly to her remarkable academic progress. Of the seven students in the study, she was by far the most proactive in searching for the information she needed and in seeking assistance from the people around her. As one of her teachers said, 'Kadi, she is not quiet; she gets what she wants' (FN 05/24/2011).

Spring Junior Year

Kadi had a very clear career goal from the very beginning: she wanted to become a nurse and work with babies and children. When she first moved to the United States, one of her older stepbrothers was attending college to become a nurse, and that was her first introduction to nursing as a profession. However, the real inspiration came when her stepsister

Debbie became pregnant and gave birth: 'When my sister have a baby to the hospital and the nurse was helping her and I was like, I wanna be like this person some days. I just love to be with kids and help them' (IN 03/08/2011).

At this point, Kadi was unaware of the different categories of nurses (e.g. nurse aide, registered nurse, nurse practitioner) and different levels of education that these qualifications entailed. Because she was unfamiliar with the necessary educational qualifications to become a nurse, Kadi was not sure whether to go straight to a four-year college or go to a community college. She was nonetheless proactive in consulting those around her about her postsecondary plans. She discussed options with her uncle and aunt, and she approached her guidance counselor. This guidance counselor, Mrs McLaughlin, who would unfortunately leave the school in the middle of Kadi's senior year, was proactive in reaching out to her charges, and Kadi reported having comfortable and relatively frequent conversations with her. It was out of these conversations that the idea of enrolling in a nursing vocational program in her senior year emerged. In typical Kadi fashion, it was her own curiosity and efforts that led her to discover the career and technical education (CTE) program. She even enlisted the help of Josephine, a close friend, to find out more about it:

> I saw my friend at breakfast in the morning. She alway—, I was asking where she go. She said she go to CTE, which I didn't even know what was CTE, so huh. And saw the packet, I asked Josephine. I was like give me—, you know what CTE. She said she have the packet and she showed me the packet. And she give it to me and I took it home and read it and go to a meeting. And then I come back to school. I think I asked one of my teacher. She's um, I have to write a letter. I went to my counselor. She give me um, paper to write essay about why I want to be in the nursing program. (IN 10/14/2011)

When she approached Mrs McLaughlin with the idea, the counselor figured out that Kadi was sufficiently on track to meeting all the graduation requirements, such that she could afford to allocate a large proportion of her class schedule in her senior year to a CTE program. They decided that Kadi should apply to the two nursing-related programs available at Brighton.

Fall Senior Year

Kadi was admitted to both of the CTE programs. One involved working in a nearby hospital and offered a modest pay, but it did not provide much training; the other involved working in a senior citizens' home without pay but would lead to a nurse aide certificate at the end of the program. Kadi was looking for a head start in training as a nurse and chose the program that would lead to a nurse aide certificate. For her whole senior year then, Kadi would take two regular academic classes at Brighton, and then at 10:30 am take a school bus to the CTE program at the County Career and Technical Education Center (CCTEC). She would stay there until 2:15 pm and then take the bus back to Brighton to catch another bus to go home. The program started with training in hand hygiene (how to wash one's hands properly), feeding patients who could not feed themselves and giving bed baths, gradually moving on to going to a senior citizens' home and working with elderly people who needed assistance.

Apart from the CTE program being a wonderful head start to a nursing career, Kadi also carefully thought of it as her college financing plan. She knew that she would not be able to count on her family to finance her college education, and she thought that her part-time work as a nurse aide would be a viable source of income. She said that she was inspired by one of the alumni of the CTE program who visited the program to talk about how she worked her way through college:

> Because this girl she came into our class and talked to us how she going, like from 5 to 11 o'clock, she work for all that time. Then 12 to 3 o'clock, she go to school and come back home 3 or 4. So, and she said the money really help her to buy her book, which her parent don't have to buy her nothing for school. Then the job help her do lot of stuff, so I was like, 'That's good.' And that's what I want to do it for. (IN 10/14/2011)

One of the additional benefits of the CTE program, in terms of Kadi's college planning, was that it led her to further resources. In October of her senior year, Kadi started attending a College Access Center run by the local county, on the recommendation of one of her CTE teachers. The center offered high school students from any schools in the region drop-in assistance with homework, SAT preparation and college planning. One could argue that the same services were available right at Brighton, and that Kadi did not have to travel all the way to the center to receive these services. But she took to going to the center, and it turned into a weekly visit for the whole fall semester.

By December of her senior year, Kadi was steeped in the CTE program and had progressed to assisting the elderly at the senior citizens' home. She said,

From Tuesday through Thursday we just go there, help them, feed 'em. Like, you know, if they need water or if they don't feel good, just tell the doctor they don't feel good. So they have to come over and check on them. (IN 12/09/2011)

Although the work she did in the program had nothing to do with children, she seemed to enjoy working with elderly people: 'I like it to help old people. It's very fun' (IN 12/09/2011).

By December too, she had completed her application to LCC while also considering several four-year colleges. As discussed in Chapter 3, she had developed a detailed college list with the help of the College Access Center back in October. Nonetheless, she seemed swayed by the information packages she was receiving and mentioned applying to Arcadia University, Cedar Crest University and, quite randomly, Virginia Wesleyan College. When I asked why she was applying to these colleges, she could not produce any reason other than that these were the colleges she heard from.

At the same time, however, Kadi was leaning toward going to LCC. She had become quite close to one of the CTE teachers, who was a registered nurse, and this teacher advised her to attend LCC to complete the first two years of college and then apply to a nursing program in a university:

And she told me that, my teacher, she said for nursing schools, she went to LCC for, to take all her classes. And for two years and then she transferred to a university. Then took, just be in the program, not the classes. I was like, that makes sense because she said, you know, you gotta take all your classes and if you transfer, you don't have to go take math, so you don't have to do none of that. (IN 10/14/2011)

The idea of completing the general education requirements at LCC at a fraction of the cost of a four-year institution appealed to Kadi. Also, the fact that her mentor had herself become a registered nurse through spending the first two years at LCC and then later transferring to a four-year college was compelling proof that such a pathway was possible.

Spring Senior Year

By late January of her senior year, Kadi had received a letter of acceptance from LCC. She was also accepted to Virginia Wesleyan College with a scholarship, but since the college had no nursing program, and she did not have any relatives in Virginia, she decided to decline the offer. Her CTE mentor continued to encourage her to attend LCC for two years and then transfer to a nursing program at a university, and by February, Kadi had decided to attend LCC.

As Kadi became clearer about which college to attend, her attention shifted to the question of how to finance her college education. She was eager to file her FAFSA. However, one complication that arose was the question of who her guardian was for financial-aid purposes. The FAFSA requires students and their families to provide not only the student's but also the parents' financial information except for those who are deemed independent students.[1] For a student like Kadi, who comes from a non-traditional family background, the process is considerably more complex. Even after consulting several people at the school, she was still unsure whether she needed to apply as a dependent of someone and if so, exactly of whom she was a dependent. With both of her biological parents deceased, her stepmother was her official guardian. However, Kadi was currently not living with her stepmother, but with her uncle and his family. Compounding the problem was that neither her stepmother nor her uncle was employed, and Kadi was not sure whether either of them filed their tax returns.

In early February, she and her uncle attended the FAFSA workshop at Brighton together.[2] An officer from the state grant office came to assist with the workshop and advised them to use her uncle's tax information for her application. By then, her uncle was able to produce his tax return, and during the workshop, they used his tax information to fill out her application. Nonetheless, confusion about her status and her guardian ensued. In the end, Kadi herself called the Federal Student Aid Information Center and talked to a customer service representative, who advised her to file her application as an independent. Ultimately, she filed her FAFSA application as an independent student.

While she was trying to figure out her financial aid application, she was also working toward obtaining her nurse aide certificate. In May of her senior year, she passed the skills evaluation administered by the National Nurse Aide Assessment Program but failed the written exam. She would have to retake the written exam before she could enroll in the Pennsylvania Nurse Aide Registry, but she said that she was going to wait until after graduation to retake the exam since she currently had too many other commitments. After graduation, she would have more time to focus on preparing for the exam.

Kadi saw her own education and career development as a way to benefit not only herself, but also her family, friends and her larger community. Once again, her stepsister Debbie, was her inspiration:

If I get a better job, I'll be able to support all these people here, for one education, go to the job, I will support everybody. Friends, family. Plus, you know, the way that I'm gonna help, I'll go back home, to my country, help those people, because my sister, she doing it right in Minnesota. She have a program in Minnesota, like, those people in Africa, not going to school. (IN 05/19/2012)

The nurse aide certificate would help Kadi support herself during her college years. Once she finished her associate's degree at LCC, her plan was to enroll in a nursing program at a university and to work toward earning her license as a registered nurse. Then she would have a professional license that would help her contribute to making the world a better place.

Notes

(1) The FAFSA considers undergraduate students under the age of 24 'independent' only if they are married, are orphaned, have children, served in the military or fall into very specific legal categories (e.g. emancipated minors) (Federal Student Aid US Department of Education, n.d.).

(2) As discussed in Chapter 3, there was a separate FAFSA workshop for EL seniors and their parents. However, since Kadi was no longer an EL, she attended a workshop that was open to any seniors and their parents.

4 Different Reasons to Choose a Community College

So far in this book, I have discussed the factors that inhibit ELs' access to four-year colleges, often pitting four-year college access against the option of attending a community college. Readers may therefore assume that I hold the belief that all students should aim for a four-year college, and that community colleges are a lesser option. That is not my belief. It is true that I came to this project espousing something akin to that viewpoint; however, through my work with these seven ELs, I have come to realize that community colleges play a vital role in making PSE possible for many ELs. I have also come to realize that not all students want or need a college degree. As I will discuss in Chapter 5, for some students, a postsecondary CTE program that leads directly to a career is a much more productive pathway than jumping on the 'college for all' bandwagon (Rosenbaum *et al.*, 2010).

Statistics show that a growing number of students begin their PSE at community colleges. In 2012, the year in which the study participants graduated from high school, 29% of high school graduates enrolled in two-year colleges immediately after high school graduation, while 37% enrolled in four-year colleges (National Center for Education Statistics, 2014). Whereas the rate of four-year enrollment has not changed significantly since 1990, the rate of two-year college enrollment has increased by 9%, indicating the growing importance of community colleges as the entry point into PSE (National Center for Education Statistics, 2019). Even those who are academically qualified to enroll in four-year colleges increasingly attend community colleges first in order to reduce the cost of the first two years of college education (Ellis, 2013; Merrow, 2007). Indeed, the price differential is clear: for 2020–2021, the mean cost of tuition and fees at a community college is $3,770 as opposed to $10,560 at a public four-year institution (instate tuition) and \$37,650 at a private four-year institution (College Board, 2020). Given the current trends toward escalating college tuition and mounting student loan debts, being able to save money in the first two years of college and then transfer to a four-year college later is an attractive option for many prospective four-year college students (Wang, 2013). Articulation agreements between community colleges and four-year institutions are a growing trend, and many community colleges now have established pathways that enable students who have met eligibility requirements, such as a certain minimal GPA and completion of an associate's degree, to be able to transfer automatically to a four-year institution.[1]

Community colleges also play a key role in giving traditionally underserved students 'a second chance' by providing them with an opportunity to fill in gaps in their academic preparation and enabling them to achieve a college degree, be it an associate's or a bachelor's. For that reason, Merrow (2007) likens community college to a 'stepladder', a tool to reach a height that one otherwise cannot reach. There is also the argument that without remedial education both at community colleges and four-year colleges, US higher education would become even more exclusive, denying access to all but those who are fully academically prepared upon high school graduation (Attewell *et al.*, 2006). Already underserved groups in US higher education, such as racial/ethnic/linguistic minority and low-income students, would bear the brunt of such a policy.

Of the seven ELs in this study, four of them ultimately decided to attend LCC: Erica, Alexandra, Josephine and Kadi. Their reasons for switching from a four-year college to a community college as their postsecondary destination varied from one student to another. Erica and Alexandra chose to attend LCC because they were intimidated by the idea of going directly to a four-year college. They enrolled in LCC without applying to any four-year colleges despite being the highest-performing students of the seven. Josephine opted for LCC after she was rejected by most of her four-year college options and upon realizing that a four-year college was out of her price range. Kadi decided to follow in the footsteps of her mentor who had become a registered nurse by completing her first two years of general education at a community college and then transferring to a nursing program at a university. In this chapter, then, I explore the different reasons and conditions that led the four students to choose LCC. I then examine the impact of Brighton's institutional habitus on the students' decisions.

Erica and Alexandra: Afraid to Go to a Four-Year College

Of the seven participants, Erica and Alexandra had the best chances of being admitted to a four-year college. Yet, in the end, both decided to enroll in LCC without submitting a single application to a four-year college. In exploring how these two students reached this decision, two elements stand out: Erica and Alexandra's own fear of failure and Brighton's lack of encouragement for them to apply to a four-year college.

Erica chose to attend LCC in part because she was too linguistically insecure to view herself as a legitimate four-year college candidate. The term *linguistic insecurity*, coined by Labov (1966), refers to the feeling of inferiority about one's own speech as measured against an exterior standard of correctness. Although Labov used the term to refer to social class differences as reflected in speech patterns among monolingual English speakers, we can also apply the notion to ELs and their anxiety about their English as compared to 'native speaker' standards (Bucci & Baxter, 1984). Erica, the highest academic achiever of the seven participants, was ironically also the student who exhibited the strongest linguistic insecurity, and it permeated many aspects of her life. Her fear of socializing with English L1 speakers made her reluctant to join clubs and sports teams at school. I asked her about it:

Yasuko: Why did you not do that?
Erica: Why I didn't do it? Because I don't know [pause]. I feel kind of lazy to do it.
Yasuko: Yeah? You're just too busy learning English and—
Erica: Yeah, and I was like, I don't know. I thought that I was not able to understand. (IN 05/22/2012)

Her linguistic insecurity similarly prevented her from challenging herself academically. Mr Woznyj shared that in senior year, Erica begged him to move her from a regular (i.e. non-EL) English course back into his EL course:

> Erica is a pretty intelligent girl ... but, I don't see the push to really achieve that goal in her. She was in regular ed. English and wasn't even doing poorly ... [but] she started saying, 'I can't do this. I don't want to'. (IN 01/06/2012)

In Chapter 2, I noted that ELs rarely contested the courses that they were assigned; this was a rare case wherein an EL exerted her agency, but to request an *easier* course. Erica was subsequently moved to Mr Woznyj's EL course.

Ultimately, Erica's decision to enroll in LCC stems from her individual habitus, which was constricted by her linguistic insecurity. She was clear that she would eventually attain a bachelor's degree. However, as she moved from junior to senior year, Erica became increasingly convinced that her English proficiency necessitated that she first attend a community college before she would be ready for the demands of four-year college work: 'If [I] go to LCC, I can study English very good. So, I can go to the university. I won't have, like, a lot of problems' (IN 09/26/2011). In leaning toward LCC because of her still developing English, Erica might have erroneously assumed that one's English had to be perfect to attend a four-year college. Such an assumption was common among ELs, observed EL teacher Ms Li: 'I know that they think college is where all these like, you know, perfect-speaking English people go. And you have to have such a great score on your SATs' (IN 01/23/2012). In this respect, Erica's low SAT scores also likely reinforced her belief that her English ability was insufficient for college-level work.

Like Erica, Alexandra similarly felt a sense of linguistic insecurity. She said, 'Sometimes I'm afraid to speak. [Yasuko: Why?] 'Cause I don't feel like I'm speaking well, like other people. Like when I had to speak with Americans. The Americans are—, they can speak well' (IN 04/20/2011). In addition, Alexandra's hesitation to begin the actual college application process derived not only from her linguistic insecurity, but more broadly from her general sense of being unprepared. She knew all along that she had to take the SAT in order to apply to Penn State. However, her aversion to taking the exam, based on her feeling unprepared to take it, was so strong that she kept on deferring. When the last possible exam deadline arrived, she failed to register:

Yasuko:	And why didn't you take the SAT? You could have taken the one in November, right?
Alexandra:	It passed already.
Yasuko:	Yeah. I know, but I mean, you knew you could have—, you were talking about taking it in October, but—
Alexandra:	Yeah. But, I missed it.
Yasuko:	The deadline? In October? Hm. And why did you miss the deadline?

Alexandra: Want to take it, but I think I'm not prepared. Maybe I am, but I need practice. 'Cause I don't know what's on the SAT. (IN 11/21/2011)

Elsewhere in the same interview, Alexandra attributed this missed deadline to a careless mistake. She simply forgot, she claimed: 'When people told me, [I thought] oh my God' (IN 11/21/2011). However, in the above excerpt, she hints at more intentionality: she let the deadline pass because she felt unprepared.

I remember at that time being very surprised by Erica and Alexandra's decision to enroll in LCC. I was more than a little frustrated that they did not even try to apply to any four-year colleges. However, upon reflection, part of their feeling unprepared, it seems to me, derived from their own internal standards, their own sense of the kind of academic ability and English proficiency that college students should possess. If they were not prepared to meet those standards, they were not going to try. Both of them had been academically top students in their countries of origin, and I believe it was difficult for them to take the risk and potentially see themselves fail or face rejection.

However, it is important not to reduce these ELs' lack of confidence to their personal weakness and to recognize the influence of both the larger societal language ideology and Brighton's institutional habitus on the students' individual habitus. As a nation, the United States is deeply monoglossic in its language ideology (García & Torres-Guevara, 2009: 184), where 'English monolingualism has been constructed as the only acceptable language use of loyal and true United States citizens'. This monoglossic ideology funnels down to individual schools and influences the way schools position multilingual students in their midst. During the three years of fieldwork, I never heard any educator at Brighton describe ELs as 'bilingual' or 'multilingual'. Many spoke of ELs' language proficiency, but always in terms of 'less than': less than native speakers, less than what is necessary to take challenging courses, less than what was expected of four-year college students. For example, Mr Burke, Director of Guidance, explained some teachers' rationale to recommend remedial courses for ELs based on their English proficiency: 'This is kind of the regular level versus remedial. So, some teachers might say, "OK. Well, this EL is still developing reading and communication skills in English. So, therefore, I'm going to put him in remedial"' (IN 10/03/2011). Although such statements – and there were many – may at first glance sound neutral and reasonable, it becomes clear that they reflect a deficit orientation based on a monoglossic ideology. Any counter-discourse, such as the following, was entirely missing at Brighton: 'These are multilingual students with cognitive advantages thanks to their multilingual proficiency[2] and rich intercultural experiences, and they should be placed in higher level courses in which cognitive flexibility and the ability to see multiple perspectives are critical'. Thus, the fact that Erica already spoke three languages (Spanish, English and French) and was adding a fourth (Italian) to her repertoire, or that Alexandra was the first student in the history of Brighton High School to be inducted into the Sociedad Honoraria Hispánica – these are all linguistic accomplishments – did not seem to alter the teachers and counselors' view of where they should go to college. They were still first and foremost 'English learners', an identity so deeply entrenched in the school's institutional habitus that it dictated the staff's assumptions about their appropriate postsecondary destinations.

Under such conditions, it is not at all surprising that Erica and Alexandra came to espouse acute linguistic insecurity and a general sense of being unprepared. They might have been top students back in their countries of origin; they might speak multiple languages; but in the context of this country and this high school, they were ELs who were assigned to average- or remedial-level courses. They were also recent immigrants who were getting used to an entirely new education system. Under those circumstances, it is not hard to imagine self-doubt creeping into an 18-year-old's mind. In other words, Erica and Alexandra's individual habitus about what PSE options were within their reach was strongly influenced by their positioning within the context of Brighton's institutional habitus.

When Erica and Alexandra began to second-guess their ability to reach a four-year college, teachers and counselors failed to encourage them to stay the course and at the very least try applying to four-year colleges. Instead, the staff presented LCC as a good entry point that would eventually lead to a four-year college. Erica and Alexandra came to integrate this advice into their own narratives of what was a reasonable course of action without having to give up on their original aspirations of obtaining a bachelor's degree. Erica shared that she had consulted Mr Woznyj about going to LCC and seemed reassured by his endorsement: 'He was saying like, um, if I go, I go two years to LCC, I can um, ca-, transfer? [Yasuko: Transfer. Yes.] transfer … to university' (IN 11/21/2011). In other words, rather than thinking that they missed the critical opportunity to reach a four-year college, they were able to take comfort in the idea that their ultimate goal of obtaining a bachelor's degree had not fundamentally changed and that they were simply taking an alternative route to the same destination.

Josephine: A Four-Year College Was Out of Reach – For Now

Unlike Erica and Alexandra, Josephine did not hesitate to apply to four-year colleges. As someone who had been schooled in English in Ghana and who had already been reclassified by the time of this study, Josephine was much more comfortable speaking English than more recent arrivals such as Erica, Alexandra and Ken. Having been at Brighton since the beginning of ninth grade, she was also relatively more integrated into the school community, regularly attending the EL homework club and belonging to a couple of student clubs.

Likewise, Josephine was more proactive in her college planning than Erica and Alexandra and was on track with her college applications according to the timeline suggested by the school. She was able to name several colleges of interest in the spring of her junior year and took the SAT in June of her junior year. In the fall of her senior year, she prepared her application materials and submitted them to several colleges before Thanksgiving, just as the guidance counselors suggested. In other words, a critical difference between Josephine's college access experience and those of Alexandra and Erica is that Josephine actually applied to four-year colleges, while Alexandra and Erica did not.

Nonetheless, Josephine was rejected by all the colleges she applied to except Virginia Union University, which she had little intention of attending. There were several reasons why her four-year college application was not successful despite her consistent planning efforts and timely submission. First, for a candidate who wanted to major in science, her transcript did not present a rigorous set of math and science courses or stellar performance (Table 4.1). Her math courses, while all at the grade level in their sequence (algebra 1 in ninth grade, geometry in 10th grade, etc.), were also all at remedial level. Similarly, her science course sequence showed EL science courses followed by science electives typically taken by lower-track students. For a student aspiring to major in science, the conspicuous absence of chemistry and physics on her

Table 4.1 Josephine's math and science courses at Brighton

Year	Math	Grade (%)	Science	Grade (%)
9th	Remedial Algebra 1	80	EL Physical Science	81
10th	Remedial Geometry	82	EL Biology	85
11th	Remedial Algebra 2	82	Earth Science (elective)	89
12th	Remedial Probability and Statistics	89	Life Science (elective)	79
			Human Anatomy (elective)	83

transcript presented a costly gap. In fact, her science coursework was exactly what Brighton's program of studies recommended college-bound students *not* to follow. According to Brighton's program of studies, 'a strong foundation in Biology, Physics, and Chemistry is recommended for college. Anatomy and Physiology and/or Environmental Science are useful additional courses of interest, *but should not be substituted for the three basic science courses*' (emphasis added). And yet, Josephine was allowed to follow a non-college-bound science track, likely because, once again, in the context of Brighton's institutional habitus, an EL with a mid-range academic performance was not seen as four-year college bound.[3]

Also, Josephine's grades were not particularly high in those courses. In math, her grades ranged from 80% to 89% with a mean of 83.25%, while her science grades ranged from 79% to 89% with a mean of 83.4% (Table 4.1). We should remember that this is a student who arrived in a new country just before ninth grade and began high school as an EL. Considering those circumstances, it is a remarkable achievement to earn a B average. However, on an absolute scale, coupled with a math SAT score of 370, her academic qualifications were unimpressive for a prospective science major in a four-year college.

Second, as discussed in Chapter 3, her lack of college knowledge did not improve her likelihood of college admission. Her exclusive choice of private colleges would have likely resulted in attending LCC even if she had been admitted to more colleges because of the high cost of a private college education. In addition, her college essay, which could have appealed the hardships that she had overcome as a recently arrived immigrant from a low-income home with a single parent did not effectively communicate her resilience and strengths.

Ultimately, for Josephine, two aspects of the college application process led her to the conclusion that LCC was the best option for her: the cost of college and the viability of transferring from a community college to a four-year college. Although she was aware of her family's financial situation, she had not connected it with the actual cost of college as evidenced by private colleges. It was during her college and FAFSA applications, that it finally dawned on her that she needed to consider college affordability if she were to complete a four-year college education: 'Because if you go straight to a four-year college, you're paying like, about $30,000 a year, and when you go to community college, you can save more than—, that money you can use to pay for the other two years' (IN 05/31/2012).

Note in the above excerpt that Josephine was assuming that she was going to transfer to a four-year college later, and that idea took hold during the actual college application process. She applied to several four-year colleges she wanted to attend, but none accepted her. While she was going through this process, she also saw her brother, who had attended a community college, apply to transfer to a four-year college.[4] Her brother's example presented to her, in the most concrete way, an alternative pathway to a bachelor's degree. The fact that Brighton educators also consistently spoke of LCC as a pathway to a four-year college also likely influenced her perception that this was a viable option. Thus, Josephine, an EL from a low-income family with immigrant optimism (Kao & Tienda, 1995), with her individual habitus, accepted the outcome and concluded that given her current situation and her hopes for the future, attending LCC was the best option available.

Kadi: Following in the Footsteps of Her Mentor

Kadi's case presents yet another example of why an EL might enroll in a community college: to follow in the footsteps of her CTE mentor and complete two years at a community college before transferring to a nursing program at a university. I believe it is fair to say that Kadi's pathway to LCC was the most positive of the four cases in this chapter, and several factors contributed to this positive outcome.

First, Kadi's own initiative and self-advocacy made a difference. While most of the other participants tended to shy away from actively seeking the guidance of their teachers and counselors, Kadi had no such hesitation. She discovered CTE through a chance encounter with a friend at school breakfast one day, enlisted the help of Josephine to learn more about it and then went to her guidance counselor to explore the possibility of enrolling in the program herself. This is entirely in keeping with Kadi and her stepsister Debbie's remarkable help-seeking ability. Ever since they arrived in the United States, they had been approaching people around them – neighbors, family doctors, teachers – to ask for information and enlist their help. Given that Kadi started out as a student with no formal education, she would not have come as far as she did without an ability to effectively seek help and make use of whatever resources were around her.

However, it is also the case that Kadi's academic circumstances worked in her favor. When Kadi transferred from a high school in Minnesota to Brighton in 11th grade, she had already been reclassified as English proficient, and she was able to transfer a large number of credits from her previous high school. In other words, she no longer had any EL course requirements, and she had already met many of her graduation requirements through her transferred credits. As a result, in her senior year, Kadi could afford to leave Brighton after the first two blocks in the morning for the County Career and Technical Education Center (CCTEC). This point is important. All CCTEC classes counted as electives; thus, in order to qualify for the CCTEC programs, students must have completed the majority of the graduation requirements beforehand because CCTEC students only had two blocks in the morning to complete the remaining required courses. ELs who had arrived from another country in the middle of high school, such as Ken and Erica, and those who had failed multiple courses and had numerous required courses to pass in senior year, such as Eddie and Carlos (see Chapter 5), would not have been eligible to enroll in CCTEC programs. Fortunately for Kadi, that was not the case.

Further, in a classic pattern of 'social capital begets more social capital', Kadi's enrollment in the CCTEC program led to more resources and support. Working closely with instructors at CCTEC, Kadi was put in touch with the College Access Center of the local county and was able to receive one-on-one guidance on college planning. As discussed in Chapter 3, through the mentoring she received at the center, Kadi produced a much more systematic list of colleges along with the required application materials and deadlines than any other participant in the study. At CCTEC, she built a relationship with a teacher/mentor who recommended that she spend two years at LCC to complete her general education courses, and then to transfer to a university to pursue a nursing degree because that was how this teacher had done it. It is notable that Kadi was the only student in the study who had a stable mentor with a US college degree whom she could consult on a regular basis. Because Kadi was certain about her career choice, and she had a mentor who could show her a viable and affordable pathway to that career, choosing LCC became a straightforward choice. Her story then represents an EL who took the initiative to marshal the resources and social capital within her reach to negotiate a postsecondary pathway that would lead her to her career goal.

The Influence of the Institutional Habitus on Students' Choices

So far, I have related four ELs' decision-making processes to attend LCC. Although the ultimate decisions to attend LCC were the students' own, the school's institutional habitus had a strong bearing on their decisions. In particular, 'going to a community college first is an economically smart way to earn a college education, and you can always transfer to a four-year college later' was a prevalent institutional discourse that Brighton educators frequently employed. In the remainder of this chapter, I highlight Brighton's institutional habitus and its impact on the four students' college decisions.

The most salient aspect of how Brighton educators talked about LCC was that it was an economical way to pursue a college education. As a high school that served a largely working-class community, its educators were highly aware of the importance of college affordability. This view was explicitly articulated by the school principal, Mr Lawrence. As I already discussed in Chapter 3, the principal strongly endorsed the community college pathway to earning a bachelor's degree:

> To go [to a community college] and have something a little more finan-cially affordable for a year, a year and a half, two years, and then go on to a traditional four-year school, finish and obtain a degree, I think is becoming a much more financially realistic path for all students. (IN 01/24/2012)

This is an important acknowledgement of the rapidly changing landscape of US higher education, wherein many students, including those who would not have considered going to college in the past, now want a bachelor's degree. At the same time, the cost of a four-year college education is skyrocketing, making student loan debt a significant social problem in the United States (Adelman, 1999, 2006; Cappelli, 2015; McCormick, 2003).[5] Every guidance counselor I spoke with mentioned the critical importance of LCC as a more affordable choice.

Another salient characteristic of Brighton's institutional habitus as it relates to the community college is that its educators consistently presented it, not as a place to obtain an associate's degree as one's terminal degree, but as a pathway toward a bachelor's degree. In other words, when Brighton educators recommended LCC, there was always an added message, 'You can always transfer to a four-year college later'. In Mr Lawrence's previous remark, we can see that this was very much the position he took; he did not present the community college as a good place to earn an associate's degree but as a stepping stone to a bachelor's degree that is realistic and within reach for Brighton students. With respect to ELs in particular, Mr Woznyj took a similar position. One day in class, he presented this alternative pathway to ELs in the following way:

> [Mr. Woznyj] emphasized how much money it costs to go to college and went into considerable detail about how it may be a good idea for people

to go to a community college first and then transfer to a university. He did a quick calculation of the price difference between four years of Temple [University] versus two years of LCC and then two years of Temple. (FN 09/28/2010)

Mr Woznyj's stance on community colleges was important because as the Chair of the EL Department, he was one teacher with whom ELs had regular contact. As Erica's comments above illustrated, he had a direct influence on ELs' decision-making. He too presented the community college as an economical and pragmatic pathway to a four-year degree.

Some of Brighton's educators presented community colleges as a good postsecondary option without specifying *for whom* it was a good option. However, Brighton's institutional discourse also revealed a deficit orientation toward community colleges: namely, 'a community college was appropriate for those who were in some way behind'. Counselor Mrs Salomon's statement reflects this discourse:

> We do really push LCC for a lot of students. ... It's a very, very good option um, economically for a lot of kids. And also, you know, some of the kids do need that extra year to kind of develop their work ethics and the kids that sometimes wake up in January and wanna do it. Sometimes they may be a good fit for LCC because they are a little bit behind in maturity maybe with wanting to go to college. And it may be good for them if they do need any remedial courses to take them while it's cheaper. (IN 11/09/2011)

Again, the primary reason she lists for recommending LCC is cost savings. Beyond that, however, the list of students that Mrs Salomon thinks should attend LCC – students who lack a work ethic, students who are behind in college planning, students who are immature and students who will need to take remedial courses in college – reveals her implicit bias that community college is for students with deficits. Mrs Meyers, career and college counselor, was even more blunt about the function of the community college by stating, 'Community college is a great solution to many of our problems here if it can be used appropriately' (IN 05/06/2011). When I asked her what she meant by 'our problems', she elaborated:

> Well, number one, a lot of students ... the seniors think about, 'OK, I need to go to college, now what do I do?' They do it too late so that's, so

community college is the only [option]. So, it's the problem of procras-
tination. Another problem of low SAT scores. Another one, just plain,
not having the intellect, not being smart enough to go to a four-year college. Another one being afraid to go to a four-year college. Or parents,
and, and this is I think possibly quite true of EL students, EL parent not
necessarily encouraging their kids to college. And, of course, the financial
problem. (IN 05/06/2011)

In other words, although many educators endorsed LCC as a good
postsecondary option, it was implicitly recommended to those
students who were seen as having deficits. ELs at Brighton were widely
conceptualized as significantly behind, either in their English proficiency,
their academic knowledge or both, and these were seen as the students'
own deficits, rather than the school's failure to prepare them for college.
With the majority of ELs also being low-income students, all these factors
fit perfectly into the schema of Brighton's institutional habitus about who
should go to LCC and why.

ELs, who were on the receiving end of the endorsement of LCC,
however, did not know this implicit bias in the endorsement. Rather,
they took to heart the institutional discourse, 'You can always transfer
to a four-year college later'. All four students spoke of transferring to
a four-year college from LCC as if it were part and parcel of attending
LCC. For example, when Alexandra realized that she had lost the option
to apply to Penn State because she did not have any SAT scores, she still
reasoned, 'But, I didn't [take the SAT], so now I don't have choice. So,
that's why I decide to go to LCC instead and for one year or two and then
transfer' (IN 02/29/2012). In this excerpt, she talks about transferring to
a four-year college after one or two years at LCC as if it would simply
happen as long as she wanted it. The way Alexandra and the other three
students talked about the transfer from LCC to a four-year college,
however, is simply mirroring the educators' discourse about attending
LCC. They were the ones who promoted the institutional discourse,
'Going to a community college first is an economically smart way to earn
a college education, and you can always transfer to a four-year college
later'.

The problem with this institutional discourse is that it is simply inac-
curate – at least the second part: one can*not* always transfer from a community college to a four-year college. A large percentage of students who
enroll in community colleges leave without earning an associate degree or
transferring to a four-year college. Nationwide, over 80% of community
college students aspire to earn a bachelor's degree (Jenkins & Fink, 2015).

In reality, however, only about 33% of first-time, full-time, degree-seeking community college students transfer to four-year colleges within six years of first enrollment. Moreover, only 20% of those who first enrolled full-time in community colleges ultimately earned a bachelor's degree within six years (National Student Clearinghouse Research Center, 2019).[6] The challenges that many community college students face in staying in college and making progress toward their degree are well documented. According to the US Department of Education (2017), 51% of students who first entered community colleges during 2010 and 2011 needed remediation, meaning that they were essentially taking high-school-level courses in community colleges. Many community college students need to work to support themselves and/or have significant family responsibilities (e.g. having a child), engaged in a constant study–life balance (Ma & Baum, 2016). Additionally, community college students who are non-native speakers of English may also be saddled with English as a second language (ESL) remedial course requirements if they do not meet the college English language proficiency standard (Bunch & Endris, 2012; Hodara, 2015). Li's (2021) qualitative case studies followed the transfer experiences of four community college ELs who were enrolled in healthcare programs. She found that all of them fell short of their original transfer aspirations. Furthermore, these ELs were required to undergo prolonged ESL and mathematics remedial education during the first year of community college, so that by the time they were ready to take mainstream college courses, they had forgotten what little science they had learned in high school and found themselves wholly unprepared for college-level science. They also lacked sufficient college knowledge to navigate the transfer process and consequently made costly mistakes such as transferring to a four-year program in which very few of the community college credits they had earned were counted. In short, then, yes, it is true that some community college students successfully transfer to a four-year college and go on to obtain a bachelor's degree, but it is a small segment of community college entrants. Transfer to a four-year college is far from guaranteed.

I do not believe that Brighton educators knowingly misled students about the likelihood of transferring from a community college to a four-year college. Rather, I believe that they too thought that transfer was, if not automatic, entirely realistic for students who wanted it, based on the good reputation of LCC and the number of articulation agreements that it had with four-year colleges. In fact, when I pointed out to Mrs Salomon that the transfer rate of community college students was low, she sounded somewhat offended and argued that while that might be the case with community colleges *in general*, LCC was different:

My experiences with LCC has been very positive, and I don't know whether that um, yeah, that's just anecdotal and that's not real scientific. But, I, I'm curious to see if what LCC's figures—, they keep really good records on, of, you know, where kids go after three and five years and all of that sort of thing. So that may be something that we can look at. (IN 11/09/2011)

However, LCC's graduation and transfer rates are no different from the national average. According to LCC's website, the three-year graduation rate for first-time full-time students was 18% in 2018 while 23% transferred to other institutions without graduating. It is important to note that not all 18% of LCC graduates went on to four-year colleges and not all 23% of transfer students transferred to four-year colleges, because the transfer rate includes transferring to other community colleges as well. The comparable national figures are a three-year graduation rate of 25% and a transfer-without-graduation rate of 18% (National Center for Education Statistics, 2019). We can see that compared with the national data, LCC students are slightly more likely to transfer out without graduation and slightly less likely to earn an associate degree, but its combined graduation/transfer rate (41%) is similar to the national rate (43%). Thus, as far as these rates are concerned, and contrary to Mrs Salomon's claims, LCC is no better than other community colleges.

Not knowing, however, allowed Brighton educators to continue holding onto the belief that community colleges are great equalizers, providing access to four-year colleges to students who were academically behind in high school. And the presence of LCC as Plan B for those students who needed it, I would argue, lessened Brighton educators' sense of urgency to make all their students college ready by the end of high school: there was always LCC to serve as 'Grade 13' for underprepared students.

Thus, ultimately, the community college served as a double-edged sword for ELs at Brighton. It certainly gave access to a college education for ELs such as Kadi and Josephine who otherwise would not have been able to access it. It is indisputably the case that students who start out at a community college are in a much better position to eventually complete either an associate's or a bachelor's degree than students who do not enroll in any postsecondary institution upon high school graduation (Kanno & Cromley, 2013). By having the option to enroll in LCC, Josephine and Kadi retained at least some chances of attaining a college degree, be it an associate's or a bachelor's degree. At the same time, precisely because LCC provided a middle ground between the two extreme options – going straight to a four-year college and not going to college at all – its availability allowed Brighton educators to relegate the responsibility of making students college ready onto LCC.

Meanwhile, for higher-performing ELs such as Erica and Alexandra, LCC provided a safer option than a four-year college. Consistent with the way they had recommended lower-track courses to ELs, Brighton educators tacitly steered high-performing ELs like Alexandra and Erica away from a four-year college to LCC in the name of 'protecting ELs': they hoped to prevent ELs from setting themselves up for failure. Alexandra and Erica, who had been reminded of their linguistic 'handicap' all along, in turn came to accept LCC as the best PSE choice for now. With their diminished individual habitus, they took to heart the institutional discourse, 'You can always transfer to a four-year college later', and found in LCC a solution to their dilemma of wanting a four-year college degree while being afraid of attending a four-year college immediately.

Summary

This chapter inquired into how and why four of the EL participants who originally planned to attend a four-year college switched to attending a community college. The two highest-performing students, Erica and Alexandra, chose to attend LCC because they lacked confidence in their English language proficiency to succeed at a four-year college and were too afraid to try and ultimately be found inadequate. Josephine switched to LCC after being rejected by all four-year colleges she was interested in attending and after realizing that the cost of a four-year college education was beyond her family's reach. Finally, on the advice of her CTE mentor, Kadi opted to enroll in LCC as a viable pathway to a nursing program.

Although ultimately these were the four students' own decisions, the influence of Brighton's institutional habitus was unmistakable. Brighton educators presented the community college as an affordable and smart pathway to a bachelor's degree, especially to students they perceived as not college ready. With the deficit positioning of ELs in the school and their low-track course placements, ELs were primary examples of students who were not college ready. In recommending community colleges, the educators themselves appeared to be unaware of community college students' low retention and transfer rates and the challenges many of these students face. But this uninformed advice resulted in ELs' choosing LCC on the erroneous assumption that they were nearly guaranteed transfer to a four-year college after two years of studying at the community college.

Notes

(1) However, Anderson *et al.*'s (2006) analysis of state articulation agreements between community and four-year colleges found no statistical effect on the actual increase in transfer. Thus, such agreements may be creating the perception among high school students, their families and school personnel that transfer is now more possible and easier than before, but without delivering any actual impact.

(2) Scientific evidence for the so-called 'bilingual advantage' is less than conclusive (e.g. Blom *et al.*, 2014; Morton & Harper, 2007; Paap & Greenberg, 2013). However, the point is that given that the idea of the bilingual advantage has spread in the media and has entered mainstream education discourse, it is reasonable to expect at least some educators would express this viewpoint. I find it telling that such a counterdiscourse was total absent at Brighton.

(3) Another possible explanation is that this was a simple oversight. As I discuss in Chapter 5 with regard to Carlos and Eddie's coursework, errors in the participants' coursework and fulfillment of graduation requirements were noticeable. Harklau (2016) points out that bureaucratic dysfunctions are common in public schools and that underserved students take the brunt of such dysfunctions.

(4) However, I do not know the outcome of Josephine's brother's transfer application. I did not obtain information on whether he actually enrolled in a four-year college.

(5) Despite the traditional image of college attendance as enrolling in one four-year college and graduating from it in four years, the reality is that there are now multiple patterns of college attendance. In addition to transferring from a community college to a four-year college, *swirling* (moving back and forth among multiple institutions) and *double-dipping* (attending two institutions at once), among others, are also common (Adelman, 1999, 2006; McCormick, 2003).

(6) It is important to add that part-time community college students fare much worse than full-time students. Only 5% of part-time students transfer to four-year colleges and 0.3% attain a bachelor's degree within six years of first enrollment (National Student Clearinghouse Research Center, 2019).

Eddie's Story

Eddie first struck me as a quiet, gentle person. Although I have since heard his teachers and counselors speak of him as 'very social' and having 'fallen into the wrong crowd', I still think of him as a quiet, polite and shy person. Eddie was born in the United States, which makes him a US citizen, but he moved to Mexico with his parents when he was three or four and attended elementary and middle school there. In 2008, his father passed away after an illness, which prompted Eddie's relocation to the United States. It was Eddie's own decision to move to the United States in search of a better life. He said, 'There's, like, hard then [pause], you know, 'cause I'd have to like get a job and you know, stop going to school' (IN 05/06/2011). His mother and his older sister, who were not US citizens, remained in Mexico. Eddie moved in with his uncle's family who lived in the Brighton area.

Unlike the previous stories in this book, which focus much more on making the transition to PSE, Eddie's story is of an 'at risk' youth who was never sure until the very end whether he would even graduate from high school. As far as his conversational English was concerned, he was much more fluent and at ease than Ken, Erica or Alexandra. Because of his conversational fluency, I had assumed that he had been in the United States for five or six years and was surprised to learn that he had arrived only three years prior. When he first arrived at Brighton, he spoke very little English, to the point where his guidance counselor, Mrs Salomon, needed Mrs Hernandez, a Spanish speaker, to serve as a translator. Given Eddie's near zero proficiency in English at the start, Mrs Salomon called his English language development 'phenomenal' (IN 11/09/2011). However, his academic work was consistently weak, and his attendance sporadic. One of the special education teachers I spoke to was worried about Eddie's reading skills and suspected that he might have a learning disability, although he was never referred for formal evaluation. Math also seemed to be a major weakness. Mrs Anderson, an EL teacher, and Eddie's study hall period teacher, explained that he was a respectful person but was not interested in school work: 'Last semester I was able to pull him in by himself because how my schedule was with his study hall. ... And he was always willing to come in but, if I didn't help him with things, he wouldn't do them. ... He's very social. He likes to socialize before doing his work' (IN 06/02/2011).

Spring Junior Year

Eddie was clear about what he wanted to do in the future: he wanted to become a car mechanic. He explained that this interest started while he was growing up in Mexico and helping his father fix cars. He was particularly drawn to a type of car called a lowrider. He would often search the web to find cool-looking lowriders and post them on his Facebook page. But in terms of how he would receive the formal training to become a car mechanic in the United States, Eddie was extremely vague. Initially, he talked about enrolling in the automotive technology program at a community college but then changed his mind and thought about attending a trade school (a postsecondary institution designed to provide job training in a specific skilled career, such as a car mechanic or welder) only to revert back to the idea of going to a community college soon after. He had not spoken to any of his teachers or his guidance counselor about his PSE plans, and had not looked up the automotive technology programs in the area.

It is safe to say, however, that the priority of making postsecondary plans was displaced the spring of his junior year with a far more pressing issue. In the spring, he had a baby with his girlfriend, Paola, a second-generation Latina student at Brighton. Eddie himself was not even 18. Understandably, both sets of parents/guardians were upset and angry: 'Well, they [Paola's parents] were mad, too. Yeah, were so mad' (IN 09/26/2011). Eddie himself was confused and scared. Some of his friends suggested leaving his girlfriend and fleeing to Mexico, but he stood his ground: 'I wasn't feeling good, like, to do that for her, and you know, it wasn't gonna be right for her. You know, I know it was my fault, too, and whatever happened, it was between me and her' (IN 05/30/2012).

Eventually, the arrangement was made for baby Jorge to live with Paola and her parents, with Paola's mother as the primary caregiver. Eddie reported spending several hours after school every day with

Jorge, to the point where he sometimes talked about practically 'living' at Paola's parents' house. However, Paola's mother was not always available to take care of the baby, and Eddie and Paola sometimes had to take turns staying home and caring for him, resulting in absences from school. Eddie's attendance was never good to begin with – the whole pregnancy incident took a toll – and his performance in class was never strong. But the added parenting responsibility made it even more difficult to attend school regularly. In the end, he was absent 20 days in the spring semester of his junior year, and failed EL US History, Remedial Algebra 1 and PE/Health. He earned only 16 credits in 11th grade, as opposed to 37 credits in 10th grade and 35 in ninth grade.

Fall Senior Year

Eddie was advised to attend summer school in order to make up for the classes he failed in the spring, but much to Mrs Salomon's chagrin, he did not, because in the Brighton school district, students have to pay to attend summer school. Once his senior year started, however, Eddie seemed more focused on graduation. He said, 'Yeah, now I'm doing more work because I know my—, this my senior year and I gotta … get good grades' (IN 09/26/2011).

Although having a baby is often a risk factor for dropping out and not continuing further education (e.g. Bridgeland *et al.*, 2006; Shuger, 2012), Eddie took his parenting role quite seriously and wanted to provide for Jorge and support Paola, who was planning to stay at home after graduation to look after the baby. For this reason, going to college took on added importance: 'Well, I think that's why I want to go to college, so can get a better job' (IN 09/26/2011). The adults in Eddie's life also rallied around his pursuing further education. His uncle, though generally uninvolved in his postsecondary plans, indicated to Eddie that he should go to 'a real college' (IN 09/26/2011) and that 'if it's about education … they help me' (IN 01/10/2012). His girlfriend's parents also strongly encouraged him to pursue a college education so that in the long run, he would be better able to support his new family.

Thus, graduating on time was important to Eddie, as was pursuing further education to become a car mechanic. But the execution of these ideas was a different matter. Although his attendance improved somewhat in the fall, he was still absent at least once a week, according to Mr Woznyj. He still had not consulted any teachers or counselors about his PSE plan and seemed unaware of community colleges in the region. In other words, by the end of the fall semester, when many of his peers in the senior class had already applied to colleges, Eddie had not taken any concrete step toward his PSE.

Spring Senior Year

In the spring of his senior year, with graduation looming large, Eddie was more focused on working toward graduating on time: 'I'm trying to do everything I can to graduate, do my best' (IN 01/10/2012). Yet, at the same time, no better arrangement had been made for the care of baby Jorge, and both Eddie and Paola continued to miss school regularly to take care of him. To make matters worse, in February of his senior year, he was briefly hospitalized for kidney stones – a familial genetic trait – and although he was on medication, he was often in pain and sometime missed school because of it. Had he explained to his classroom teachers about his situation, at least the absences because of his illness could have been excused and would not have hurt his grades. But Eddie seemed unaware of, or uninterested in, how to protect himself from undue institutional penalties by advocating for himself. When asked whether he had told his teachers about his illness and his resultant absences, his response was: 'Well, not really because I haven't, well, they haven't talked to me about it' (IN 01/10/2012). Virtually all his teachers I spoke with observed that Eddie's work ethic had vastly improved and that he was much more serious that year than the previous year. But they were also concerned that he might not be able to graduate because of his frequent absences.

In January, Eddie expressed an interest in a trade school that specialized in automotive technology, located in a nearby city. He had heard about the school from one of his friends at Brighton, but when I asked him the name of the school, he could not remember: 'Um [pause], I forgot the name. But, it's like about, about cars and stuff' (IN 01/10/2012). It was also around this time that he started talking about going back to Mexico for a couple of months after graduation. He explained that his paternal grandfather was aging and unwell and had expressed a desire to see him. Technically, visiting Mexico for a couple of months in the summer after graduation would not have affected his plans for the fall, but Eddie seemed to use this trip as a delaying tactic for making his postsecondary plans. He reasoned, 'If I decide to go to one place and come back, I will think about, probably want to do something else' (IN 01/10/2012).

Indeed, around this time Eddie seemed rather overwhelmed trying to balance parenting and schoolwork. He had always reported having a good relationship with his uncle and his family, and had never complained about them, but he admitted that living with relatives was not the same as living with one's own parents:

> Sometimes it's just hard for me 'cause I got to do my things on my own 'cause I am not living with my parents. So, it's kind of difficult for me to be focused on something, like school or [pause]. I mean, it's mostly myself that I gotta think about my own. (IN 01/20/2012)

It is important to note, however, that although Eddie continued to struggle with his schoolwork, he did not feel alienated from school. He expressed that he was coming to school not because he had to, but because he liked school and enjoyed learning. He believed that education was important:

> Education is like, the most important thing too 'cause, you know, without education, you're not gonna be able to do well in your life, so I think that's important too. Like, school too, 'cause, you know, you have be ready like or, you know, learn things and so, you will, you know, become what you want. (IN 04/20/2012)

He also perceived his Brighton teachers as caring: 'If I need help, or I ask, they really want to help me. Like, they really want to make me understand what's going on' (IN 04/20/2012). Thus, although he was frequently absent, when he did come to school, he seemed to find his place in this community.

In April, Eddie talked about going straight to work after graduation for the first time. He said that he had helped Paola's brother fix cars and do some landscaping and that he could see himself doing that for a while. He still wanted to pursue further education by going to a community college: 'I still wanna go to a community college. Yeah, look something, you know, something like big and like something that can help me get a better job' (IN 04/20/2012). However, increasingly he talked about it as a future plan, rather than something he envisioned doing right after high school.

In the end, he was absent 42 days in his senior year. He failed Algebra 1 again in the fall and had to do credit recovery during the second semester, and failed Human Anatomy and Remedial Algebra 2 in the spring. He was not able to graduate in June with his class – he was notably absent from the graduation ceremony – but after completing his failed courses in summer school, he graduated in August. When I asked him what he would do differently if he were to do high school all over again, he said that he would be 'more responsible' and 'pay more attention, doing things right' (IN 05/30/2012). He never went to Mexico and at the time of graduation, and he had no concrete plans for what he would do next, work- or education-wise. But he clearly imagined a future in which he was an established car mechanic and a good role model for his son, who, it was clear, brought him a lot of joy:

> Yeah, like, every time we, like, go over there, like, we come from school and we go over there. Like, when we see him, he starts smiling and talking like, you know, telling us, like, what, what he did. Like, that's, that what we think. 'Cause, and he, like, be making all these like, he be talk, like, he be talking like with his hands and stuff. (IN 05/30/2012)

I asked him what he thought he would be doing in 10 years, when he was 28, and his response was this: 'I think, first of all, well, have a good job doing mechanic stuff, and have my own place. Yeah. Be there for my son' (IN 04/20/2012).

Carlos's Story

Carlos, seen as a low achiever and chronic absentee, fundamentally thought of himself as a good student. My relationship with Carlos had an on-again, off-again quality, because during much of my fieldwork period, he skipped school so often and for such long stretches at a time that I could never assume that he would show up for our interviews. But periodically he would show up at school, and when he did, he would always claim that now was different, he was 'doing good' and that he was going to attend school more regularly – until he lapsed again.

Of the seven EL students in this study, Carlos had been in the United States the longest and was the only long-term EL in this study. By the time I met him in 11th grade, his English language proficiency was already quite high (ACCESS score: 5.1), certainly high enough to trigger reclassification consideration. However, at the time of this study, reclassification in Pennsylvania required meeting both English language proficiency criteria *and* academic criteria (e.g. achieving at least 'Basic' in the state academic standardized tests), and because he never met the academic criteria, he was never reclassified. Yet, Carlos was not always a low achiever. Back in Ecuador, he attended school regularly and was a good student – or so he claimed. He also added that he remembered his teachers in Ecuador being more caring: 'I don't know, like back in Ecuador, like everybody used to be caring. Here, it's like [pause], you know' (IN 05/29/2012). It was only after his immigration to the United States that he began sliding academically.

Carlos immigrated to the United States with his older brother when he was 10 to join his parents, who had left Ecuador eight years earlier to work in the United States. Carlos and his brother had been brought up in the interim by his grandmother. He believed that his parents immigrated to the United States to find better job opportunities for themselves and to provide their children with a better future. His parents had wanted both boys to go to college, but his older brother dropped out of school at 15 when he had a baby with his girlfriend. Consequently, Carlos knew that his parents wanted him to go to college ''Cause they don't want me to be like my brother' (IN 05/03/2011). His father worked as a contractor, and his mother was a janitor at a nearby university, but the family struggled financially, and Carlos often talked about feeling guilty about having his parents pay for his expenses.

Spring Junior Year

When I first asked Carlos about his postsecondary plans, he expressed trepidation about life after high school and noted that he had an interest in attending college: 'I don't really know 'cause I'm like, scared about what's gonna happen when I'm alone. Under the world. But uh, I guess, yeah. I wanna go to college' (IN 05/03/2011). At that point, he was curious about the nursing profession, which one of his aunts had suggested: 'My aunt. She told me about it 'cause, it's more, like, it's something that I like and, like you get pain and you get through the pain and stuff. Take care of people stuff' (IN 05/03/2011). But he also mentioned he was thinking of E-Tech Institute (pseudonym), a trade school in a nearby city with programs in computer technology and electronics. While he expressed an interest in going to college, the trade school option also seemed to hold certain attractions for Carlos because of the prospect of getting a job right after the program.

However, Carlos's actual talent lay in something else: fine art. When I observed him in Mr McGrath's Power and Transportation class, I watched him draw his design for a minicar with ease and precision. I jotted in my field notes: 'Carlos is actually quite good at drawing. His lines are smooth, and he draws lines without hesitation and with a flow' (FN 03/28/2012). Carlos later shared that he enjoyed drawing and that art was the only subject for which he received an A: indeed, at 94%, his final grade for visual arts was a marked anomaly in a sea of Cs, Ds and Fs. However, he did not seem to make any connection between his artistic talents and career options – except for a fleeting consideration to become 'a tattoo artist' (IN 06/02/2011). All the potential career choices he named – e.g. nursing, electronics – were those that were suggested by his family members and were relatively familiar to him.

With all that said, however, making PSE plans was probably not Carlos's priority as of May of his junior year: much more pressing was the risk of dropping out of high school. He had already failed Remedial

Algebra 1 twice in ninth grade and 10th grade, and he was working on passing it the third time around in 11th grade. He acknowledged that his grades consisted mostly of Cs and Bs, but added, 'I am doing really good this year' (IN 05/03/2011). Indeed, relatively speaking, his junior year was academically an all-time high for him with an overall GPA of 69.7% (70% is the passing grade in Brighton). But there was no question that he failed many classes; although he finally passed Algebra 1 with a grade of 74%, he failed Remedial American literature, Remedial US history and Life Science. Because there would be no PSE if he did not graduate from high school, Carlos – and, as described in Chapter 5, the educators around him – seemed much more concerned about his completing high school than making PSE plans.

Fall Senior Year

I did not see Carlos at all during the fall semester of his senior year because he skipped school most of the time. He failed all of his courses in the fall. It was not any life-altering circumstances that kept him from school. When he reappeared in the spring, he likened chronic absenteeism to addiction. 'It's kinda like, it feel like an addiction, like the more you do, like you don't nothing in school, like it's like laziness or something' (IN 03/27/2012). Cutting school was not new to him; he had certainly done that before. In fact, he explained that he was much worse in middle school: 'I was like really, really bad. Like really bad' (IN 03/27/2012). Back then, not only did he skip school, but he also stayed away from home for days on end, sometimes staying with his aunt, other times staying with his friends. Fights with his parents were frequent. His relationship with his father was particularly strained. Comparatively speaking, then, Carlos's absenteeism this time around was rather tame because he was at least staying home. But even he acknowledged that his absences were getting out of hand: 'I took it to the next level' (IN 02/29/2012), he said.

His mother left for work early in the morning and at that time, his father was away in New York with his construction job. His parents were not even aware that Carlos was skipping school until the school contacted them. In response, his parents told him to keep on attending high school so that he could at least graduate, warning that his options would be limited if he failed to obtain a high school diploma. Carlos himself was aware of the need to graduate from high school, as he said, 'I need a high school degree to do something … I can't just drop out' (IN 02/29/2012).

As a result of his failing all his fall semester courses, it was determined that Carlos would have to attend summer school, and that in addition, he would have to come back the following fall to take two more courses. The best-case scenario at this point was to graduate in January 2013, a half year later than the rest of his class. Naturally, if he was not able to graduate from high school, PSE would be a moot point.

Spring Senior Year

At the beginning of the spring semester of his senior year, Carlos began attending school more regularly, to the point where I was actually able to meet with him for an interview. He claimed that he had changed his attitude – 'Now, it's—, I'm going good' (IN 02/29/2012) – and indeed, for a while he seemed to have settled into a good rhythm of coming to school every day. I would see him in the hallway in passing, and he would wave at me or greet me with, 'How are you, Miss?' In other words, I did not always see him when I expected, and he stood me up more often than any other participant, but when I did see him, he was unfailingly polite and friendly.

By the second half of his senior year, the idea of becoming a nurse, if it ever was seriously entertained at all, had all but disappeared. At this point, Carlos had very low self-efficacy; he explained the reason for giving up on the idea of becoming a nurse:

Carlos: Maybe 'cause if I'm lazy in school, I'm gonna be lazy in college.
Yasuko: It's just a matter of attitude, isn't it? It's all up to you.
Carlos: I don't know if I—, I don't have that attitude. (IN 02/29/2012)

In this and other instances, Carlos often sounded as if he was commenting on someone else's life over which he had no control.

By March, Carlos was lapsing again. He took two weeks off to visit New York with a group of friends who had already dropped out of school. As someone who has always liked school and was good at academics, it was beyond my comprehension how a high school student could randomly take a two-week break from school for a little trip to New York in the middle of March, especially when his chances of graduating were already vanishingly slim. So, I asked him to explain the psychology of cutting school, to which he responded:

> I put myself to test and stuff. Like, I'm doing good, but then I just fall over, and I do the same. Like, I see things around. Like, I start doin' good and then, like, I fall over. (IN 03/27/2012)

Carlos was aware that he was repeating the pattern of coming out of a period of chronic absenteeism pledging to do better and then getting derailed by one temptation or another. One of the temptations that kept him from school was his friends outside of school. Carlos used to be an avid soccer player and was a member of the school's varsity team. 'I was raised with soccer' (IN 05/03/2011), he said. However, his grades had dipped too low, and he had lost his eligibility to play varsity.[1] He also started smoking, which made it harder to play without running out of breath. By the spring of his senior year, he had not played soccer for more than a year. Outside of school, he was spending more time with his older brother's friends who were working, and his friends from middle school who had dropped out. Socializing with friends who were no longer attending school might have made school seem less relevant to Carlos. Certainly, if he had primarily socialized with peers who attended school regularly, temptations such as a trip to New York would not have arisen.

Furthermore, Carlos continued to express a very low sense of self-efficacy. On the one hand, he categorically denied that he would drop out because, 'I'll break my mom's heart if I dropped out' (IN 03/27/2012). He was aware that it was a matter of coming to school every day and doing the work. On the other hand, he seemed not to trust his own ability to persist: 'I'm scared I might start slacking. Umm, something might come up' (IN 03/27/2012).

May of his senior year was academically the lowest point of his high school life. Earlier in the month, he received a suspension because he failed to serve a detention for skipping a class: 'I just went to McDonald's and eat and then came back. And they caught me' (IN 05/29/2012). Unfortunately, the day he was suspended and not allowed to come into school was also the day when he was supposed to work on credit recovery to make the last-minute effort to salvage some of the classes he was failing:

Yeah, my absences for this semester are like, they're not that much, it's like 15. I was on this pink paper and um—, I had to like, if I did the little pink paper, it will say like 2 days out of, those things and next week too. But then, that day I was doing the pink paper, that's the day they suspended me. And so when they suspend you, you can't do that no more. (IN 05/29/2012)

Being absent on this critical day resulted in failing grades in two more courses, in addition to the four he knew he had already failed. Carlos appeared much less sure of the prospect of ever graduating. Up to this point, regardless of the gap between his words and his deeds, he had always insisted that he would graduate. Now he was no longer certain:

Yasuko: In your opinion, how likely is it for you to graduate from high school? Would you say it's 50%? 80%? 100%?

Carlos: At this point? It's [pause] like, [pause] nah, 20%. (IN 05/29/2012)

Moreover, when I asked him how much he *wanted* to graduate, he responded that it was about 30%.

On the home front, however, his relationship with his father had improved somewhat. Carlos reported that he had had a heart-to-heart talk with his father about the future. 'First time, you know' (IN 05/29/2012), he said, adding that he felt good about it. Also for the first time, he mentioned that he wanted to attend a trade school to train as an electrician and eventually start a business with his father: 'He said he was going to change but I have to change too. I told him, yeah' (IN 05/29/2012).

In the end, Carlos failed all nine courses he took in his senior year. Two of his teachers gave him 1% for his grade; another teacher gave him 5%. He did not graduate in June 2012 with his class.

Repeat Senior Year

It was a while later that I had a chance to interview Carlos again. Much to his credit, he did come back to school the following year to repeat the courses he had failed. He had been advised to attend summer school in the previous summer, but he decided not to do so. Rather, he chose to come back for another full year of school in the fall, since students had to pay to attend summer school whereas school during the academic year was free.

I cannot say that during his repeat senior year Carlos was a dramatically different person from the previous years. Just like before, he was often absent or tardy, and he was scraping by with his classes. The key difference, however, was that at least this time, he was passing all his classes – just barely, but passing nonetheless. His better performance seemed to boost his confidence too: 'Yeah, I'm really confident. My classes are really, not that hard' (IN 02/22/2013).

Carlos also began working part-time. He had always been keenly aware that his family struggled financially and had expressed his desire to lessen their burden by achieving financial independence: 'I'm not tryin' to ask my parents for money no more. ... 'Cause my parents, like they work so much for the house and stuff. So, I'm not tryin' take money from them' (IN 02/29/2012). His desire for financial independence led him to apply for a night-shift position as a busboy at a local diner. Working the night shift from 5 pm to 3 am over Friday, Saturday and Sunday was probably not the wisest choice when his chances of graduating were already slim. At the same time, working such long hours on weekends probably kept him away from many temptations that might have lured him away from school again.

Encouraged by his comparatively regular attendance and also by his interest in applying to the electrician certification program at LCC, after our February interview, I suggested that we meet a week later to start his online college application. However, on the day we were supposed to meet, Carlos was absent from school, and when I contacted him, he told me that he had to stay home because his little sister was sick and needed someone to stay home with her. A month later, I reached out again and asked whether he was still interested in filling out the LCC application. He responded by saying that he was not going to apply to LCC after all because he was now planning to go back to Ecuador after graduation and spend some time there.

By June 2013, his plans had changed once again, and he was not going to Ecuador after all. He reverted back to the idea of attending the electrician certification program at LCC. He appeared more aware that time was slipping by and that he was not getting any younger. He said, 'Yeah, 'cause I mean, I really don't want to waste my time 'cause [pause] years go fast and I'd really like to try and get that done' (IN 06/06/2013). In addition to learning about electricity, another thing he wanted to do at college was pick up soccer again. He seemed to associate playing soccer with a productive life: 'Trying to change my life' (IN 06/06/2013), he said.

In the end, Carlos had to stay for summer school after that academic year to complete Remedial Algebra 2, but at the end of summer 2013, he successfully graduated from Brighton. Together, we started his LCC online application process in June, but he ultimately never followed through. He continued to work as a busboy at the diner. There was no indication that he was going to pursue PSE.

Notes

(1) Many public high schools in the United States have a requirement for varsity players to keep a certain level of academic performance in order to maintain their privilege to play on a varsity team.

5 Not Career Ready

In the previous three chapters, I have largely focused on the experiences of ELs who are college bound. In this chapter, I want to switch gears and examine the career readiness of those ELs who are *not* going to college. To be clear, I believe ELs who want to go to college should have equal access to college as their English first language (L1) peers. However, not all students – ELs or non-ELs – are college bound, and neither should they be. Some students are not interested in an academic degree or they want to become financially independent as soon as possible. As Roberto, one EL senior I was informally mentoring at Brighton[1] told me, 'You know, Dr. Yasuko, I'm just not academic. I want to go to a technical school and get a job'. Ensuring that those high school students who are not college bound become career ready, then, should receive the same priority as making college-bound students college ready. Yet, because of the overwhelming emphasis on college going and a general ethos of 'college-for-all' (Rosenbaum *et al.*, 2010), helping non-college-bound students become career ready has received short shrift.

This chapter examines the educational experiences of Eddie and Carlos, the two lowest-performing students of the seven, and inquires into how they were left to graduate from high school without becoming either college or career ready. When I originally asked Mr Woznyj to help me find a set of participants, I told him that I did not want to have just high-performing EL students at Brighton; rather, I wanted some high-performing students, some low-performing students and those in-between. Mr Woznyj, who understood my goals, recommended that I work with Carlos and Eddie, two 'at-risk' students whose prospects of graduation were far from assured. These two students were chronically absent, failed multiple courses and presented major challenges to the counselors and teachers who wanted to help them graduate. Unlike the other five participants, Carlos and Eddie never seriously entertained the notion of obtaining a college degree; rather, they were interested in earning a vocational certificate either at a community college or at a trade school, and working as soon as possible, so they could contribute financially to their families. Both students had strengths they could have leveraged in building promising careers. As discussed in their narratives, Carlos was artistically talented, and Eddie had a strong interest in becoming a car mechanic. And yet, because of the school's institutional habitus, which espoused both strong college-for-all aspirations *and* a deficit orientation toward at-risk students, Eddie and Carlos graduated from high school without any concrete guidance on how to build a postsecondary career.

Recall from Chapter 1 that career readiness involves foundational cognitive and non-cognitive skills as well as career-planning skills (Clark, 2015). Just as a high school diploma does not automatically translate into college readiness (ACT, 2017; Kirst, 2004), it also does not guarantee career readiness unless foundational skills are intentionally cultivated during the high school years. In reality, however, in this era of college-for-all, those students who are not interested in pursuing a college education and would rather enter the workforce as soon as possible tend to be low-performing students who are at risk of dropping out. The education of non-college-bound students, then, often focuses exclusively on drop-out prevention, reengagement efforts and the remediation of low academic skills rather than crafting a well thought-out CTE pathway. In too many cases, instead of becoming career ready, non-college-bound students exit high school barely meeting high school graduation requirements, if at all, and no career prospects other than entry-level minimum wage jobs.

In the remainder of the chapter, I inquire into how Carlos and Eddie, who were low achieving to be sure, but who had notable strengths and a desire to engage with school, nonetheless never benefitted from CTE and graduated from high school without becoming career ready.

'So Many Strange Things' in Their Curricula

As their stories illustrated, Eddie and Carlos exhibited chronic absenteeism, which, combined with their general low academic performance, led to a number of failed courses. As Figure 5.1 shows, there is a general inverse relationship between the number of absences and grades. Carlos's grades had hovered around just below 70% (70% was the passing grade at Brighton) until the end of 11th grade and plummeted to 24% when his absences skyrocketed in 12th grade. Similarly, Eddie had

(a)

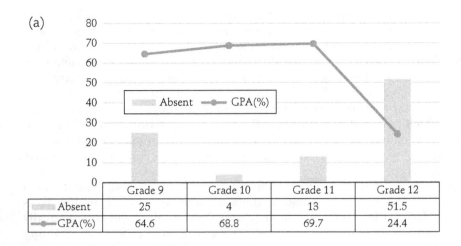

	Grade 9	Grade 10	Grade 11	Grade 12
Absent	25	4	13	51.5
GPA(%)	64.6	68.8	69.7	24.4

(b)

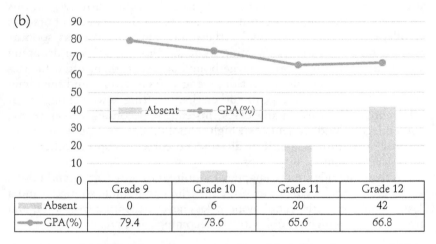

	Grade 9	Grade 10	Grade 11	Grade 12
Absent	0	6	20	42
GPA(%)	79.4	73.6	65.6	66.8

Figure 5.1 Carlos and Eddie's absences and GPAs. (a) Carlos's absences and GPAs. (b) Eddie's absences and GPAs.

been achieving a GPA of above 70% in ninth and 10th grade, but when his absences increased in 11th grade, his GPA dipped below passing. Table 5.1 shows the same pattern from a different angle. During the first two years of high school, Eddie failed only one course – an elective computer course. However, in 11th grade, all of a sudden he began failing core courses. Carlos, who had failed two or three courses in each

Table 5.1 Eddie and Carlos's failed courses

	Eddie	Carlos
Grade 9		Remedial Algebra 1 Remedial General Science
Grade 10	Desktop Publishing	Remedial Algebra 1 (repeat) Remedial Biology
Grade 11	Remedial Algebra 1 EL US History EL Biology Physical Education	Remedial American Literature Remedial US History Life Science
Grade 12	Remedial Algebra 1 (repeat)[a] Remedial Algebra 2 Remedial Human Anatomy	Remedial English Skills and Composition Remedial US History (repeat) Remedial Human Behavior Remedial Algebra 2 Remedial Probability and Statistics Remedial Human Anatomy Physical Education Power and Transmission Chorus
Repeated Grade 12		Senior Seminar

[a] (Repeat) indicates courses that they repeated and failed again.

of the years prior, failed essentially all courses in 12th grade. Put another way, in both cases there is an identifiable momentum of failure, and it corresponds with a sudden increase in absences.

These extensive patterns of truancy and failed courses presented a major challenge to their guidance counselors, who set and reset Eddie and Carlos's coursework in an effort to help them meet the graduation requirements. Mrs Salomon, Eddie's counselor, lamented,

> He's definitely been the most challenging. And scheduling has been a nightmare with him because he's failed EL courses, which are not offered all the time and are so specific. And so, I have had to do so many strange things with his schedule to try to get him in a position that he could potentially graduate. (IN 11/09/2011)

Indeed, an analysis of the two students' transcripts revealed that the counselors' efforts to squeeze in the graduation requirements, in the face of multiple failed and repeated courses, resulted in a low-level, patched-up curriculum. For example, Carlos passed Reading EL 9 and Remedial English 10 in the first two years of high school, fulfilling half of the English graduation requirements (Figure 5.2). However, the other half of the graduation requirement was to complete two English electives

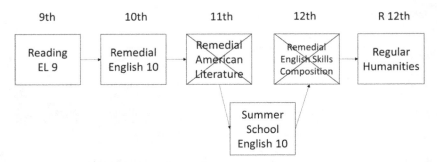

Figure 5.2 Carlos's English courses. *Note*: X indicates a failed course; R12th indicates Carlos's repeated 12th grade.

in 11th and 12th grades. For these requirements, Carlos took Remedial American Literature in 11th grade and Remedial English Skills and Composition in 12th grade but failed both. To make up for the American literature course, he took English 10 in summer school following 11th grade. However, he had already passed English 10 in 10th grade, and therefore this course should not have been repeated in summer school and certainly should not have been used as a replacement for Remedial American Literature.

Further, Carlos clearly did not meet some of the graduation requirements. For one thing, he did not take a geometry course, which was a graduation requirement, instead moving directly from Remedial Algebra 1 to Remedial Algebra 2.[2] Somehow incongruently, Carlos took Probability and Statistics, which is a higher-level course than Remedial Algebra 2 and was *not* a graduation requirement in 12th grade. Moreover, all Brighton students were required to complete a senior graduation project, which was a Pennsylvania Department of Education requirement. Carlos failed senior seminar, in which students wrote the papers for their graduation projects, during his repeated senior year. Yet, Carlos's transcript has a notation 'Grad Project, EX', suggesting that he was somehow exempted from completing his graduation project. Harklau (2016: 602) points out that schools are bureaucratic institutions that make numerous random errors and that such errors disproportionately affect Latinx students' education: 'These mistakes have less in common with sociological visions of inexorable institutional social reproduction and more in common with Kafkaesque visions of random bureaucratic dysfunction'. I too believe that these inconsistencies and omissions in Carlos's graduation requirements are bureaucratic errors of a system that has to monitor more than 2,500 students' academic progress; nonetheless,

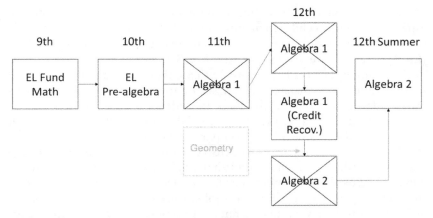

Figure 5.3 Eddie's math courses. *Note*: X indicates a failed course.

they did detract from Carlos's right to receive a meaningful high school education.

Eddie's transcript also shows that although he technically graduated from high school, he was by no means career ready. What is noticeable about Eddie's coursework is that he began high school at below-grade level and only reached about 10th-grade-level courses by the end of high school. For instance, Eddie began ninth grade with EL Fundamental Math, one level lower than prealgebra; most ninth graders start with algebra 1 (Figure 5.3). That is, at the beginning of high school he was already two years behind grade level in math. He went on to take EL Pre-algebra in 10th grade and only reached Remedial Algebra 1 in 11th grade. However, he failed Remedial Algebra 1 twice and had to take a credit recovery program, an on-line course that allowed struggling students to earn credits for the course they failed. After passing Remedial Algebra 1 through credit recovery, Eddie took Remedial Algebra 2 in the second half of 12th grade but failed it too. He had to attend summer school after 12th grade to repeat Remedial Algebra 2. In all the other core subjects, his coursework was similarly low level.

Like Carlos, some graduation requirements are also inexplicably missing from Eddie's high school transcript. Similar to Carlos, Eddie did not take a geometry course, moving directly from Remedial Algebra 1 to Remedial Algebra 2. Furthermore, he also skipped Government and Law, which most students took in 10th grade and was a graduation requirement. This is alarming given Callahan and colleagues' (Callahan *et al.*, 2008; Callahan & Muller, 2013) finding that high school social studies credits have a direct impact on the subsequent civic engagements, especially voting, of children of immigrants. Similarly, in science, although the graduation requirement was 20 credits, Eddie only completed 15 (EL Physical Science, EL Biology and Life Science).

To summarize, it is hard to make a case that Eddie and Carlos's high school diplomas translated into a set of foundational cognitive skills that made them career ready. Even if students are not college bound, to become career ready, they need a solid academic foundation. In an influential 2006 report, ACT compared two of its own assessments: WorkKeys, an assessment of workforce readiness, and the ACT college entrance exam. The study found that the levels of reading and mathematical skills that test takers needed to achieve Level 5 in WorkKeys, the level required for middle-skills jobs, were comparable to a score of at least 21 on the ACT, its benchmark for college readiness. More concretely, both college-ready and career-ready students needed to be able to identify the main idea in a paragraph, to solve multistep arithmetic problems and to express and interpret quantitative data in table, graph and chart forms (ACT, 2006). In other words, the foundational academic skills required for career readiness may not be so different from those associated with college readiness. If at-risk students such as Carlos and Eddie are led through an incoherent string of courses just for the sake of fulfilling graduation requirements, even ignoring some required courses in the process, they are likely to suffer the consequences in their subsequent careers.

Deficit Thinking: 'Eddie is Limited and Carlos is Lazy'

While Brighton educators were concerned about Eddie and Carlos's academic performance and expended considerable time and energy trying to keep them both in school, fundamentally they blamed the students for their predicaments. Rather than examining the ways in which the school was failing to meet their needs, the educators identified certain traits in Eddie and Carlos – and in their families – and attributed these students' failures to these traits, thereby engaging in quintessential deficit thinking: 'The student who fails in school does so because of internal deficits or deficiencies' (Valencia, 1997: 2).

In Eddie's case, teachers pointed to his lack of cognitive abilities as well as his limited English proficiency. Mrs Anderson, an EL teacher who had Eddie in her classes, noted: 'Eddie's skills are limited. ... I know he does struggle in school. I know he's struggling in math and he's also struggling with reading and writing as well' (IN 06/02/2011). As I noted earlier, a special education teacher who pushed into one of Eddie's classes also commented on his struggle with reading, adding that he might have a learning disability. However, he was never referred for a formal evaluation.

Eddie's teachers and counselors focused on his English proficiency, limited academic preparation in his home country and complicated family background. When I asked Mrs Salomon to comment on Eddie, she started out by stating, 'Eddie is someone who may not graduate' (IN 11/09/2011). She then elaborated:

> When he started here ... I couldn't communicate with him at all. I mean nothing. [Yasuko: Because of English?] Because of Eng—, I mean he knew nothing. And I believe he was someone who did not have a lot of [academic] background in his other country, and I, um, gosh, I don't know how to put it. I think his father had a—, he's living, I think, with an uncle here. Um, there's some social issue stuff. (IN 11/09/2011)

Mrs Salomon then went on to commend Eddie for his 'phenomenal' progress in English. However, the overall tenor of this conversation was why Eddie might not graduate, and it was striking that the factors she immediately identified as contributing to his 'at-risk' status were those associated with his background, including his family. Nothing about the quality of education he had received since his arrival in the United States was mentioned.

Teachers did, at least, note that Eddie periodically put forth some effort. With graduation looming large, Eddie began his senior year with a renewed resolution to graduate on time, saying, 'Yeah, now I'm doing more work 'cause I know, my—, this my senior year, and I gotta get good grades' (IN 09/26/2011). Several teachers approvingly noted his improved work ethic. Among the teachers, then, the shared discourse was that Eddie made an occasional effort but struggled because of his limited abilities.

Carlos, on the other hand, was seen as a student who was plenty intelligent but lazy. Mrs Anderson described Carlos as, 'He's smart, but does not want to do the work' (IN 06/02/2011). Carlos himself seemed to have internalized the identity of a 'lazy student' who could not maintain consistent effort. As I described in his story, Carlos told me that he did not have the persistence to follow through with a nursing degree. He reasoned, 'Maybe 'cause if I'm lazy in school, I'm gonna be lazy in college' (IN 02/29/2012), indicating how the school's positioning of him as a lazy student had seeped into his own self-image. Of all the EL participants,

Carlos by far exhibited the weakest sense of individual autonomy. He often talked about his future as if he were a bystander. In March of his senior year, I asked him to predict what he would be doing in 10 years, to which he replied, 'If I keep going to school I see myself doing good. If I don't, I see myself workin' in construction, I guess' (IN 03/27/2012), as if the two fates had equal odds of happening, and he had no control over which way his life would turn. At that point, feeling disconcerted and more than a little frustrated, I launched into a long pep talk about how it was within his power to shape his destiny, very much reminiscent of the pep talk that Mr Burke gave at the 'Act Now!' event for undecided seniors (see Chapter 3). Carlos humored me and agreed that he 'gotta work hard', but in the end went right back to his lack of control: 'I'm scared I might start slackin'. Something might come up' (IN 03/27/2012).

Once students reached a certain level of underachievement, educators started sending not so subtle messages about their at-risk status and let them know that the school could assist them only so much. In his senior year, Eddie took Remedial Algebra 2 – he had passed Remedial Algebra 1 on his third try. In one observation, I heard Mr Savage, his math teacher, comment offhandedly, 'I believe in you mostly; the rest of the school doesn't believe in you so much' (IN 03/26/2012). I looked up in astonishment, wondering what it takes to make an educator so jaded. But ironically, this teacher was on point in articulating Brighton's institutional habitus. Indeed, the school did not much believe in the capabilities of students like Carlos and Eddie.

Even more sympathetic teachers at some point gave up on their 'at-risk' students and interpreted their failures in deficit terms. Mr McGrath, whose CTE electives Carlos took and enjoyed, was initially sympathetic and encouraged Carlos to continue and graduate. However, seeing Carlos's continuing truancy, by the end of May of the senior year, even he had given up on him. One day at the end of May, I ran into Mr McGrath, and I asked how Carlos was doing:

> Mr. McGrath said that Carlos has totally checked out, and said, 'I dearly hope that he will graduate, but if he doesn't he is another dropout.' He also said that if you are here for a long time, you can tell whether kids will graduate or not, and unfortunately, Carlos is one of the latter. (FN 05/29/2012)

Two characteristics are of note here. First, by stating, 'He's another dropout', Mr McGrath is articulating the institutional discourse that allows a student, especially an underachiever, to be transformed from a unique individual to a mere statistic for the school. Second, by categorizing students into those who will graduate and those who will not, Mr McGrath is assuming that it is the student attributes, rather than the school attributes, that lead to dropout. Absent in his comments is any reflection on 'how schools are institutionally implicated in ways that exclude students from optimal learning' (Valencia, 2010: xvii). This was another salient theme in Brighton's institutional habitus. There was a strong sense among the educators that they were doing everything they could to educate the children of a working-class, increasingly transient community; therefore, if students did not live up to their expectations, it was their fault.

Another assumption that disadvantaged both Eddie and Carlos was the educators' notion that if a male student started cutting school, then he was socializing with 'the wrong crowd'. This institutional discourse was pervasive, and it impacted more than just how Eddie and Carlos's truancy was perceived. Rather, all male students in this study were subjected to this suspicion to varying degrees. Even the most academic of my male participants, Ken, was not immune from this prejudice, and when he started skipping some classes in 12th grade, educators began to talk about him mixing with the wrong crowd. For example, after commenting, 'Eddie has just, has sort of fallen into the wrong crowd', Mrs Salomon, who was also Ken's guidance counselor, added, 'Ken, I'm worried is … going the same route' (IN 11/09/2011). However, since Eddie and Carlos's truancy was extreme, these two students received the greater brunt of educators' suspicion of mixing with the wrong crowd. Brighton educators never elaborated on what they meant by 'the wrong crowd'. It was used as an all-purpose code word for anything ranging from socializing with other truants to actual gang involvement.

Educators' reliance on the institutional discourse of 'hanging out with the wrong crowd' to make sense of Eddie and Carlos's absenteeism was harmful because it prevented them from identifying the underlying cause of their absenteeism. Although the educators clearly knew that Eddie had a baby, there is no evidence that any counselor or teacher reached out to him to ask how he and his girlfriend were managing; nor did they know that he suffered from a kidney stone problem because Eddie never told them and no one approached him. In other words, had the staff not made an automatic assumption that prolonged absences meant socializing with undesirable peers, they might have approached these students individually to ask what was going on in their lives.

The educators' deficit orientation did not end with students, but expanded to their parents (Moll *et al.*, 1992). The lack of parental involvement – not just with the parents of ELs, but parents in general – was a major source of complaint across the school. Mrs Salomon was clearly frustrated by the lack of communication with Eddie's uncle: 'Sometimes I can get a hold of the uncle. And, and last year I remember trying to ca—, call numerous times at the end of the year about his status. And no one ever calls back' (IN 11/09/2011). In other words, when a student was perceived as 'at risk', in addition to pointing to the deficits within the student, educators also pointed to the deficits in the attitudes and support of his family.

Not all teachers dismissed Carlos and Eddie as lost causes. For example, Mr Woznyj, EL Department Chair, recognized both Carlos and Eddie as individual students with unique strengths, perhaps because he was among the first to teach them when they arrived at Brighton. He noted Carlos's resolve:

> I taught him as a freshman when he first started and uh, he struggled, but he would come in some days, 'I'm turning around Mr. W.' You know … and he even said some really, like wise thing once. I'll never forget. I know he has problems with his dad or had problems at home. And he said, 'You know, I don't even care about my dad making me do this anymore. I'm doing this for me.' And he was a freshman. You know, I, I, it's like, 'Alright Carlos. You can do it. You just get to work'. (IN 01/06/2012)

Likewise, Mr Woznyj recognized Eddie's intellectual curiosity: 'He's a very nice guy. He's interesting. He comes up, he comes up after class with an interesting, insightful question or something like, "What kind of stuff do you like to read?"' (IN 01/06/2012).

Nonetheless, even in his position as Chair of the EL Department, Mr Woznyj seemed either unable or unwilling to push back against the deficit orientation espoused outside the protective 'ESL bubble' (Przymus, 2016). He was frustrated by how his ELs, once they had completed EL sheltered courses and were placed in remedial courses, became acculturated into the negative ethos of the remedial class (see Chapter 2, where he discussed Josephine's academic plateau in this regard). At the same time, knowing how his colleagues who taught remedial classes were already stretched thin to meet the needs of their struggling students, Mr Woznyj felt constrained from making more demands on them:

> I talk with teachers in my position too about, you know, when the kids are failing. I say, 'Wh—, what can you do differently?' They say, 'Look at my room. I have 30 students. Twenty of them, you know, haven't

done their homework tonight.' And it, so it's this whole, and, and with the regular ed. teachers who aren't trained in EL, sometimes they're not sensitive to it or even aware of what might be going on to this EL student. (IN 01/06/2012)

In all, then, the majority of educators attributed the struggle of students such as Eddie and Carlos to their own deficits, instead of questioning the ways in which *they* as educators were not meeting these students' needs and how the school was systemically directing its resources to certain kinds of students and not to others (Venezia *et al.*, 2003). On the other hand, the small number of teachers who did recognize these students' unique strengths and needs did not speak up to question their colleagues' deficit assumptions about these students. As a result, these teachers also became part of the school's institutional habitus that overwhelmingly viewed Carlos and Eddie as 'at risk'.

Unrecognized Strengths and Aspirations

As I was learning how teachers and counselors interpreted Eddie and Carlos's underachievement and 'at-risk'-ness, I was simultaneously getting to know the students – and their strengths and aspirations. And what they had to say about their high school experiences and their future stood in great contrast to their educators' deficit views about them. They were not at all 'checked out'; in fact, they were quite worried about their high school graduation. They held themselves accountable to their families and wanted to start careers to support them. To be sure, they had limited knowledge of what career options were within their reach; they nonetheless wanted to make something of themselves. For example, Eddie had clear career aspirations: he wanted to work in the automobile industry as a car mechanic. In fact, of the seven participants in this study, Eddie and Alexandra had the clearest career aspirations at the beginning of the study. Alexandra wanted to be an immigration lawyer and Eddie a car mechanic. Eddie was already informally fixing up relatives and friends' cars and enjoyed the work. In his mind, fixing cars was strongly associated with fond memories of his deceased father. Also, now that he had a baby, Eddie took his parenting role seriously and wanted to provide for his girlfriend and their baby son. His situation was by any measure very difficult: his high school graduation was by no means assured; he was living with relatives; and he and his girlfriend had just had a baby. And yet, he had a remarkable clarity about what he wanted to do with his life and how he might support his young family.

Similarly, Carlos's artistic talents could have been turned into a career. Some teachers were aware of his talents as Mrs Anderson told me, 'Carlos is very artistic' (IN 06/02/2011). However, no educators at Brighton ever suggested to Carlos that he might want to consider a career that could use his artistic talents such as web designing or computer graphics. When I asked Carlos whether he had ever considered pursuing a career which utilized his artistic talents, he simply said, 'I never thought about it' (IN 03/27/2012).[3] Since no one in his immediate or extended family had ever worked in design or technology, it is highly likely that Carlos was simply unaware that something he was good at could, in fact, lead to a viable and highly remunerative career. Moreover, he was probably not informed that the County Career and Technical Education Center (CCTEC), the CTE center with which Brighton was affiliated, had a program in Interactive Multimedia and Design. Instead, when he attempted to make future plans, he first thought of nursing, which one of his relatives suggested, and then electronics, which was familiar territory given his father's job in construction.

Also, in contrast to the institutional habitus that framed these students as limited, lazy and 'checked out', Eddie and Carlos were eager to learn and wanted to present themselves as good students when they were in school. In contrast to teachers' general perception that Eddie had low academic abilities, he in fact expressed his intellectual curiosity. For example, Eddie took Remedial Human Anatomy in his senior year, and he said that through this course, he became much more aware of how the human body worked:

> I'm really learning this stuff, but, you know, I didn't thought about it that, you know, like about myself, like, about me, like my body, you know, like sometimes we … I just do things, but I don't really know about it. Yeah, like, parts of my body or my brain, like if you got into an accident or hit your head or something, you may … maybe not gonna be able to be normal 'cause, there's like certain spots in your head that, you know, they're like, yeah, important for you. (IN 04/20/2012)

In other words, Eddie was able to make a connection between class content and his own experiences and reflect on how he needed to take care of his body. In this particular interview, we went over each course he was taking, and he was able to articulate his personal 'take away' from each class, demonstrating that he was, in fact, engaged with his academic learning.

Carlos did not express the joy of academic learning that Eddie did, but he too was eager to project the image of being a good student.

In Mr McGrath's class, the teacher was explaining how to use the band saw, and Carlos was listening intently:

> [Mr. McGrath] explains how to use the guard with an eighth of an inch above the block of wood they are cutting. He tells students to stay three feet away from the guy who is using the machine, adding that this is a good class that is respectful, while his fourth block [class] scares the hell out of him because they mess around. When he says that this class is respectful, Carlos pats his chest lightly, as if to say, 'That's me'. (FN 03/28/2012)

Given the number of classes he had missed, Carlos could hardly claim to be a model student. However, in front of Mr McGrath, whom he perceived as caring, Carlos nonetheless wanted to come across as an eager and respectful student. In other words, both Carlos and Eddie, far from being 'checked out', did care; they wanted to engage with their school and the learning that was happening there.

Further, in spite of the institutional discourse that located the source of the problem not only in the students but also in their families, Carlos and Eddie in fact benefitted from the support of their immediate and extended family members for their schooling and further education. Family mattered to them, and their families' support helped them persist through graduation. Carlos's parents made it clear that he had to at least graduate from high school. This was part of the reason why he came back in the spring of his senior year after a long absence in the fall. 'I'll break my mom's heart if I dropped out' (IN 03/27/2012), he said. Similarly, despite Mrs Salomon's lament about the lack of family engagement, Eddie's uncle and even his girlfriend's parents communicated to him that they would support his further education. Eddie told me that his uncle offered to support him financially if he wanted to pursue PSE. His uncle, who had a high school education and worked as a cook in a restaurant, had two young children of his own. Given that he and his wife had their own children's educational expenses to consider, their offer to help financially with Eddie's PSE shows their commitment to their nephew's well-being and future. Eddie's girlfriend's parents also strongly encouraged his to pursue a college education: 'Actually my girlfriend's parents, they don't mind if I go to college. They actually want me to go to college' (IN 09/26/2011). In other words, although Carlos and Eddie's families may not have actively sought out communication with the school, at home they clearly impressed upon these youth the importance of education, which the students incorporated into their own individual habitus.

Finally, Eddie and Carlos were proficient bilingual speakers, capable of shifting fluidly and appropriately back and forth between two languages as the situation required. At school, their *lack* of English proficiency was constantly emphasized, compared against the monolingual English standard, while their Spanish proficiency was virtually ignored. Yet, it was by virtue of their bilingualism that Eddie and Carlos were able to maintain close ties with their families and kin and to benefit from the rich familial capital from their community. Carlos and Eddie were able to persist through graduation because they could fully communicate with their families in Spanish and understood their parents and relatives' expectations.

High School Diploma without Career Readiness

In this chapter, through the experiences of two low-performing ELs, I explored how non-college-bound ELs are educated in high school. What became immediately apparent was that Brighton did very little for students like Carlos and Eddie except help them to graduate. Within the institutional habitus of the school, it was assumed that high school graduation was the best educational outcome that low-achieving ELs could attain (Callahan & Gándara, 2004). This is not to say that Brighton educators did not invest in supporting Eddie and Carlos: they were willing to set and reset their schedules in a way that fit all the required courses; they reached out to their parents/guardians; and if necessary, they were willing to forgo some of the graduation requirements. As a result, the two students did graduate, and therefore came out of high school measurably better off than 17% of ELs who leave high school without a diploma (Kanno & Cromley, 2015). Having a high school diploma is no small matter. In virtually every economic indicator one can think of, individuals who do not have a high school diploma perform measurably worse than those who hold a high school diploma (Ma *et al.*, 2019). Thus, the importance of the support that Brighton educators provided to help Carlos and Eddie graduate cannot be overstated.

Beyond a high school diploma, however, Brighton offered them very little. Carlos and Eddie's academic experiences illustrate that they did not fully develop the foundational cognitive skills a high school diploma is supposed to warrant. They were confined to the lowest-level classes that Brighton offered and were exposed to extremely basic instruction, constant disruptions and tense relationships between teachers and students in remedial classes. Brighton's practice of moving even high-performing, college-bound ELs to remedial courses once they completed EL sheltered courses had a cascading effect on lower-achieving, non-college-bound ELs. Students like Carlos and Eddie went through their entire high school careers with little or no opportunity to rise above the remedial track.

However, the foundational cognitive skills that a high school diploma is supposed to guarantee are not just relevant for college-bound students; rather, they are also critical for career readiness since they 'serve as a basis—the foundation—for supporting more advanced skill development' (Clark, 2015: 4). While these cognitive skills may not be needed for some entry-level jobs, they are critical for further advancement in one's career. Consequently, 'when workers in the lowest-level jobs lack basic academic skills, as they often do, they are stuck in those jobs' (Rosenbaum, 2001: 118). Ultimately, receiving a high school diploma is better than not receiving one, but a diploma without the accompanying foundational cognitive skills creates a long-lasting setback to students' economic prospects. A school that is operating with the institutional habitus of expecting certain groups of students to reach high school graduation but nothing more ultimately becomes an agent of social reproduction, wherein such students are firmly segmented back into the low SES background from which they came.

At the same time, 'college-for-all' *was* another prominent aspect of Brighton's institutional habitus, and therefore, ironically, those students who were neither planning to pursue a college education nor enrolled in CTE programs received virtually no help in building their career-planning skills (Clark, 2015). Although the other college-bound participants' contacts with their guidance counselors were generally minimal, the school offered a number of college-planning orientations, which were mandatory for all students to attend. This meant that although their college knowledge remained underdeveloped (Chapter 3), comparatively speaking, college-bound ELs did develop some awareness of what they needed to do in order to go to college. In contrast, there were no equivalent school-wide orientations on how to become career ready. Rather, data from Kadi's experience suggest that concrete training and guidance to become career ready took place within the confines of the CTE program for those students who chose CTE pathways. Thus, students like Eddie and Carlos, who were neither college bound nor enrolled in CTE programs, were left completely in the dark about how to prepare and plan for a post-high-school future. Such lack of guidance is particularly devastating to immigrant ELs. Because they lack exposure to a wide range of career options, immigrant ELs from low-income families tend to hold a binary view of their vocational choices: 'that is, getting a job at McDonald's or going to college' (Gándara, 2008: 81). Carlos's example of thinking of becoming a tattoo artist as the only way he could use his artistic talents speaks volumes about his lack of familiarity with career options. Educators, in part, failed to provide the guidance Carlos and Eddie needed because they attributed the two students' problems to their own deficits and remained largely unaware of the institutional structures that limited their opportunities to learn. Being acutely aware of the students' and their families' shortcomings while being oblivious to institutional inequities, I would argue, shaped Brighton's institutional habitus and educators' expectations for what low-performing ELs were capable of. Brighton educators saw themselves as 'helping' low-performing students, who, in their minds, were causing their own demise, as opposed to being part of a system that reduced their opportunities to learn. If we believe that,

> Some children are at a deficit because of race, poverty, culture, behavior, home language, and so forth, and therefore, are incapable of performing at high levels, we lower our expectations for them. ... These students, thus, often receive a less rigorous curriculum, are held to lesser standards, and often times are placed in special education or lower level classes. (McKenzie & Scheurich, 2004: 603–604)

Because Brighton educators saw Carlos and Eddie as 'at-risk' students who were failing because of their own deficits, they lowered their expectations and prioritized the students' high school graduation at the expense of everything else, as if that was the best that could be expected of them.

Further, I do not think it is a coincidence that of the seven EL participants, Eddie and Carlos received the lowest expectations from educators. In addition to being ELs, these two students were also young Latino men. In the context of US society, Black and Latino men are subjects of particularly negative stereotyping, as Harper and Williams (2014) describe:

> They are to be feared, stopped and frisked, and mass incarcerated, as they are the antithesis of law-abiding citizens. When they show up to school (which isn't very often), administrators and teachers should expect them to be disengaged, disrespectful, unprepared, underperforming, and violent. (Harper & Williams, 2014: 5)

When Black or Latino male EL students underachieve, the deficit thinking toward them correspondingly increases: their being male students of color may become one more ready explanation, in addition to being ELs from low-income families with non-college-educated parents, for their underachievement.

Lack of Access to CTE

The great irony of Eddie and Carlos's high school education is that Brighton offered CTE programs that would have matched their interests. As I mentioned in Chapter 4, some of the CTE programs were offered in-house while others were offered in affiliation with CCTEC. These programs were the principal ways through which Brighton educated a subset of its students to become career ready. CCTEC's Automotive Technology would have enabled Eddie to acquire the necessary qualifications to become a car mechanic while its Interactive Multimedia and Design might have paved the way for Carlos to use his artistic talents in his career (Table 5.2).

However, accessing those CTE programs required a certain degree of cultural capital on the part of the student: namely that the student had to be making good progress in fulfilling graduation requirements in order to enroll in a CTE program because all CTE courses counted as electives. As discussed in Chapter 4, Kadi was able to enroll in CCTEC because she had already completed the majority of her graduation requirements and was therefore in a position to be able to leave Brighton after two morning blocks to travel to the CCTEC campus and spend the rest of her day at her CTE program. To have sufficient impact and to make enrollees truly career ready, Brighton's CTE programs required this level of intensive training in a dedicated block of time. But this feature also limited the pool of CTE-eligible students to those who were making on-grade progress toward graduation.

For those advocates of CTE who want to destigmatize CTE and see the status of CTE elevated, there may be nothing wrong with limiting CTE program entry. They would probably like to see more students

Table 5.2 CTE programs offered at CCTEC

Divisions	Examples of programs
Construction	Carpentry, Landscape and Greenhouse Operations
Power and Transportation	Automotive Technology, Collision Repair Technology
Health and Human Services	Health Occupations, Culinary Arts and Hospitality
Technology Academy	Computer Integration and Support, Interactive Multimedia and Design

like Kadi enrolled. Also, while a number of careers do not require a bachelor's degree, many of them, such as registered nurses, air traffic controllers, police officers, real estate brokers and dental hygienists, do require some level of PSE (National Skills Coalition, 2017). Thus, CTE needs to ensure its students acquire a solid academic foundation that will enable them to gain access to and be successful in postsecondary programs (Hodge *et al.*, 2020). In other words, more than ever, college readiness and career readiness converge. To be career ready in the early 21st century is to check the many boxes of what it means to be college ready. Yet, one unintended consequence of the convergence between career readiness and college readiness is that severely underperforming students like Eddie and Carlos who are attending a comprehensive high school that offers both academic rigorous courses and an array of CTE options nonetheless end up leaving high school without having had an opportunity to benefit from either.

Summary

In this chapter, I examined the experiences of two low-performing students who were *not* going to college. In the era of 'college-for-all', high schools do not offer many options for students who are so low-performing that college going is not realistic. As Carlos and Eddie accumulated absences and failed more classes, educators' attention turned increasingly and more exclusively toward their high school graduation. These two students had interests and talents, but such strengths remained largely invisible to those educators who attributed the students' failure to their and their family's own deficits. CTE programs that could have engaged their interests and nurtured their talents were inaccessible to them because they had failed so many classes and could not afford to take CTE courses, which were all electives. Thus, Carlos and Eddie did graduate, but without any specific plans or skills with which to build a career after high school.

Notes

(1) While I was continuing the data collection through Year 3 in order to see Carlos through graduation, I started informally mentoring some EL juniors and seniors about college planning during 2012–2013. Roberto was one such student.
(2) The usual math course sequence in high school is algebra 1, geometry and algebra 2.
(3) As I mentioned in his story, at the end of his junior year, Carlos had said, 'I was thinking about being a tattoo artist. Like, tattooing people' (IN 06/02/2011). This is not entirely surprising because through the three years I worked with Carlos, I noticed an expanding collection of tattoos on his body, some of which were absolutely beautiful.

He took to wearing loose-fitting tank-top shirts to show off his tattoos on his chest and shoulders. And indeed, becoming a tattoo artist may have been a promising venue to pursue. That said, it is telling that the only career that he could name that would use his artistic talents was to become a tattoo artist. It illustrates the narrow range of familiar career options within which low-income immigrant students like Carlos and Eddie were developing their future plans.

6 ELs' Access to Postsecondary Education

Federal law requires that schools and districts must provide sufficient language and academic support services to ELs, so that they 'can participate meaningfully and equally in educational programs' (US Department of Justice and US Department of Education, 2015: 2). Importantly, this mandate does not extend to PSE because, while having PSE is becoming increasingly necessary for one's pursuit of a sustainable career and financial stability (Carnevale *et al.*, 2011; Ma *et al.*, 2019), it is not considered compulsory. Therefore, PSE technically remains a 'privilege' and does not have to be accessible to everyone. However, it is the case that ELs' limited access to PSE is a consequence of an inequitable K-12 education. In other words, ELs' low advancement to PSE happens because they are not provided with opportunities to participate 'meaningfully and equally' in K-12 educational programs as federal laws demand.

All seven ELs in this study had originally hoped to attend PSE after high school. Five of them wanted to enroll in a four-year college while the other two were interested in a trade school or a CTE program at a community college. Dishearteningly, none of them reached the postsecondary destination they had envisioned. Table 6.1 summarizes the students' initial PSE aspirations, the PSE schools to which they applied and were admitted, and the actual outcomes, along with the salient factors that shaped each participant's PSE outcome. Of the five students aiming to enroll in a four-year college, four of them (Erica, Alexandra, Josephine and Kadi) decided to attend a community college. The only student who reached a four-year college, Ken, was admitted to a non-selective institution as an undeclared major on the condition that he attend a summer bridge remedial program – far from a slot in a nursing program he was hoping to attain. Meanwhile, two students, Carlos and Eddie, who were considering a CTE-related

Table 6.1 Seven participants' PSE aspirations and actual outcomes

Students	Original PSE aspirations	College applications submitted	Colleges admitted	Actual PSE destinations	Salient factors shaping the outcomes
Erica	4 year, CC	LCC	LCC	LCC	Linguistic insecurity Father's preference for CC
Alexandra	4 year	LCC	LCC	LCC	Reluctance to take the SAT Lack of trust in educators
Ken	4 year	Drexel Penn State Rutgers Widener	Widener	Widener	Strong 4-year college orientation Weak STEM preparation
Josephine	4 year	Drexel USciences Cedar Crest Virginia Union LCC	Virginia Union LCC	LCC	College cost Older brother's CC transfer
Kadi	4 year	Virginia Wesleyan LCC	Virginia Wesleyan LCC	LCC	Self-advocacy CTE mentor's suggestions
Eddie	CC, trade school	None	None	No PSE	Parenthood Lack of career guidance
Carlos	CC, trade school	None	None	No PSE	Chronic absenteeism Lack of career guidance

Note: CC: Community College; LCC: Local Community College.

certificate program did not reach any PSE at all. This study, then, was an investigation of how and why, in this day and age where ELs represent 10% of the US public school population, access to PSE remains such an elusive goal for them.

In what follows, I first discuss the main findings of the study. The findings described in the previous chapters are theoretically expanded and presented in the following thematic categories: (a) Brighton High School's institutional habitus; (b) ELs' individual habitus and self-elimination; (c) the myth of community college transfer; and (d) access to a CTE. I then offer several concrete implications that emerge from the findings.

Brighton High School's Institutional Habitus

In a recent theoretical exploration, byrd (2019) argues against previous conceptualizations of institutional habitus (e.g. McDonough, 1997; Reay *et al.*, 2005) that assert that a school develops its particular institutional habitus solely because it serves students of a particular social class. Rather, she posits that a school's institutional habitus is also generated out of the social position that the school itself occupies relative to other schools and related institutions (e.g. colleges) within the arena of education. Conceptualizing institutional habitus this way, there are several factors that shaped Brighton High School's institutional habitus.

First and foremost, Brighton was a public high school that served a largely working-class community. As a *comprehensive* high school, as opposed to a magnet school,[1] it accepted all middle-school graduates in its catchment area and strove to meet the needs of a broad spectrum of students. As such, it never aimed to be an elite public school that sent the majority of its students to selective four-year colleges. At the same time, the Brighton school district was situated near a larger school district with persistent underachievement. Brighton High School prided itself on the contrast: the school provided a better education in a safer and more stable environment to students of similar demographics.

Brighton's collective sense of appropriate and realistic PSE options for its students, then, was part of the school's institutional habitus. This habitus emerged out of the school's status vis-à-vis other schools and colleges, and in its relationship with the local and broader communities. As Principal Lawrence articulated, the school was not solely focused on four-year colleges. Taking advantage of the presence of LCC nearby, Brighton educators took the position that state colleges such as Temple University and Penn State were excellent choices for high achievers, whereas for students who were not ready to advance directly to a four-year college or who could not afford a four-year college education, LCC was a fine choice, too.

But a school's institutional habitus about appropriate postsecondary destinations is not always uniform across different student subgroups: 'Even students in the same school may actually experience different institutional habitus on the assumptions and practice embedded into the institution and enacted by its agents' (byrd, 2013: 20). As illustrated in Figure 6.1, if Brighton educators recommended state colleges for high achievers and LCC for mid to low achievers among non-ELs, they lowered the expectations for ELs by one notch: they recommended LCC for high- and mid-achieving ELs and focused on high school graduation for low achievers. Had Brighton been an elite public high school where the vast majority of its graduates went to selective institutions, then the expectation for ELs may have been mid-level four-year state colleges. Conversely, if Brighton had been a persistently underperforming school where the top students went to community colleges, the best outcome that ELs could be expected to achieve might have been high school graduation. In other words, Brighton's overall institutional habitus

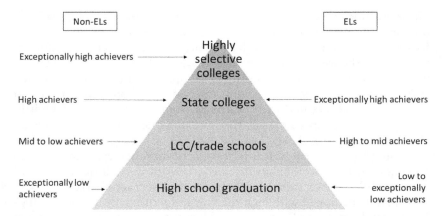

Figure 6.1 Brighton's differential expectations for EL and non-ELs' postsecondary destinations

regarding its graduates' PSE destinations influenced ELs' PSE destinations, but the range of options recommended for ELs was lower than that for non-ELs.

Lower academic preparation

Brighton's institutional habitus, which positioned ELs as 'lesser' than English L1 students, had two major consequences for its practice with ELs: (a) limited access to advanced college preparatory courses; and (b) lack of sufficient guidance and information about PSE options.

With regard to ELs' coursework, educators' assumption was that if ELs were going to a community college at best, there was no point in pushing them into advanced courses at the risk of failure. It was a much safer choice to place them in remedial- and regular-level courses that they knew ELs could pass, thereby making steady progress toward meeting graduation requirements. The seven EL students in this study, students of a wide range of academic capability, were all placed in low-track courses. Once ELs completed the sheltered classes, they were almost always placed in remedial-level courses of the same subject regardless of their performance in the sheltered courses. As a result, the students in this study had no access to advanced-level courses – except for AP Spanish.

Brighton educators defended this practice, citing the need to 'protect ELs' from failure – one of the most pervasive discourses of Brighton's institutional habitus. By stating that advanced courses were for students who were independent and tenacious learners capable of managing large amounts of reading and writing outside of class, the 'protecting ELs' discourse characterized ELs as dependent, passive learners incapable of academic challenges. It also created a vicious cycle: the absence of ELs in advanced courses led to a lack of EL support in these classes, which in turn led to guidance counselors' reservations about sending ELs to advanced classes because they lacked EL support. The lack of built-in EL support in advanced classes then became one more reason to steer ELs away from these classes.

Behind this rationale was a false logic of meritocracy. The only students qualified to enroll in advanced coursework were those who would be successful in the existing model of advanced instruction: students who were already equipped with high reading and writing proficiency in English. EL students' lack of academic and linguistic capabilities was pointed to as the cause of their ineligibility to enroll in advanced courses, whereas structural inequities that made these classes inaccessible to ELs never surfaced as underlying causes. In a quintessential pattern on deficit thinking (Valencia, 2010), the cause of limited academic access was seen as residing in the students themselves.

Clearinghouse approach to college guidance

A second consequence of the school's institutional habitus regarding ELs was the lack of sufficient information and guidance about PSE choices. Stanton-Salazar (2001: 215) points out that since schools' resources are finite, 'they are … charged with reserving their best resources, including social capital, for those who are deemed "most deserving"'. From this perspective, ELs' PSE access was simply not a priority for Brighton; there were many more 'promising' students who could, with educators' guidance and help, reach solid state colleges and even beyond. ELs were certainly given the information and guidance offered to everyone across the school, but they never received tailored guidance that fit their specific needs.

As discussed in Chapter 3, Brighton took a clearinghouse approach (Hill, 2008) to PSE guidance. The school hosted many information sessions both for students and parents and informed them of the resources available at the school; however, the school left it up to individual students and families to make use of these resources. Those students who took the initiative were praised for taking ownership of their PSE access, and educators then readily offered individualized support. Thus, when Kadi wanted to explore CTE options and approached her guidance counselor, the counselor was more than willing to sit down with her, help her apply to two programs and, after she was accepted to both, help her select the one that best fit her needs.

But it is hard to seek help if one does not even know where to begin. All the PSE guidance at Brighton assumed a baseline knowledge about the US higher education system. If students and their families did not share this background knowledge, the guidance information that was provided en masse would have been incomprehensible. For example, as I discussed in previous chapters, on a number of occasions, many educators told my participants that it was a good choice to enroll first in a community college and then afterward to transfer to a four-year college. But I never heard them backtrack and explicitly explain the differences between community colleges and four-year colleges and exactly what transferring from a community college to a four-year college entailed. As a result, some of the EL participants, even in their senior year, were unclear about the distinction between the two types of colleges and what exactly they needed to do at a community college in order to transfer.

I suspect that much of the college information given out to students was also lost on many non-EL students who were the first in their families to attend college. However, for ELs, there was the additional challenge of processing unfamiliar information in a language they were still learning. Behind numerous new and unfamiliar labels that guidance counselors routinely peppered in their talks were concepts specific to US colleges, e.g. *FAFSA, common application, college essay, grade point average (GPA), SAT/ACT, loans* vs. *grants, early decision* vs. *early action, fee waiver*, etc. As Stanton-Salazar (2001: 215) points out, 'Access to an institution's human resources is reserved for students who have learned to *decode the system*, even when the "codes" appear arbitrary or as fetishes of those in charge' (original emphasis). In the case of ELs, even the 'codes' in the literal sense of the term, meaning the language in which PSE discourses were couched, were opaque to begin with. When so much is unfamiliar and yet so much is assumed to be known, it is hard for individual students to come out and admit that they need help.

On the other hand, the information that was specific to EL and immi-grant students was provided in neither student assemblies nor parent orientations. Given that some Brighton EL students were undocumented, it would have been helpful for them to learn about PSE and scholarship options for undocumented students. Also, some of the participating stu-dents wondered if they needed to take the Test of English as a Foreign Language (TOEFL) in addition to the SAT/ACT in order to apply to four-year colleges. This information was never provided to them. In fact, educators themselves seemed unclear about the role of the TOEFL in US-educated (as opposed to international) ELs' college applications.

Nonetheless, ELs' lack of help-seeking and, as a consequence, their lack of college knowledge were once again attributed to their own deficits. As far as Brighton was concerned, the school offered a number of PSE resources and made them available to all students equally. Thus, if individual students failed to utilize the resources, that was because they were too passive or not serious enough. EL teacher Ms Li commented on how much of the information that was given to students in assemblies was incomprehensible to ELs. However, she also added, 'I know that EL students *who are really serious* about going to colleges can take all the information, understand it, and do something about it. But, a lot of them, it just goes over their heads' (IN 01/23/2012, added emphasis). Ms Li was a former EL herself, and yet now as a teacher, she too seemed to have internalized the deficit orientation toward ELs and reduced their access to college information to a matter of motivation and seriousness.

ELs' Individual Habitus and Self-Elimination

A school's institutional habitus provides an overall framework within which its students negotiate their PSE access. But a school's institutional habitus does not affect all students the same way because students bring their own individual habitus to the table. Students with relatively more cultural capital may assume that they deserve to attend top-level PSE institutions, and they demand the most individualized support that the school can offer. In contrast, students who possess little cultural capital may recognize the resources available at the school but may simply assume that they are not for them.

In this study, ELs for the most part fell into the second type of student. Positioned as less capable than their English L1 peers, they internalized some of Brighton's institutional habitus about what they were capable of and what they deserved. They neither challenged the structural inequalities nor expected much help from educators. Bourdieu (1991; Bourdieu & Wacquant, 1992) would classify this as an example of symbolic violence, whereby the marginalized misrecognize the cultural capital they lack as inherently valuable and thus come to accept their own marginalization. The symbolic violence in this case is the perpetuation of the primacy of English monolingualism, making it seem as if multilingualism was a real handicap that limited students' PSE options. The misrecognition of the 'meritocracy' in which they came out 'lesser', I would argue, constricted ELs' individual habitus and led to two forms of self-elimination: (a) self-elimination from the four-year college race and (b) self-elimination from seeking institutional help.

Self-elimination from the four-year college race

Before I began this project, I had naively assumed that ELs applied to four-year colleges just like non-ELs, but that they were either denied admission or unable to find the financial means to attend. I had predicted that those two reasons accounted for ELs' lower college enrollment rate than that of their English L1 peers. Among my participants, one student, Josephine, fit this pattern. She applied to several four-year colleges but was rejected by most of them. She therefore decided to enroll in a community college instead. In all likelihood, even if she had been admitted to any of her preferred choices, she would not have been able to afford it because they were all private colleges.

But I learned through conducting this study that there was another pattern which diverted ELs from the four-year college trajectory: self-elimination from applying. Alexandra and Erica, with their academic qualifications, might have been able to enroll in a four-year college had they insisted on it. But by November of their senior year, they had switched to attending LCC. That the two highest-performing students in the study both opted for a community college without trying out their competitiveness in the four-year college race speaks volumes about ELs' individual habitus and how it is influenced by their school's institutional habitus.

Bourdieu (1982, as cited in Bourdieu & Wacquant, 1992) argues that one's linguistic habitus, formed through one's past experiences with various linguistic markets, leads one to anticipate the value of one's linguistic competence in a future market:

> This anticipation ... is the deed of the linguistic habitus, which, being the product of a primordial and prolonged relation to the laws of a definite market, tends to function as a sense of the acceptability and of the probable value of its own linguistic products and those of others on the different markets. (Bourdieu & Wacquant, 1992: 145–156)

Both Erica and Alexandra knew that they were multilingual; however, their past experiences at Brighton – and indeed in the United State at large – had amply taught them that their multilingualism counted for very little as linguistic capital. In fact, their lack of native English proficiency in the market of US K-12 education pulled them down so much more than their multilingualism lifted them up. Then, why would they expect the value of their linguistic capital to be any different in the market of US higher education? When Erica said, 'If [I] go to LCC, I can study English very good. So, I can go to the university. I won't have, like, a lot of problems' (IN 09/26/2011), on the surface, it sounds like a pragmatic and sensible decision of an immigrant student who recognized the need to improve her English language proficiency before she could be successful in four-year college-level work. But from the point of view of her linguistic habitus, it can also be read as her anticipation of her lack of linguistic capital in US higher education and its potential negative consequences, based on her experiences so far with K-12 education. These examples demonstrate that ELs' own individual habitus can be a powerful barrier to their own four-year college access.[2]

Self-elimination from seeking help

A second way in which ELs' own individual habitus led to self-elimination was in the area of seeking PSE guidance. If educators at Brighton did not reach out and offer the specific PSE guidance that ELs needed, neither did the ELs in this study reach out to seek help. None of the EL participants was in a position to receive sufficient PSE guidance from their family; they definitely could have used some help from the school. Yet, none of them, with the exception of Kadi applying to CTE programs, took the step to approach their guidance counselors or teachers to seek assistance. In fact, they seemed to prefer to fly under the radar and tried to find the information they needed by themselves.

I would argue that high school students' own individual habitus affects the ease with which they can make use of the resources available at school. If students believe that school resources, including educators' time and attention, are theirs to use, they are more likely to seek out what they need and even demand help. I have worked with students – ELs in fact – who approached their high school resources this way. For example, Mickey was a participant in a qualitative study that colleagues and I conducted on ELs who were admitted to a selective public university (Kanno & Varghese, 2010; Varghese, 2013). She assumed that she was entitled to school resources as much as any other student once she discovered them:

> I knew what a counselor was, someone who can helps you. I didn't know it was someone you could go and say, 'I don't know what I am doing actually; should I take this class? Or da-da-da.' I didn't know that stuff

until I was in my junior year of high school. That's when I realized that *all this information was available to me and that's when I started making use of it*. I went to my counselor and said, 'Hi, my name is Mickey. I don't believe you met me before, but you have been my counselor for two years. But anyway, we are going to be friends now'. (Varghese, 2013: 155, added emphasis)

Mickey initially lacked the college knowledge to locate the support that was available, but once she did, she assumed that it was for her to use. This sort of disposition was wholly absent in most of the EL participants in this project.[3] I believe that to a certain extent, the EL participants had internalized the school's positioning of them as marginal. Consequently, when support was not readily accessible, they simply gave up, interpreting it as a reflection of their marginality. When Alexandra went to seek her guidance counselor and was told that he was not available right at that moment, one way to interpret the situation was that he just happened to be busy at that moment and that she could come back another time. If Alexandra had assumed, as Mickey had, that she was worth his attention and that *of course* he was going to help her, she might have come back for assistance. Instead, she took his unavailability as another example of how the school failed to care about her, consequently believing that she had no choice but to go it alone.

Unfortunately, the ELs' lack of self-advocacy had the effect of reinforcing Brighton's institutional habitus. Educators saw that the students expressed interest in attending a four-year college but did not aggressively self-advocate for support. This, in turn, confirmed educators' belief that these students were not yet mature and autonomous enough to pursue a four-year college education and inclined them further to recommend LCC as an alternative. In this way, the school's institutional habitus regarding ELs' PSE choices went uninterrupted.

The Myth of Community College Transfer

Although Brighton educators collectively argued that community colleges were a good choice for many of their graduates, their institutional habitus was such that their endorsement of community colleges did not imply that their graduates' education should stop there. Rather, they overwhelmingly spoke of community colleges as a stepping stone to a bachelor's degree. 'You can always transfer from a community college to a university', was an institutional discourse embraced by many Brighton educators.

I remain puzzled by why Brighton educators adhered to the 'you can always transfer' discourse without verifying the actual transfer rates or communicating to students the challenges involved. I do not believe that they knowingly misled the students. The absolute conviction with which many of them – from the principal, to guidance counselors, to the EL department chair – claimed that students could transfer from LCC to a university indicates that they genuinely believed that it was possible and highly likely.

One possible explanation for why Brighton educators collectively put so much stock in what I call 'the myth of community college transfer' relates to high school educators' aversion to dashing their students' hopes for their future. Today, 'over 80 percent of community college students intend to earn at least a bachelor's degree' (Jenkins & Fink, 2015: 1). To inform community college goers that, realistically speaking, they have a slim chance of attaining a bachelor's degree is to deflate their ambitions. For educators who want the best for their students, it is an uncomfortable task to tell them that their goals are unrealistic. Rosenbaum *et al.* (1996) argue that the open-door policy of community colleges has provided educators with a way out of this dilemma:

> In the past, college admission standards compelled counselors to confront students' unrealistic college plans. Now, however, admission standards are practically nonexistent. ... Since any student who can find a way to pay tuition can attend, counselors no longer need to discourage unprepared students from making college plans. (Rosenbaum *et al.*, 1996: 259)

I would argue that high school counselors – or rather high schools – continue to function as gatekeepers through their institutional habitus. They highlight certain PSE options more than others; within each school, educators stratify students into different PSE pathways, placing some students in advanced tracks and others in remedial tracks starting in ninth grade (or even earlier). Nonetheless, it is true that when the time comes for actual college advising, educators seem highly reluctant to explicitly crush individual students' aspirations.

Thus, among themselves and with me, Brighton educators characterized attending a community college as a lesser option, suitable for students with significant challenges, be they academic underpreparation, low SES or lack of sufficient English language proficiency. In other words, they were steering certain groups of students to LCC for a reason – because they did not anticipate those students would be successful at four-year colleges. But the educators' messaging to students about community colleges was remarkably upbeat: they highlighted the possibility of transferring from LCC to a four-year college. By accentuating the potential for four-year college transfer, the educators could avoid hurting students' feelings by telling them that they were underqualified for four-year college enrollment while also allowing the students to maintain their original ambitions.

Finally, there is a strong disconnect between K-12 education and PSE in the United States, which keeps educators in each sector blithely uninformed about what goes on in the other sectors (Kirst, 2004; Venezia *et al.*, 2003). Very few high schools – not just Brighton – keep track of their graduates' persistence and degree attainment in PSE in any systematic manner. Rosenbaum *et al.* (2010) point out that this information is, in fact, hard to come by for high school educators:

> Most counselors cannot get authoritative information about their graduates' college outcomes. Data on college's graduation rates are rarely provided, and whatever numbers are available usually do not apply to the graduates of any one particular high school, since several high schools usually feed into each community college. (Rosenbaum *et al.*, 2010: 6)

Without an obvious way to track their graduates' PSE attainment and given the long-standing divide between K-12 education and PSE, it is not surprising that many high school educators feel that while their students' PSE *access* is their responsibility, their graduates' PSE *success* is not. It is indeed striking how few Brighton educators spoke about how their students' academic preparation in high school directly impacted their success in PSE – although the link between the two has been well established (Adelman, 2006; Cabrera *et al.*, 2005; Kanno & Cromley, 2013). Rather, they spoke of how students' academic preparation and qualifications affected their college *admission*. The inclination to believe that their graduates' success in PSE was not their primary responsibility might have made it easier for Brighton educators to tell their students, 'You can always transfer later', without verifying the actual process and the likelihood of transfer.

However unintentional it may be, the consequences of this misinformation about transfer are clear. The four students in this study – Erica, Alexandra, Josephine and Kadi – who switched from a four-year college pathway to a community college pathway, all decided to do so with the firm conviction that they would later transfer to a four-year college. Just like their educators, those students also spoke of their later transfer as a given – that is, '*I* can always transfer'. Lacking other authoritative sources of information, these students had no independent means to verify the veracity of this claim. Would they have pushed themselves harder to apply to enroll in a four-year college had they been informed that the rate of transfer from a community college to a four-year college was generally very low? This is impossible to ascertain given that it is counterfactual. However, I do know that they were all very firm in their aspiration to earn a bachelor's degree. None of them adjusted their ultimate goal when they switched to the community college pathway.

Access to CTE

At the outset of this study, I was going to focus on ELs who had the intention of attending college (either a two-year or a four-year college) and explore what their college access experiences were like. Once I began the fieldwork, however, I quickly realized that a study of ELs' going to college also had to be a study of ELs' *not* going to college if it was to present the whole picture. After all, nearly half of high school ELs do not go on to PSE (Kanno & Cromley, 2015). Given the statistics, Carlos and Eddie's stories are not unique among ELs.

Once again, I reiterate my position that not all students need to go to college. However, by the time they graduate from high school, all students need to have gained foundational academic knowledge and skills as well as concrete ideas for how to move forward with their lives after high school. The fact that Carlos and Eddie did not go to college is not what is deeply troubling, but rather, that they graduated from high school without career readiness or concrete PSE plans.

Despite the long-standing stereotype of vocational education as 'dumping grounds for students who couldn't cut it in college prep' (Newman & Winston, 2016: 58), I found that access to today's CTE, a more recent and elevated form of vocational education, in fact requires a significant amount of cultural capital – in many ways similar to the cultural capital required for access to college. For students like Eddie and Carlos, who were clearly not college bound because of their low academic performance, CTE was likewise inaccessible. Since all CTE credits were treated as electives, students who specialized in CTE first needed to be making on-grade progress toward fulfilling graduation requirements. Students like Carlos and Eddie who had failed multiple required courses stood no chance of getting into CTE programs regardless of their interests. Students had to be more like Kadi, who had transferred in many credits from her previous high school and also passed all her classes since arriving at Brighton, to be eligible for a CTE program.

Thus, public comprehensive high schools like Brighton today are, in reality, not divided into a college track and a vocational track; rather, they are divided into (a) a college track, (b) a CTE track and (c) what Deil-Amen and DeLuca (2010) call *the underserved third*:

> This 'underserved third' group is likely to depart from high school having taken classes mainly from the high school general curriculum in which they are at risk of receiving low-quality instruction, lower levels of academic preparation, and little to no job preparation or guidance. (Deil-Amen & DeLuca, 2010: 28)

Neither college nor career ready, the underserved third students are by far the worst off of all high school students. I would argue that ELs who come into high school with the least amount of cultural capital are at a significant risk of becoming members of the underserved third.

In recent years, CTE educators and policymakers have worked hard to gain the recognition and respect that CTE deserves, emphasizing how CTE in high school prepares students for PSE (Hernández-Gantes & Blank, 2009; Hodge *et al.*, 2020). By aligning career readiness with college readiness and by focusing on pathways to PSE, however, CTE educators may have unwittingly placed CTE out of the reach of the underperforming students who could most benefit from it. There are signs that this is not just an issue for Brighton, but an emerging trend. A recent investigative report by *The Boston Globe* (Gay, 2020) found that CTE schools in Massachusetts are becoming much more selective in their admissions criteria, so much so that they are now becoming a new battleground for equity, not because traditionally underserved students are overrepresented in these schools, but because such students are now *under*represented. The limited access has become so extreme that two dozen mayors in the state have jointly submitted a letter to the Massachusetts Department of Elementary and Secondary Education, urging them to require some CTE schools in the state to abandon their selective admissions criteria and switch to a lottery system. Citing an example of a Latina student who wanted to attend a CTE school but, because of a suspension record in her middle-school transcript, was subsequently denied admission, the report argues:

> Many of the state's 37 vocational schools have come under fire recently for using their admissions criteria to screen out struggling students like Sanchez—exactly the sort of non-college-bound striver they were built to serve. Over the past two decades, the schools have been transformed

from their blue-collar roots into high-tech training centers that prepare students equally for college or for well-paying jobs in the trades. Today, some are better funded than nearby public schools, and they have become increasingly selective in who they admit. (Gay, 2020: A16)

This, then, is hardly the picture of a program for students 'who couldn't cut it in college prep', but rather, yet another enrichment program from which many ELs are excluded.

EL students who *can* access CTE and are placed in programs that are oriented to PSE might reap the benefit of future capital accumulation. There is no question that Kadi gained specialized training which led to a qualification (an important form of cultural capital) and received mentoring (social capital) through her CTE program. She made a wise move in choosing to enroll in CTE in high school, and her college access was enhanced by this choice. In contrast, Brighton did not have much to offer to students like Carlos and Eddie who qualified for neither college nor CTE. For them, the focus shifted to high school graduation and dropout prevention. Callahan and Shifrer (2016) point out that some educators believe that high school graduation is good enough for ELs:

> Some educators justify high school graduation as the end goal for EL students because, according to their interpretation of EL status, limited English proficiency precludes full participation. As a result, learning the language and the culture is considered 'enough' for EL students to make it in adulthood, leaving them at a perpetual disadvantage. (Callahan & Shifrer, 2016: 487)

I would not claim that this was the expectation for *all* ELs at Brighton; higher-performing ELs were expected to go to college. However, for low-achieving ELs, high school graduation was indeed considered 'enough' – or rather, the best outcome for which one could hope.

Implications for Educational Practice

A number of implications can be drawn from this study, even though I am fully aware that this is a single-case study of one school, and thus its generalizability is limited. However, every case study is a case study of a broader, more universal issue and reflects some of the universal qualities of that issue. Erickson (1986: 130) articulates this principle in the context of studying teachers: 'Each instance of a classroom is seen as its own unique system, *which nonetheless displays universal properties of teaching*. These properties are manifested in the concrete, however, not in the abstract' (added emphasis). Similarly, I would argue that although the Brighton High School I studied is a unique school situated in a particular community at a particular point in time, it nonetheless exhibits some of the universal properties of EL education in the United States.

The implications for educational practice that I offer below, then, are in response to some of the most persistent challenges that I witnessed at Brighton, with the hope that some of them will be useful to other educators who are grappling with similar issues in their own schools or districts.

Run equity audits on ELs' coursework

This study found a clear pattern of unequal access to advanced-level courses by language status – a finding that has been corroborated by a number of studies, both qualitative and quantitative (Callahan & Shifrer, 2016; Callahan *et al.*, 2010; Johnson, 2019; Kanno & Cromley, 2015; Thompson, 2017; Umansky, 2016a). But educators at individual schools may not be aware that such inequities are happening within their own school, or they may not be aware of the extent of the inequities. One way to prompt a conversation is to run *equity audits* (McKenzie & Scheurich, 2004: 617): '"auditing" the school's or district's data for inequities' between student subgroups. For example, a school can run an analysis of the percentage of ELs enrolled in honors and AP courses and compare them with the percentage of non-ELs in these courses. When I told Brighton educators that 15% of all seniors took at least one AP course while no EL seniors did so except for AP world language courses (e.g. AP Spanish), they were genuinely surprised because no one had run such an analysis. Yet, all it took was a simple cross-tabulation of the current list of ELs and the current roster of AP courses.

Once such patterns become public knowledge within a school, two things can happen. First, educators can then further investigate where the blockage is happening. For example, they might find an academic trajectory that leads from EL sheltered courses to remedial-level courses of the same subjects, as I found at Brighton. Or they might discover that ELs spend so much time learning English in the first half of high school that they simply run out of time to reach high-level courses by the end of the 12th grade. Once they have identified the sources of the blockage, they can begin to address them.

A second possibility is that equity audits might open up uncomfortable but honest conversations about whether such unequal access is justified. Even when an equity audit reveals differential access between ELs and non-ELs, some educators might very well argue that it is a legitimate consequence of meritocracy. Others might find such differential access along language status unacceptable. These would be potentially unsettling conversations to have, revealing deeply held ideologies, level of trust in meritocracy and attitudes toward language and racial minoritized students. However, for some schools, even the ability to have such a dialogue is progress over unquestioningly continuing to place ELs in lower-level courses because that has been the practice all along.

Place ELs in advanced courses and provide training to advanced course teachers

Simply put, ELs must be given the same opportunity as English L1 students to learn the college preparatory curriculum. This is consistent with a policy recently jointly reaffirmed by the US Department of Justice and the US Department of Education (2015: 21): 'School districts may not categorically exclude EL students from gifted and talented education (GATE) or other specialized programs such as Advanced Placement (AP), honors, or International Baccalaureate (IB) courses'. But, of course, in order for ELs to reach honors and AP courses by the end of high school, they first need access to advanced-level courses in earlier grades that will lead to honors and AP courses. Stopping the practice of automatically placing ELs who have completed EL sheltered courses in remedial courses of the same subjects would be a step in the right direction. Beyond that, rather than assuming that ELs are incapable and subsequently creating many safety nets to prevent failure, educators should err on the side of placing ELs in too advanced courses rather than too low-level courses, trusting that they will rise to the challenge.

But if we place ELs in honors and AP courses, the teachers of these courses must be ready to support them; we cannot simply place ELs in advanced courses and let them sink or swim. Recall that part of the reservation that Brighton guidance counselors had about placing ELs in advanced courses was that teachers who taught these courses were not equipped to provide linguistic support for ELs. When I say that ELs will rise to the challenge if educators give them a chance, it is with the assumption that those who teach the advanced courses are skilled and prepared to support ELs' learning. High school ELs' burden of 'double the work' (Short & Fitzsimmons, 2007), i.e. learning English while also learning advanced academic content through English, should not fall solely on the students; it should also be shared by the teachers who teach honors and

AP courses. Specific training on how to embed linguistic support in the delivery of academic core content must be provided.

Install EL-specific bilingual guidance counselors

Installing bilingual guidance counselors who specialize in working with ELs is another policy that can make a real difference to high school ELs' access to PSE. At Brighton, guidance counselors were mechanically assigned to students by grades and by students' last names. Theoretically, by starting with the same students from ninth grade and going up by grade every year with them, guidance counselors were supposed to build close relationships with their charges. That might have happened with some students, but it certainly did not happen with any of the EL participants in this study. If a school designates bilingual guidance counselors to ELs, ELs might more readily approach their counselors, and the counselors in turn can advocate for their needs and rights. Such counselors should be proficient in ELs' L1s and should have training in dealing with common equity and access issues that ELs tend to encounter. They should have specialized expertise on issues that affect ELs, such as immigration status and its relationship to financial aid, additional college application requirements such as the TOEFL and where to find targeted scholarships to which ELs are eligible. This way, the responsibility of advocating for ELs' educational opportunities does not fall solely on the students or the EL teachers, but can also be shared by bilingual counselors who are keenly aware of how ELs are underserved in educational structures that assume English L1 students as the norm.

Switch to a brokering approach to promoting college knowledge

In order for EL students to exert their agency and navigate their college choice effectively, they need to be equipped with much more college knowledge. They need to be informed of the system of academic tracking in high school and its consequences for their college options. They also need to be much more explicitly educated about the steps they need to take in the college application process. A clearinghouse approach (Hill, 2008), making resources available and expecting interested students and parents to make use of them, is clearly inadequate. Instead, a brokering approach is needed to ensure that available resources and guidance reach the students who could use them the most.

One such model already exists – at the community college level. The idea of 'intrusive academic counseling' (Grubb, 2006: 18; also see Karp *et al.*, 2008) is to *require* traditionally underserved students to receive structured academic guidance, such as regular meetings with advisors and an introductory course on how to navigate college (Karp *et al.*, 2008). We can expand the idea and spirit of intrusive counseling to high school, and even to middle school: to actively seek out and direct resources to those ELs who are the least likely to initiate help-seeking. If a school adopts bilingual counselors, they can provide intrusive academic counseling starting in ninth grade, requiring ELs to meet with them on a regular basis. Guidance counselors can also push into EL study hall periods or even EL sheltered classes to provide college and career guidance that is tailored to ELs' specific needs. Working closely with EL teachers, bilingual counselors can also identify, in ninth grade, those underperforming and/or chronically absent ELs who are at risk of dropping out and increase their regular meetings with them.

Start building partnerships with EL parents well before high school

Schools need to make a more concerted effort to reach out to EL parents/guardians and treat them as equal partners in their students' PSE planning. But to realize such a goal, relationship building must start well before high school. For a variety of reasons (e.g. fear of the unknown, lack of English proficiency or in deference to teachers), ELs' parents tend to distance themselves from their children's schools (e.g. Arias & Morillo-Campbell, 2008; Han & Love, 2015). Unless schools make a concerted effort to cultivate trusting relationships with them, ELs' parents' alienation from US schools is firmly established by the time their children reach high-school age. Brighton did host a FAFSA meeting specifically for ELs and their parents, but the turnout was disappointing. ELs' parents did not attend as the educators had hoped because, I believe, by the time their children reached 11th grade, they had settled into a pattern of non-involvement. When high school educators start inviting them to participate halfway through high school, it is already too late. If schools are to work with ELs' parents, efforts must begin much earlier, preferably in elementary school, so that by the time ELs are in high school and need to seriously consider their PSE options, relationships of trust have already been firmly established. Also, part of this outreach should also involve educators going into the community, rather than always expecting parents to come to the school. Efforts such as home visits and holding meetings at a community church or a neighborhood coffee shop (e.g. The Community Café Collaborative, 2020) would go a long way to earning the trust of the community.

Do not treat community college as grade 13

Community colleges have contributed to expanding access to PSE to underserved populations, including ELs. However, as Bunch and Endris (2012) caution, community colleges' 'open access' policy does not mean open access to college-level courses or four-year college transfer. Students who are not college ready may be granted admission to community colleges as long as they hold a high school diploma, but they will be required to take remedial-level work before they are allowed into college-level courses. These remedial requirements can add years to the students' community college tenure, reducing the likelihood of their retention and graduation (Hodara, 2015; Li, 2021; Park, 2019; Rodriguez *et al.*, 2019). Further, unlike public high schools, remedial education at community colleges is not free, adding an extra financial burden on ELs, many of whom are low-income students.

Yet, because community colleges have an open access policy, some high school educators seem to believe that if students do not complete the academic preparation necessary for PSE, they can simply carry on in 'grade 13' at community colleges, where they will have another chance at getting college ready. This mindset is especially likely to be applied to ELs since their English development is often considered a prerequisite before their high school academic preparation can commence (Rodriguez & Cruz, 2009). However, as Cabrera *et al.* (2005: 199) remind us, the responsibility for preparing students for the rigors of PSE resides with K-12 education institutions, not with community colleges: 'Holding community colleges responsible for creating academic resources, which evolve throughout middle and high school, is misplacing a responsibility that lies at the middle and high school levels'. After all, community colleges are institutions of higher education, not an extension of high school.

High school educators need to have a more heightened sense of urgency to accelerate ELs' language and academic preparation. The promise of four-year college transfer is only likely to be fulfilled if students enter a community college with a solid academic foundation and advanced English language proficiency so they can start college-level courses right away – in other words, only if they are college ready. Also, if high schools become more committed to making ELs college ready by the end of high school, more ELs will have the option to enroll in four-year colleges directly, and educators will no longer have to make the empty promise, 'You can always transfer to a four-year college'.

Make CTE available to ELs

Another clear implication of this study is the need to take the aspirations and talents of non-college-bound ELs seriously and expand their access to CTE programs. Part of the challenge of working with non-college-bound ELs is that virtually all of us who are involved in high school education – from policymakers, to district administrators, to classroom teachers, to university researchers like myself – are college educated. Careers that do not involve a bachelor's degree are unfamiliar territory and many of us are hesitant to venture into them. We are much more comfortable inviting high school students into our world – the college-educated world – where we feel at home. But our lack of familiarity with career trajectories that do not involve a college degree must not limit the options for students who want to do something other than go to college. We must pay more than lip service to the adage 'Going to college is not the only option youth can choose after high school', and actually ensure that there are indeed other viable options that will lead to fulfilling careers and financial independence.

Our current preoccupation with sending as many students as possible to college has left few alternatives for students like Carlos and Eddie who do not fit into the college-going mold. As Newman and Winston (2016) argue,

> We cannot ignore the profoundly uneven educational outcomes that are plain to see, and that presently offer few meaningful alternatives that will help today's youth become productive workers with decent jobs. ... Students from working-class and poor communities need options that traditional forms of higher education may not provide, and they need them now, not thirty or forty years hence. (Newman & Winston, 2016: 6)

Although ELs are by no means the only group of students who could benefit from alternative pathways to productive careers, their unique set of needs, I would argue, make CTE a particularly pressing issue. Many ELs come from low-income families; having watched their immigrant parents struggle, many ELs want to contribute to the family finances as soon as possible (Gándara, 2008). Many secondary-level ELs who have recently immigrated also face additional challenges such as being overage, having had significant interruptions to their formal education and not having sufficient time to catch up academically or linguistically by the end of high school (Short & Boyson, 2012). Some are undocumented immigrants, who are not eligible for federal student aid to attend college (National Conference of State

Legislatures, 2020).[4] In short, the idea of going to college may not be of interest to some ELs or may not match the financial, educational and legal realities they are currently living. Yet, we offer such limited options to these students, allowing many of them to fall into the underserved third because we fundamentally cling to the belief that going to college and earning a bachelor's degree is the best outcome for any student, with all other outcomes being compromises. But that itself is a form of arrogance that ignores the varied ways that people in different occupations, including plumbers, car mechanics, barbers, hairstylists, nurse aides, movers, cooks, upholsterers, police officers, sanitation workers, among others, contribute to society.

A more productive solution, I believe, is to create CTE pathways that students can start exploring from ninth grade. Within CTE programs, students should be able to choose career options that match their interests, as opposed to a selection process determined by placement tests or past academic achievement. Career options that are too popular to accommodate all students should determine their enrollment by a lottery rather than an academic assessment because studies show that ELs are again disadvantaged in such a system (Emerick, 2019; Salerno & Kibler, 2015). Core academic curricula (e.g. math, English) should be designed and delivered in the context of CTE, emphasizing how those foundational skills are related to students' chosen careers (Hernández-Gantes & Blank, 2009). This way, students in CTE programs might be more invested and engaged in their academic learning. Concurrently, students should receive guidance on how to pursue their career (i.e. career-planning skills; Clark, 2015), with specific pointers on what jobs would be available within their field right after high school graduation, and how their options might expand if they further pursue a postsecondary certificate program or a four-year college degree.

Following a CTE pathway today does not mean being condemned to a lifetime of low-skill jobs and low wages. The middle-skill job sector, which many CTE programs feed into, is where jobs are and will be plentiful (National Skills Coalition, 2017). It is thus critical to take the interests of non-college-bound ELs seriously and create CTE pathways that will enable them to pursue the middle-skill jobs that match their interests. Furthermore, accessible CTE pathways will go a long way toward ending the false binary choice between going to a four-year college and working at a McDonald's.

* * *

In making the above recommendations, I could not underscore enough the importance of making *systemic* changes. It cannot be a matter of individual teachers or guidance counselors making heroic efforts to level the playing field for ELs, because to expect individual educators to step up and take on the work of expanding PSE access for ELs is to fall far, far short of condemning and eradicating the structural inequities that are deeply embedded in the current educational system. Thus, I am not advocating bilingual guidance counselors taking on the entire burden of earning the trust of linguistically minoritized families and communities; or AP teachers sitting down after school with individual ELs day after day, going over the content the students did not learn before reaching the AP class; or CTE teachers personally calling up PSE institutions to make a case that their ELs deserve a spot in their programs. While I have personally witnessed the impact that exceptionally equity-minded educators can make on ELs' trajectories, such impact tends to be localized, limited to the domains in which the educators have influence, and affecting only a few ELs at a time who are fortunate enough to have such mentors and advocates in their lives. What we need, instead, are wide-ranging systemic reforms, such as those recommended above, that interrogate how and why coming from a non-English L1 background must have such a deleterious impact on students' educational opportunities in the United States and go on to remove each and every structural barrier that lies between ELs and PSE access.

Summary

This final chapter revisited the major themes that emerged in the previous chapters and theorized them in terms of Brighton High School's institutional habitus and EL students' individual habitus. On the one hand, I see a school that consistently lowered expectations for ELs. This, in turn, led to limited access to advanced coursework and less than adequate guidance and information on four-year college planning and application. On the other hand, I also see EL students, internalizing the school deficit orientation toward them. They have acquiesced to an educational hierarchy in which they were definitely positioned lower than English L1 students and in which they did not expect or demand any more help than the little that was given. In a structure that was essentially not designed to make ELs college ready, none of the five students who initially hoped to enroll in four-year colleges reached the destination of their choice.

Almost paradoxically, however, Brighton High School's 'college-for-all' institutional habitus offered few viable options for underperforming ELs. These ELs' academic performance made four-year college entry unrealistic, and they were disqualified from enrolling in the school's own CTE programs. Educators took it upon themselves to help such non-college-bound ELs graduate from high school by arranging and rearranging the lowest possible courses that would meet graduation requirements into their rosters. However, a high school diploma earned under such circumstances guaranteed neither the foundational academic skills nor the career-planning skills to navigate postsecondary career options. Non-college-bound ELs such as Carlos and Eddie, then, fell into the underserved third (Deil-Amen & DeLuca, 2010) instead of becoming career ready.

Notes

(1) In the United States, some school districts have magnet schools that select their students based on an admission exam and past academic records. There are also high schools that specialize in certain areas, such as arts and sciences. The vast majority of US public high schools, however, are comprehensive high schools that take in all students who live in the catchment areas.

(2) It does not take an astute reader to notice that the only one of the five four-year college aspirants who actually enrolled in a four-year college was a male student, Ken. Given the small number of participants and given that the other two male students were struggling to graduate from high school, it is impossible to conclude with any degree of certainty that gender played a role. Nonetheless, the way Ken never applied to a community college and insisted on going to a four-year college, compared with the way the four women readily shifted their gears to LCC, indicates that there is some gender difference in their habitus: what they thought was within their reach and what was their rightful place in the world.

My conjecture is that it had something to do with what two journalists, Katty Kay and Claire Shipman (2014), call *the confidence gap*. Describing mostly the business world, they argue that the reason why women are still outpaced by men in promotion and are underrepresented in leadership positions is not that women are less qualified or less competent than men, but rather that women's lack of confidence holds them back from seizing opportunities the way men do. 'The natural result of low confidence is inaction', they write. 'When women don't act, when we hesitate because we aren't sure, we hold ourselves back' (Kay & Shipman, 2014: 22). Perhaps some similar confidence gap was at play in how Ken on the one hand and Erica and Alexandra on the other pursued their PSE options. The three students were more or less comparable in their academic performance and English language proficiency; if anything, Erica and Alexandra were slightly higher performing than Ken. Yet, Ken judged his qualifications as good enough to attend a four-year college whereas Alexandra and Erica judged theirs as insufficient. Clearly, how female and male ELs view their academic qualifications, choose their PSE destinations based on their individual habitus and who and what factors contribute to this potentially gendered process are subjects that deserve further investigation.

(3) Mickey's case provides good disconfirming evidence that not all ELs internalize marginalized positioning. But of course, that itself raises another question: What constricts some ELs' individual habitus but not others'? It seems to me that ELs who are able to resist internalization of marginality often have access to some key form of capital:

They (a) come from a financially well-off family (at least prior to immigration), (b) have college-educated parents or extended family members, (c) received a solid school education prior to immigration and/or (d) have a parent/guardian who has an uncommon degree of tenacity and resourcefulness. In Mickey's case, her father had a combination of immigrant optimism that there was a bright future ahead of them and the tenacity to look for resources that could help them. Mickey held her father as a role model and adopted his approach that help was available if one sought it.

(4)   Undocumented immigrant students, students who do not have legal status in the United States, are not eligible for federal Pell grants. Currently, 19 states (Arkansas, California, Colorado, Connecticut, Florida, Illinois, Kansas, Maryland, Minnesota, Nebraska, New Jersey, New Mexico, New York, Oklahoma, Oregon, Rhode Island, Texas, Utah and Washington) allow undocumented students to pay instate tuition rates to attend public colleges, and just seven states (California, Colorado, Minnesota, New Mexico, Oregon, Texas and Washington) provide state financial aid to undocumented students (National Conference of State Legislatures, 2020). These restrictions make it extremely challenging for undocumented students to attend college (Suárez-Oroco et al., 2015).

Appendix: Method

This is an ethnographic, longitudinal, single-embedded case study of English learners' (ELs) access to postsecondary education (PSE). It is a *single-embedded case study* (Yin, 2017) in that it is simultaneously a case study of how one public high school in the United States prepared its students for PSE, and how seven ELs within the school navigated the transition to PSE. In other words, the unit of analysis was both the school and each of the students. It is an ethnographic study because it investigates the school culture – or institutional habitus (byrd, 2019; McDonough, 1997; Reay *et al.*, 2005), to put it in terms aligned with my theoretical framework – and how it shaped the EL students' PSE access. And finally, although I imagine that most scholars would agree that three years of data collection amply qualifies my study as longitudinal, this is a longitudinal study not just because it took a long time but because it sought to document change over time (Saldaña, 2003). I wanted to explore the PSE aspirations that high school ELs initially held for themselves and how those aspirations, as they meshed with various barriers and opportunities through the last two years of high school, translated into actual outcomes.

The fieldwork lasted from May 2010 to August 2013, during which I visited the school 70 times. Originally, my plan was to conduct two years of fieldwork, following a set of ELs for two years, from Grade 11 through graduation. However, since Carlos did not graduate in June 2012 and had to repeat his senior year, I stayed at the school in order to see him through.

The Setting

Brighton High School was chosen as the study site because it was 'typical' (Merriam & Tisdell, 2016) of the public schools that ELs across the country attend. Although determining what is typical is admittedly hard, past research suggests that ELs (a) tend to be segregated to a relatively small number of schools, (b) attend schools that also have large representations of Black and Hispanic students, (c) are taught by relatively inexperienced and less qualified teachers and (d) are concentrated in low-achieving schools measured by annual standardized testing (Consentino de Cohen *et al.*, 2005; Fry, 2008; García *et al.*, 2008; US Department of Education, 2018b). Brighton High School was staffed by well-qualified educators, that is, teachers, guidance counselors and administrators possessed full qualifications to serve in their respective roles, and teachers were teaching subjects they were certificated to teach. In this respect, it was not typical of the schools that ELs attend. In other respects, however, it fit the profile of a typical 'EL school'.

EL Participants

Originally, my plan was to work with six students. Six seemed like a large enough sample size to include sufficient variation within the sample (Patton, 2015) but small enough for me to handle longitudinal data collection by myself. However, Mr Woznyj, Chair of the EL Department, noting that ELs in the Brighton area were a transient population, recommended adding a couple more students in case one or more participants withdrew or relocated before the end of the data collection. Following his advice, I decided to start with eight students. In the end, much to my delight, all eight students stayed with the project, and although it increased the data collection and analysis workload, I am confident that the eight students together represented sufficient diversity to capture ELs' experiences of PSE access at Brighton.

As noted in Chapter 1, the three main selection criteria were that (a) when they entered high school, they were classified as ELs, (b) they wanted to pursue PSE and (c) the eight participants together represented a wide range of ELs' academic performance at Brighton. Academic performance took precedence over SES, race/ethnicity and gender in student selection for the following reasons. Although race/ethnicity and gender have certainly been treated as important components of college access (e.g. Baker *et al.*, 2018; Dwyer *et al.*, 2013; Jacobs, 1996; Perna, 2006; Riegle-Crumb & King, 2010), as far as ELs are concerned, once their academic preparation in high school is taken into account, the effects of gender and race/ethnicity tend to disappear (Kanno & Cromley, 2013, 2015). In contrast, the effect of SES does not completely disappear even after controlling for academic performance; nonetheless, its impact on ELs' college access and degree attainment is smaller than their high school academic performance (Callahan & Humphries, 2016;

Kanno & Cromley, 2013, 2015). Thus, I sought to diversify the sample in terms of SES, race/ethnicity and gender only after the main three criteria were met.

I solicited Mr Woznyj's assistance in selecting and recruiting participants. As EL Department Chair, he knew the EL students at the school very well. At the beginning of the fieldwork, I discussed the objectives of the research project and selection criteria with him. Based on this conversation, Mr Woznyj drew an initial list of 16 potential participants. Through information sessions after school and approaching students individually, I interviewed 11 of the students on the list and ultimately chose 8 of them as participants. The goal was to achieve maximum variation (Patton, 2015) within the sample along academic performance, SES, race/ethnicity and gender—in that order.[1] Additionally, at the suggestion of Mr Woznyj, I included two students who had entered high school as ELs but had already been reclassified as English proficient. Mr Woznyj believed that reclassified students might be allowed to take higher-level courses and have a higher chance of reaching four-year colleges than those who were still in the EL program. These predictions turned out to be false, but this sampling strategy made sense in light of the recent scholarship that points to the importance of following ELs longitudinally even after they have been reclassified (e.g. Kieffer & Thompson, 2018; Saunders & Marcelletti, 2013).

For this book, I focus on seven of the eight students. An eighth student, Sam, turned out to be a monolingual speaker of English from Liberia. Even after finding out that he only spoke English, I kept Sam in the larger project because he presented a 'control' case of sorts to observe how an English L1 student would navigate college access. Nevertheless, I take the position that as a monolingual speaker of English, he should not have been classified as an EL in the first place – I am writing a separate paper on this topic (Kanno, 2021). Thus, I am excluding his case from this book, focusing on the other seven students who were bona fide multilingual students.

One last piece of information I should add is that all the EL participants had legal status in the United States, i.e. none of them were undocumented students. This was a deliberate decision on my part. I knew that I was going to collect intimate details of these students' lives for an extended period time. Knowing that if ever required by the Immigration and Customs Enforcement (ICE), I might be forced to disclose the data, I did not want to collect information from undocumented students and increase their risk of deportation. Thus, although there are well-known challenges to undocumented students' access to PSE, such as ineligibility for federal funding and sometimes even state grants (National Conference of State Legislatures, 2020), my participants did not experience these constraints.

Data Collection

Data collection, typical of an ethnographic project, consisted of interviews with students and educators, classroom observations and document collection.

Student interviews and classroom observations

Each EL participant was interviewed five to seven times at regular intervals between the spring of their junior year and their scheduled graduation in June 2012 (Table A.1). The exception to this pattern was Carlos because he did not graduate in June 2012. As a result, his interviews extended through academic year 2012–2013 during his repeated senior year. Interviews lasted about 30–40 minutes and took place during the students' study hall periods or after school. The interviews focused on ELs' experiences in their coursework, the progress made so far in college planning and changes over time in their PSE plans.

I also observed each student three or four times in their classes during the data collection period. The purpose of these observations was two-fold: (a) to observe the students' participation in their classes and (b) to examine the instruction that took place in those classes. In the majority of cases, these were non-participant observations: I sat at the back of the room with my iPad in front of me and took copious notes. No recording device was used in order not to interrupt the classes and to avoid making teachers and students self-conscious. The reactions to my presence varied from class to class: some teachers introduced me at the beginning of class and invited students to ask any questions they had about me, my work as a university professor or my study; some classes proceeded as if I did not exist at all; and still in others, teachers noted that the class was more animated or students acted out more than usual because they had a guest. The EL study participants generally stayed away from me during the first couple of observations, wary of being singled out. However, as we got to know each other, most of them started to say 'hello' or wave to me when they saw me, and toward the end they routinely came up to me to chat for a few minutes to update me on what was happening with their PSE plans.

Along with observations, I analyzed the ELs' course rosters early in the data collection process and found that the participants were confined to EL, remedial- and regular-level courses. During the second half of

Table A.1 Data collection with seven EL participants

Erica
- Interview 1 — 05/06/2011
- Observation: Regular Algebra 2 — 05/24/2011
- Observation: Remedial American Literature — 05/24/2011
- Interview 2 — 09/26/2011
- Interview 3 — 11/21/2011
- Observation: Regular Government & law — 02/08/2012
- Interview 4 — 02/26/2012
- Interview 5 — 05/22/2012
- Observation: Conceptual Chemistry — 05/22/2012
- Interview 6 — 05/16/2012

Alexandra
- Interview 1 — 03/07/2011
- Interview 2 — 04/20/2012
- Observation: Regular Geometry — 05/19/2011
- Observation: EL Reading 10 — 05/17/2011
- Interview 3 — 09/28/2011
- Interview 4 — 11/21/2011
- Observation: Introduction to Accounting — 02/13/2012
- Interview 5 — 02/19/2012
- Observation: Baking and Confections — 05/01/2012
- Interview 6 — 05/16/2012

Ken
- Observation: EL Reading 10 — 05/17/2011
- Interview 1 — 05/19/2011
- Observation: Engine and Technology — 05/22/2011
- Interview 2 — 05/26/2011
- Interview 3 — 11/14/2011
- Observation, EL English 5 — 11/14/2011
- Interview 4 — 02/27/2012
- Interview 5 — 06/08/2012

Josephine
- Interview 1 — 03/08/2011
- Interview 2 — 04/04/2011
- Observation: Remedial US History — 05/17/2011
- Interview 3 — 09/19/2011
- Interview 4 — 10/31/2011
- Interview 5 — 02/10/2012
- Remedial Human Development — 02/27/2012
- Interview 6 — 04/10/2012
- Observation: Introduction to Food — 05/09/2012
- Interview 7 — 05/31/2012

Kadi
- Interview 1 — 03/08/2011
- Interview 2 — 04/04/2011
- Observation: Earth Science — 05/23/2011
- Observation: Remedial Algebra 2 — 05/23/2011
- Interview 3 — 10/14/2011
- Interview 4 — 12/09/2011
- Interview 5 — 02/03/2012
- Observation: Modern American Literature — 03/18/2012
- Interview 6 — 05/08/2012

Carlos
- Interview 1 — 05/03/2011
- Observation: Remedial American Literature — 05/24/2011
- Interview 2 — 06/02/2011
- Interview 3 — 02/29/2012
- Observation: power and transmission — 03/27/2012
- Observation: Remedial Human Development — 03/27/2012
- Interview 4 — 03/27/2012
- Interview 5 — 05/29/2012
- Interview 6 — 02/22/2013
- Interview 7 — 06/07/2013

Eddie
- Interview 1 — 05/06/2011
- Interview 2 — 09/26/2011
- Observation: EL English 5 — 11/14/2011
- Interview 3 — 01/10/2012
- Observation: EL Biology — 02/10/2012
- Observation: Remedial Algebra 2 — 03/26/2012
- Observation: Remedial Human Development — 03/27/2012
- Interview 4 — 04/20/2012
- Interview 5 — 05/30/2012

the data collection, therefore, I began observing honors and advanced placement (AP) courses to see the type of instruction available to high-achieving Brighton students, but not to the EL participants because of academic tracking. Handouts distributed during the observed classes were collected and filed together with the observation notes. In all, 37 classes were observed.

Educator interviews

Four EL teachers, the district EL coordinator, the school principal, three guidance counselors (including the Director of Guidance) and the college and career coordinator were each interviewed once. These formal interviews lasted 45–90 minutes and involved conversations about their views on EL education at Brighton, the challenges ELs faced in their transition to PSE and the procedures for EL course selection. In addition to these formal interviews, during the fieldwork, I had repeated informal conversations with those educators who emerged as key informants: Mr Woznyj, Chair of the EL Department; Mr Burke, the Director of Guidance; and Ms Vaughn, the District EL Coordinator. Classroom observations also often afforded opportunities to speak briefly with classroom teachers. During these brief conversations, teachers made comments about ELs' performance in their classes and what they thought about having ELs in their classes. These comments were recorded in the field notes together with the observations of the classes.

Document collection

The EL participants' high school transcripts, the Pennsylvania System of School Assessment (PSSA; standardized state academic assessment) scores in 11th grade and Assessing Comprehension and Communication in English State-to-State for English Language Learners (ACCESS; English proficiency test) scores were obtained from the school. The EL participants' SAT scores, when available, were provided either by the school or by the students themselves. Demographic information about EL students at Brighton was provided by Ms Vaughn, and rosters of AP courses were provided by Mr Burke. Other miscellaneous information about the school was gathered from the school and district websites, and if necessary, from Mr Burke.

Data Analysis

Since this was a longitudinal study, data analysis began while I was still collecting data and progressed in tandem. I regularly reread the materials that had been collected thus far and wrote analytical memos on emerging themes and interpretations. I periodically shared these provisional interpretations with students and teachers for member checking (Lincoln & Guba, 1985). I also chose particular classes to observe or collected additional documents in order to confirm or reject emerging assertions. For example, initially I did not pay too much attention to students who would not pursue PSE, but as it became clear that Carlos and Eddie were highly unlikely to graduate from high school on time, let alone enroll in PSE, I intensified data collection around the issue of how the school dealt with underachieving students whose chances of attending any PSE were slim.

Once the data collection was completed, I shifted to a more intensive data analysis phase. This phase of data analysis was guided by Fereday and Muir-Cochrane's (2006) *hybrid inductive-deductive approach*, looking at the data deductively through the lens of my theoretical framework while also inductively allowing themes to emerge from the data. During the first-cycle coding, I focused more on letting themes (codes) emerge from the data, regardless of whether or not they were directly related to individual or institutional habitus, or whether they were likely to contribute to the overall assertions I would be making. At that stage, my approach was, 'Let's see what is in the data'. In contrast, during the second-cycle coding, I became more selective in the codes I focused on. Drawing much more heavily on my theoretical framework at this point, I grouped related codes into larger themes in order to formulate my assertions. Put another way, my focus at this point was, 'What assertions about the relationship between EL's individual habitus and their school's institutional habitus can I make that are substantiated by my data?'

First-cycle coding

I first read the entire data set several times and then carried out the first-cycle coding (Saldaña, 2015) of the data using the constant comparative method (Glaser & Strauss, 1967): I uploaded all the data into ATLAS .ti and examined each document line by line to identify and sort the relevant parts of the data into similar codes. Since the unit of analysis was both the school and the students, I developed both the codes that pertained to the school and the codes that pertained to the students. Tables A.2 and A.3 show the codes that had more than five 'quotations' or entries to illustrate the codes that were used in building the main assertions.[2] While the frequencies of each code did not dictate the subsequent analysis, they do indicate how some codes became central to my assertions over others.

Table A.2   First-cycle analysis codes for school

Codes	Frequencies
Coursework:	
Course selection process	59
Remedial/regular courses: low-level instruction	51
Remedial/regular courses	42
AP/honors courses	28
Course sequence	17
AP: ELs in AP	11
Advanced courses	9
Remedial courses: checking the meaning of vocab	8
Course leveling	7
Remedial teachers' tough demeanor	7
Remedial courses: special ed teachers pushing in	6
Remedial courses: teacher low expectations	6
AP has a lot of reading and writing	6
Chicken and egg: lack of support or lack of ability	5
Quality of instruction:	
Disruptive students/sleeping students	101
Discipline in class	73
Quality of instruction	42
Differentiated instruction	21
Higher-order thinking skills	17
CTE courses: students engaged	6
College application:	
Lack of college knowledge	58
LCC (local community college)	28
College cost	20
Financial aid	14
College fairs	13
College application timeline	12
College visits	12
Scholarships	10
College knowledge	9
College essays	8
GPA	7
Narratives change quickly	7
Tests:	
SAT/PSAT	32
Test scores	16
TOEFL	9
School support:	
Counselor–student relationships	18
Brighton HS provides lots of information	14
Brighton HS is a big school	7
English learners:	
EL classroom participation	175
ELs' limited access to high level courses	39
ELs' lack of self-advocacy	33
ELs quiet in class	29

(Continued)

Table A.2   First-cycle analysis codes for school (*Continued*)

Codes	Frequencies
ELs on task	24
Language barriers	20
ELs' lack of confidence	13
EL-specific events	13
Want to protect ELs	12
Teacher comments on EL participants	11
EL classes: low standards	10
Motivation sags/'Americanized'	10
EL teachers as counselors	9
EL classes: attention to language	5
ELs' lack of social involvement	5
ELs: 'I'm not ready'/'I need more time'	5
Undocumented	5
Family resources:	
Parental involvement	53
Sibs in college or not in college	22
'Community is transient, poor, and uneducated'	5
Miscellaneous:	
Memorable quotes	16
Mr McGrath	14
Facebook updates	11

Note: Codes in quotation marks are *in vivo* codes based on participants' words.

For example, the high frequency (59 counts) of 'course selection process' in Table A.2 reflects the key role that this process played in ELs' limited access to advanced courses. Similarly, the high frequency (23 counts) of 'parental involvement' in Erica's case in Table A.3, compared with lower frequencies of this code in other participants' cases, shows the central role that her father played in her college planning.

Second-cycle coding

Once I had finished first-level coding, I embarked on the *within-case analysis* (Merriam & Tisdell, 2016) of each of the EL students because 'cross-case analysis first depends on coherent within-case information' (Miles *et al.*, 2020: 132). I retrieved all the codes related to each student, grouped salient codes together into larger themes and, on the basis of these themes, wrote a lengthy narrative of the student's PSE access. In the second-cycle coding stage, I analyzed how the student's individual habitus shaped the range of PSE choices they considered, how these choices changed over time and what aspects of the school's institutional habitus influenced their decisions. Writing these narratives helped me understand each EL's PSE access and the factors that shaped it. After many iterations, these narratives eventually became the students' stories in this book.

Table A.3   First-cycle analysis codes for EL participants

Codes	Frequencies
Erica:	
Parental involvement	23
Teacher comments	15
Reasons for going to LCC	11
PSE plans	10
Previous schooling	9
SAT	6
Alexandra:	
Career aspirations	15
SAT	15
LCC	14
Quiet, loner, inscrutable	14
College choice	12
Counselor relationship	10
Academic high achiever	7
College aspirations	7
College major	6
Scholarships	6
SES	6
Teacher comments	6
Financial aid	5
Parental involvement	5
Ken:	
Moving to New Jersey	17
College application	13
SAT/PSAT	13
Parental involvement	12
Slacking off	10
College choice	9
College visits	9
Good student	9
Teacher comments	9
Widener University	9
Family structure	6
College aspirations	5
Financial aid	5
Josephine:	
Brother in college	21
College choice	20
SES	18
Career aspirations	15
SAT	14
Scholarships	13
College choice – criteria/reasons	13
Parental occupation	13
College visits	12
LCC	12
College application	9
Parental involvement	8
College rejections	7
Friends	6

(Continued)

Table A.3   First-cycle analysis codes for EL participants (*Continued*)

Codes	Frequencies
Homework club	6
Teacher comments	6
College essay	5
Colleges send me information packages	5
Transfer to four-year college later	5
Kadi:	
CTE program	30
College choice	26
Financial aid/scholarships	23
Family structure	16
Help-seeking	16
Homework club/College Access Center	15
College planning	14
Career aspirations	12
Mentor teacher at CTE	12
Counselor relationship	11
Drop out of a regular English class	11
LCC	9
Friends	0
Sister	8
Guardian involvement	7
Teacher comments	7
College application	6
'EL kids are too dependent'	6
How she caught up academically in Minnesota	6
SAT	6
SES	6
Guardian occupations	5
Religion	5
Eddie:	
At risk	25
Baby	20
College planning	19
Girlfriend	12
Teacher comments	12
Academic engagement	9
Career aspirations	8
'I am getting more serious about work'	8
Parental involvement	8
Family structure	7
Friends	7
Going back to Mexico	7
Working	7
College aspirations	6
Fond of US schools	6
Portfolio	6
Who is paying for his education	6
Carlos:	
At risk	39
Parental involvement	26
Cutting classes	21
PSE choice	17

(*Continued*)

Table A.3   First-cycle analysis codes for EL participants (*Continued*)

Codes	Frequencies
College planning (very little)	15
High school diploma	15
Locus of control	15
Career aspirations	13
Family structure	10
Friends	10
Soccer	10
2012–2013 academic performance	9
Job	8
Alienated from school	6
'I'm a serious student'	6
Artistic talent	6
Summer school	6
What I should have done in high school	6
'I was really bad'	5
Counselor relationship	5
SES	5
Teacher relationship	5

Note: Codes in quotation marks are *in vivo* codes based on participants' words.

After the within-case analyses came the *cross-case analysis* (Merriam & Tisdell, 2016), during which I identified the experiences common to all or most EL participants and the experiences that were unique to a subset of the participants. For example, limited access to advanced courses was one theme that cut across all participants, whereas the theme of *community college going* was pertinent only to the four students who went to LCC. Four major themes emerged from the cross-case analysis: (a) limited access to advanced courses, (b) underdeveloped college knowledge, (c) switching to the community college pathway and (d) career readiness of non-college-bound students – and they became the organizing structure of the book. Within each major theme, I explored how the interaction between institutional habitus and individual habitus led to either common experiences across all the participants or differential outcomes for individual participants.

Trustworthiness of the Study

To ensure a reasonable degree of *trustworthiness* (Lincoln & Guba, 1985), I incorporated several measures into the study. First, the fieldwork for this study lasted three years in total, involving 70 visits. Prolonged engagement is at the heart of any rigorous ethnographic study (Lincoln & Guba, 1985; Maxwell, 2005; Miles *et al.*, 2020), and three years was definitely long enough for me to familiarize myself with the culture of the school, to collect additional data to confirm or disconfirm emerging assertions and to member-check (Lincoln & Guba, 1985) my interpretations of events and structures with the participants.

Also, multiple sources of data – interviews, classroom observations and critical documents such as high school transcripts and standardized test scores – were collected across time and participants in as consistent a manner as realistically possible. At the data analysis stage, these multiple sources of data were frequently triangulated to evaluate the veracity of my assertions.

The choice of the school and the selection of the EL participants within the school were purposefully made to increase the internal validity of the data as well as the transferability of the findings. I chose a public high school that was reasonably representative of the kinds of schools that ELs tend to attend so that the findings from this school may apply to other public high schools in the United States. Within the school, I took care to choose a group of ELs that together represented the range of educational opportunities and PSE access that ELs at Brighton were likely to experience: I did not just 'cherry-pick' the best-case scenarios of ELs' PSE access nor exaggerate the worst-case scenarios. To assess whether the patterns that were emerging from the participants were representative of the patterns of the school as a whole, I sought and analyzed the school statistics whenever possible. For example, when it became clear that none of the EL participants had access to advanced courses except for AP Spanish, I cross-checked the list of students enrolled in AP classes with the list of current EL seniors to confirm if the pattern of limited coursework among the participants was representative of ELs' coursework at the school.

During the data analysis phase, identifying disconfirming evidence for the emerging assertions was an important endeavor in order to enhance the credibility of the study (Lincoln & Guba, 1985; Maxwell, 2005). I tried not to treat the EL students as a monolithic group. Many themes and experiences cut across the EL participants, but there were also some notable exceptions. Erica's father's close involvement in her college planning was a marked exception to the overall pattern of the absence of concrete guidance from parents. Likewise, Kadi's active help-seeking behavior to enroll in a CTE program was a noteworthy exception to the ELs' tendency to stay under the radar. These important pieces of disconfirming evidence serve as reminders that the EL participants did not behave the same all the time.

Finally, while I conducted most of the data analysis myself, for the analysis of ELs' limited access to advanced courses, I was aided by another ethnographer, Sara Kangas, when we collaborated on a paper

(Kanno & Kangas, 2014), which became the basis for Chapter 2. Sara also subsequently read every iteration of the chapters in this book, thus serving as a sustained partner in *peer debriefing* (Lincoln & Guba, 1985: 308) wherein 'the inquirer's biases are probed, meanings explored, the basis for interpretations clarified'. While supportive, she did not shy away from pointing out dubious claims and biased opinions in my drafts, and since she not only read all my drafts but was also familiar with my data, her critical eye helped to keep me honest in my assertions and reporting (Lincoln & Guba, 1985). Sara was particularly helpful in providing two perspectives that I lacked: (a) she went to college in the United States and (b) she came from a working-class background. As someone who navigated college access as a US-born, working-class and English L1 student, she helped disambiguate the influences of SES from those of being an EL on ELs' PSE access and checked my middle-class biases.

Researcher Positionality

Over the years, as I have shared the findings from this study informally with my colleagues and more formally at conferences, people have asked about the level of my personal involvement in the participants' PSE access. Some seemed concerned that my involvement in their PSE planning might have skewed the outcomes while others questioned the ethics of not intervening when I was a witness to so much inequity.

My position on this issue is extremely clear: I intervened and offered assistance whenever I could, and I wish I could have helped more. I am a former EL myself, and although the exact circumstances of my EL experiences (e.g. mine took place at a British boarding school) were considerably different from those of the study participants, I strongly identified with them. When I heard Brighton educators talk about the participants' lack of English language proficiency rather than their multilingual competence, I had flashbacks of how my high school teachers 30 years prior treated my L1, Japanese, as irrelevant and how I was made to feel inferior to my English L1 peers. When Erica told me how she tended to gravitate toward Spanish-speaking peers although she knew that she should be speaking more English, it reminded me of how we, a group of Japanese students, huddled together in one corner of the school cafeteria taking a needed respite from the constant onslaught of an unfamiliar tongue.

Thus, I never even considered intentionally withholding assistance in order to preserve the integrity of naturalistic observation. During the interviews, the participants often had questions (e.g. 'Do I need a TOEFL score?' 'Should I apply online or should I mail my application?').

I answered them to the best of my knowledge, and when I did not know the answer, I made inquiries to find out. As I got to know the participants better, I also met with them occasionally outside of the interview sessions to provide extra help. They were helping me with my data collection; it was only fair that I help them prepare for college as much as possible. Thus, for example, when Ken and Alexandra said they wanted to know how to look up admissions information on the Internet, I met with them in a computer lab in the library one afternoon to show them where the relevant information was located on college websites. Similarly, toward the end of my fieldwork, alarmed that Carlos had no PSE plans, I encouraged him to consider a CTE certificate program at LCC and we began filling out an application form together.

However, the overall impact of my intervention was minimal. There are two reasons for this. First, although the content of this book may make it sound as if I intuitively understood what was going on, it was written from the vantage point of hindsight. The patterns that I describe in this book emerged over time, and the actions and decisions of the participants were not always predictable during my fieldwork. While I now have a much clearer view of the needs of each of the participants and the kinds of assistance that would have made a difference, during the fieldwork I was figuring things out as they were.

Second, although my fieldwork lasted three years, and I was at the school once or twice a week, this does not mean that I saw each of the participants every week. Sometimes weeks went by before I saw particular students again, and with Brighton being such a large school, the chances of running into the participants and catching up with them in the hallway were slim. Sometimes, between two meetings, much would happen in their PSE planning, and I would be caught off guard. In other words, the sporadic assistance that an outside researcher who was embedded in the school part-time was not going to move the needle substantially given the multiple layers of hurdles they encountered.

Consequently and ironically, then, I can assure readers that my involvement with these seven students had little impact on their access to PSE. I certainly 'did no harm' and did not reduce their access, but I also believe that had they not participated in the study, they would likely have landed where they did all the same.

Notes

(1) In this study, more students were recent immigrants than long-term residents, reflecting the composition of the overall EL population at Brighton *and* the fact that one of the key selection criteria was that students had to be aspiring to attend PSE in

the 11th grade. The only long-term EL in the study was Carlos. However, it is important to note that nationally, a substantial proportion of high school ELs are long-term ELs, who account for 23%–74% of the secondary EL population, depending on the state (Regional Educational Laboratory West at WestEd, 2016). A number of recent studies have documented the reduced learning opportunities and stigmatization of long-term ELs (e.g. Flores *et al.*, 2015; Kibler et al., 2018; Kim & García, 2014; Menken & Kleyn, 2010; Olsen, 2010; Thompson, 2015), but so far none has specifically examined the PSE access of long-term ELs. In future research, then, it would be important to explore how long-term ELs envision and navigate PSE access and how their high schools support, or do not support, their PSE aspirations.

(2) Codes that had fewer than five quotations were eliminated from these lists because they tended to be marginal codes that appeared once or twice and then disappeared.

References

Abedi, J. (2004) The No Child Left Behind Act and English language learners: Assessment and accountability issues. *Educational Researcher* 33 (1), 4–14.

Achieve (2012) The future of the U.S. workforce: The limited career prospects for high school graduates without additional education and training. See http://www.achieve.org/files/LimitedCareerProspects.pdf (accessed 21 May 2021).

ACT (2006) Ready for college and ready for work: Same or different. See http://www.sedl.org/secc/forum/07/files/concurrent_3/middle_high_school_reform/4b_readinessbrief.pdf (accessed 21 May 2021).

ACT (2017) The condition of college and career readiness 2017. See http://www.act.org/content/act/en/research/reports/act-publications/condition-of-college-and-career-readiness-2017.html (accessed 21 May 2021).

Adelman, C. (1999) *Answers in the Toolbox: Academic Intensity, Attendance Patterns, and Bachelor's Degree Attainment.* Washington DC: US Department of Education, Office of Educational Research and Involvement.

Adelman, C. (2006) *The Toolbox Revisited: Paths to Degree Completion from High School through College.* Washington, DC: US Department of Education, Office of Educational Research and Involvement.

Almon, P.C. (2010) English language learner engagement and retention in a community college setting. EdD dissertation, Temple University.

Anderson, G.M., Sun, J.C. and Alfonso, M. (2006) Effectiveness of statewide articulation agreements on the probability of transfer: A preliminary policy analysis. *The Review of Higher Education* 29 (3), 261–229.

Arias, B.M. and Morillo-Campbell, M. (2008) Promising ELL parental involvement: Challenges in contested times. *Great Lakes Center for Education Research and Practice.* See http://greatlakescenter.org/docs/Policy_Briefs/Arias_ELL.pdf (accessed 21 May 2021).

Attewell, P., Lavin, D., Domina, T. and Levey, T. (2006) New evidence on college remediation. *The Journal of Higher Education* 77 (5), 886–924.

Bagdon, E. (2012, March) Ensuring Equal Educational Opportunities for English Language Learners. Paper presented at the TESOL Annual Convention, Philadelphia, PA.

Baker, R., Klasik, D. and Reardon, S.F. (2018) Race and stratification in college enrollment over time. *AERA Open* 4 (1), 1–28.

Battey, D. (2013) Access to mathematics: 'A possessive investment in Whiteness'. *Curriculum Inquiry* 43 (3), 332–359.

Blom, E., Küntay, A.C., Messer, M., Verhagen, J. and Leseman, P. (2014) The benefits of being bilingual: Working memory in bilingual Turkish–Dutch children. *Journal of Experimental Child Psychology* 128, 105–119.

Bourdieu, P. (1977a) Cultural reproduction and social reproduction. In J. Karabel and A.H. Halsey (eds) *Power and Ideology in Education* (pp. 487–511). New York: Oxford University Press.

Bourdieu, P. (1977b). *Outline of a Theory of Practice* (R. Nice, trans.). Cambridge, England: Cambridge University Press.

Bourdieu, P. (1984). *Distinction: A Social Critique of the Judgement of Taste*. Cambridge, MA: Harvard University Press.

Bourdieu, P. (1986) The forms of capital. In J.G. Richardson (ed.) *Handbook of Theory and Research for the Sociology of Education* (pp. 241–258). Westport, CT: Greenwood Press.

Bourdieu, P. (1991) *Language and Symbolic Power* (G. Raymond and M. Adamson, trans., J.B. Thompson ed.). Cambridge, MA: Harvard University Press.

Bourdieu, P. and Passeron, J.-C. (1990) *Reproduction in Education, Society and Culture* (R. Nice, trans. 2nd edn). London: Sage.

Bourdieu, P. and Wacquant, L.J.D. (1992) *An Invitation to Reflexive Sociology*. Chicago, IL: The University of Chicago Press.

Bowen, W.G., Kurzwell, M.A. and Tobin, E.M. (2005) *Equity and Excellence in American Higher Education*. Charlottesville, VA: University of Virginia Press.

Bowen, W.G., Chingos, M.M. and McPherson, M.S. (2009) *Crossing the Finish Line: Completing College at America's Public Universities*. Princeton, NJ: Princeton University Press.

Bridgeland, J.M., Dilulio, J.J. and Morrison, K.B. (2006) The silent epidemic: Perspectives of high school dropouts. *Civic Enterprises for the Bill and Melinda Gates Foundation*. See https://docs.gatesfoundation.org/documents/thesilentepidemic3-06final.pdf (accessed 21 May 2021).

Bucci, W. and Baxter, M. (1984) Problems of linguistic insecurity in multicultural speech contexts. *Annals of the New York Academy of Sciences* 433 (1), 185–200.

Bunch, G.C. and Endris, A.K. (2012) Navigating 'open access' community colleges: Matriculation policies and practices for US-educated linguistic minority students. In Y. Kanno and L. Harklau (eds) *Linguistic Minority Students go to College: Preparation, Access, and Persistence* (pp. 165–183). New York: Routledge.

byrd, d. (2013) Beyond Barriers to Entry – Institutional Habitus and Postsecondary Success: A Literature Review and Research. Paper presented at the American Educational Research Association, San Francisco, CA. See http://www.aera.net/Default.aspx?TabID=10250

byrd, d. (2019) Uncovering hegemony in higher education: A critical appraisal of the use of 'institutional habitus' in empirical scholarship. *Review of Educational Research* 89 (2), 171–210.

Cabrera, A.F., Burkum, K.R. and La Nasa, S.M. (2005) Pathways to a four-year degree: Determinants of degree completion among socioeconomically disadvantaged students. In A. Seidman (ed.) *College Student Retention: Formula for Student Success: Formula for Student Success* (pp. 155–214). Westport, CT: Praeger.

Callahan, R.M. (2005) Tracking and high school English learners: Limiting opportunity to learn. *American Educational Research Journal* 42 (2), 305–328.

Callahan, R.M. and Gándara, P. (2004) On nobody's agenda: Improving English-language learners' access to higher education. In S. Michael (ed.) *Teaching Immigrant and Second-Language Students: Strategies for Success* (pp. 107–127). Cambridge, MA: Harvard Education Press.

Callahan, R.M. and Muller, C. (2013) *Coming of Political Age: American Schools and the Civic Development of Immigrant Youth*. New York: Russell Sage Foundation.

Callahan, R.M. and Humphries, M.H. (2016) Undermatched? School-based linguistic status, college going, and the immigrant advantage. *American Educational Research Journal* 53 (2), 263–295.

Callahan, R.M. and Shifrer, D.R. (2016) Equitable access for secondary English learner students: Course taking as evidence of EL program effectiveness. *Educational Administration Quarterly* 52 (3), 463–496.

Callahan, R.M., Schiller, K.S. and Muller, C. (2008) Preparing for citizenship: Immigrant high school students' curriculum and socialization. *Theory and Research in Social Education* 36 (2), 6–31.

Callahan, R.M., Wilkinson, L. and Muller, C. (2010) Academic achievement and course taking among language minority youth in U.S. schools: Effects of ESL placement. *Educational Evaluation and Policy Analysis* 32 (1), 84–117.

Cao, Y. and Habash, T. (2017) College complaints unmasked. *The Century Foundation*. See https://tcf.org/content/report/college-complaints-unmasked/ (accessed 21 May 2021).

Cappelli, P. (2015) *Will College Pay Off?: A Guide to the Most Important Financial Decision You'll Ever Make*. New York: Public Affairs.

Carlson, D. and Knowles, J.E. (2016) The effect of English language learner reclassification on student ACT scores, high school graduation, and postsecondary enrollment: Regression discontinuity evidence from Wisconsin. *Journal of Policy Analysis and Management* 35 (3), 559–586.

Carnevale, A.P., Rose, S.J. and Cheah, B. (2011) The college payoff: Education, occupations, lifetime earnings. Georgetown University Center on Education and the Workforce. See http://cew.georgetown.edu/collegepayoff/ (accessed 21 May 2021).

Clark, H. (2015) Building a common language for career readiness and success: A foundational competency framework for employers and educators. *ACT Working Paper Series*. See https://www.act.org/content/dam/act/unsecured/documents/WP-2015-02-Building-a-Common-Language-for-Career-Readiness-and-Success.pdf (accessed 21 May 2021).

College Board (2019, February 15) What is the FAFSA? See https://blog.collegeboard.org/what-is-the-fafsa (accessed 21 May 2021).

College Board (2020) Trends in college pricing 2020. See https://research.collegeboard.org/trends/college-pricing (accessed 21 May 2021).

College Board (n.d.-a) 8 tips for crafting your best college essay. See https://bigfuture.collegeboard.org/get-in/essays/8-tips-for-crafting-your-best-college-essay (accessed 21 May 2021).

College Board (n.d.-b) Why visit colleges? See https://bigfuture.collegeboard.org/find-colleges/campus-visit-guide/why-visit-colleges (accessed 21 May 2021).

Conley, D.T. (2005) *College Knowledge: What it Really Takes for Students to Succeed and What We Can Do to Get them Ready*. San Francisco, CA: Jossey-Bass.

Conley, D.T. (2007) *Towards a More Comprehensive Conception of College Readiness: Prepared for the Bill & Melinda Gates Foundation*. Eugene, OR: Educational Policy Improvement Center.

Conley, D.T. (2008) Rethinking college readiness. *New Directions for Higher Education 2008* (144), 3–13.

Conley, D.T. (2014) *The Common Core State Standards: Insights into Their Development and Purpose*. Washington, DC: Council of Chief State School Officers.

Consentino de Cohen, C., Deterding, N. and Clewell, B.C. (2005) Who's left behind?: Immigrant children in high- and low-LEP schools. *Urban Institute*. See http://www.urban.org/UploadedPDF/411231_whos_left_behind.pdf (accessed 21 May 2021).

Dabach, D.B. (2014) 'I am not a shelter!': Stigma and social boundaries in teachers' accounts of students' experience in separate 'sheltered' English learner classrooms. *Journal of Education for Students Placed at Risk* 19 (2), 98–124.

Deil-Amen, R. and DeLuca, S. (2010) The underserved third: how our educational structures populate an educational underclass. *Journal of Education for Students Placed at Risk* 15 (1–2), 27–50.

Deming, D., Goldin, C. and Katz, L. (2013) For-profit colleges. *Future of Children* 23 (1), 137–163.

Dwyer, R.E., Hodson, R. and McCloud, L. (2013) Gender, debt, and dropping out of college. *Gender & Society* 27 (1), 30–55.

Ellis, M.M. (2013) Successful community college transfer students speak out. *Community College Journal of Research and Practice* 37 (2), 73–84.

Emerick, M. (2019) A critical race theory perspective on English learnres' access and equity in career and technical education. PhD dissertation, Temple University.

Equal Educational Opportunity Act (1974) 20 U.S.C. Sec. 1701–1758 C.F.R.

Erickson, F. (1986) Qualitative methods in research on teaching. In M.C. Wittrock (ed.) *Handbook of Research on Teaching* (3rd edn, pp. 119–161). New York: Macmillan.

Every Student Succeeds Act (2015) 20. U.S.C. § 6301. See https://www.congress.gov/bill/114th-congress/senate-bill/1177/text (accessed 21 May 2021).

Ewing, W.A., Martínez, D.E. and Rumbaut, R.G. (2015) The criminalization of immigration in the United States. American Immigration Council. See https://www.americanimmigrationcouncil.org/research/criminalization-immigration-united-states (accessed 21 May 2021).

Fairclough, N. (2015) *Language and Power* (3rd edn). New York: Routledge.

Federal Student Aid, US Department of Education (n.d.) For purposes of applying for federal student aid, what's the difference between a dependent student and an independent student? See https://studentaid.ed.gov/sa/fafsa/filling-out/dependency (accessed 21 May 2021).

Fereday, J. and Muir-Cochrane, E. (2006) Demonstrating rigor using thematic analysis: A hybrid approach of inductive and deductive coding and theme development. *International Journal of Qualitative Methods* 5 (1), 80–92.

Flores, N. (2015, July 6) What if we talked about monolingual White children the way we talk about low-income children of color? [Blog post]. *The Educational Linguist*. See https://educationallinguist.wordpress.com/2015/07/06/what-if-we-talked-about-monolingual-white-children-the-way-we-talk-about-low-income-children-of-color/ (accessed 21 May 2021).

Flores, N. and Rosa, J. (2015) Undoing appropriateness: Raciolinguistic ideologies and language diversity in education. *Harvard Educational Review* 85 (2), 149–171.

Flores, N., Kleyn, T. and Menken, K. (2015) Looking holistically in a climate of partiality: Identities of students labeled long-term English language learners. *Journal of Language, Identity and Education* 14 (2), 113–132.

Fry, R. (2008) The role of schools in the English language learner achievement gap. See https://www.pewresearch.org/hispanic/2008/06/26/the-role-of-schools-in-the-english-language-learner-achievement-gap/ (accessed 21 May 2021).

Gamoran, A. (2017) *Engaging English Learners with Rigorous Academic Content: Insights from Research on Tracking.* New York: William T. Grant Foundation.

Gándara, P. (2008) Immigrants and English learners: Can multiple pathways smooth their paths? In J. Oakes and M. Saunders (eds) *Beyond Tracking: Multiple Pathways to College, Career, and Civic Participation* (pp. 71–90). Cambridge, MA: Harvard Education Press.

Gándara, P. and Orfield, G. (2012) Segregating Arizona's English learners: A return to the 'Mexican room'? *Teachers College Record* 114 (9), 1–27.

García, O. and Torres-Guevara, R. (2009) Monoglossic ideologies and language policies in the education of U.S. Latinas/os. In E.G. Murillo, S.A. Villenas, R.T. Galván, J.S. Muñoz, C. Martínez and M. Machado-Casas (eds) *Handbook of Latinos and Education: Theory, Research, and Practice* (pp. 182–193). New York: Routledge.

García, O., Kelifgen, J.A. and Falchi, L. (2008) From English language learners to emergent bilinguals. *Equity Matters: Research Review Number 1.* See https://files.eric.ed.gov/fulltext/ED524002.pdf (accessed 21 May 2021).

Gay, M. (2020, March 8) Tech schools are new front line in equity fight. *The Boston Globe,* pp. A1, A16.

Giroux, H. (1983) *Theory and Resistance in Education: A Pedagogy for the Opposition.* New York: Bergin and Garvey.

Glaser, B.G. and Strauss, A.L. (1967) *The Discovery of Grounded Theory: Strategies for Qualitative Research.* New York: Aldine de Gruyter.

Grantmakers for Education (2013) Educating English language learners: Grantmaking strategies for closing America's other achievement gap. See https://edfunders.org/sites/default/files/Educating%20English%20Language%20Learners_April%202013.pdf (accessed 21 May 2021).

Grubb, W.N. (2006) 'Like, what do I do now?': The dilemmas of guidance counseling. In T. Bailey and V.S. Morest (eds) *Defending the Community College Equity Agenda* (pp. 195–222). Baltimore, MD: John Hopkins University Press.

Hamilton, L., Roksa, J. and Nielsen, K. (2018) Providing a 'leg up': Parental involvement and opportunity hoarding in college. *Sociology of Education* 91 (2), 111–131.

Han, Y.-C. and Love, J. (2015) Stages of immigrant parent involvement — survivors to leaders. *Phi Delta Kappan* 97 (4), 21–25.

Harklau, L. (1994) 'Jumping tracks': How language-minority students negotiate evaluations of ability. *Anthropology and Education Quarterly* 25 (3), 347–363.

Harklau, L. (2000) From the 'good kids' to the 'worst': Representations of English language learners across educational settings. *TESOL Quarterly* 34 (1), 35–67.

Harklau, L. (2012) How Paola made it to college: A linguistic minority student's unlikely success story. In Y. Kanno and L. Harklau (eds) *Linguistic Minority Students go to College: Preparation, Access, and Persistence* (pp. 74–90). New York: Routledge.

Harklau, L. (2013) Why Izzie didn't go to college: Choosing work over college as Latina feminism. *Teachers College Record* 115 (1), 1–32.

Harklau, L. (2016) Bureaucratic dysfunctions in the education of Latino immigrant youth. *American Journal of Education* 122 (4), 601–627.

Harper, S. and Williams, C.D. (2014) *Succeeding in the City: A Report from the New York City Black and Latino Male High School Achievement Study.* Philadelphia,

PA: University of Pennsylvania, Center for the Study of Race and Equity in Education.

Hernández-Gantes, V.M. and Blank, W. (2009) *Teaching English Language Learners in Career and Technical Education Programs.* New York: Routledge.

Hill, L.D. (2008) School strategies and the 'college-linking' process: Reconsidering the effects of high schools on college enrollment. *Sociology of Education* 81 (1), 53–76.

Hodara, M. (2015) The effects of English as a second language courses on language minority community college students. *Educational Evaluation and Policy Analysis* 37 (2), 243–270.

Hodge, E., Dougherty, S. and Burris, C. (2020) *Tracking and the Future of Career and Technical Education; How Efforts to Connect School and Work can Avoid the Past Mistakes of Vocational Educaiton.* Boulder, CO: National Education Policy Center.

Horvat, E.M. (2000) Understanding equity and access in higher education; The potential contribution of Pierre Bourdieu. In J.C. Smart (ed.), *Higher Education: Handbook of Theory and Research* (vol. 16, pp. 195–238). Dordrecht: Springer.

Horvat, E.M. and Antonio, A.L. (1999) 'Hey, those shoes are out of uniform': African American girls in an elite high school and the importance of habitus. *Anthropology and Education Quarterly* 30 (3), 317–342.

Horvat, E.M., Weininger, E. and Lareau, A. (2003) From social ties to social capital: Class differences in the relation between school and parent networks. *American Educational Research Journal* 40 (2), 319–351.

Jacobs, J.A. (1996) Gender inequality and higher education. *Annual Review of Sociology* 22 (1), 153–185.

Jenkins, D. and Fink, J. (2015) *What We Know about Transfer.* New York: Columbia University, Teachers College, Community College Research Center.

Johnson, A. (2019) A matter of time: Variations in high school course-taking by years-as-EL subgroup. *Educational Evaluation and Policy Analysis* 41 (4), 461–482.

Kanno, Y. (2021) *Classifying Language, Classifying Race: A Black Immigrant Monolingual English Speaker Identified as an English Learner* [Manuscript in preparation]. Wheelock College of Education and Human Development, Boston Univeristy.

Kanno, Y. and Varghese, M. (2010) Immigrant English language learners' challenges to accessing four-year college education: From language policy to educational policy. *Journal of Language, Identity, and Education* 9 (5), 310–328.

Kanno, Y. and Grosik, S.A. (2012) Immigrant English learners' access to four-year universities. In Y. Kanno and L. Harklau (eds) *Linguistic Minority Students Go to College: Preparation, Access, and Persistence* (pp. 130–147). New York: Routledge.

Kanno, Y. and Harklau, L. (eds) (2012) *Linguistic Minority Students Go to College: Preparation, Access, and Persistence.* New York: Routledge.

Kanno, Y. and Cromley, J.G. (2013) English language learners' access to and attainment in postsecondary education. *TESOL Quarterly* 47 (1), 89–121.

Kanno, Y. and Kangas, S.E.N. (2014) 'I'm not going to be, like, for the AP': English language learners' limited access to advanced college-preparatory courses in high school. *American Educational Research Journal* 51 (5), 848–878.

Kanno, Y. and Cromley, J.G. (2015) English language learners' pathways to four-year colleges. *Teachers College Record* 117 (12), 1–44.

Kao, G. and Tienda, M. (1995) Optimism and achievement: The educational performance of immigrant youth. *Social Science Quarterly* 76 (1), 1–19.

Karp, M.M., O'Gara, L. and Hughes, K.L. (2008) Do support services at community colleges encourage success or reproduce disadvantage? Community College Research

Center, Teachers College Columbia University. See https://ccrc.tc.columbia.edu/publications/do-support-services-encourage-success.html (accessed 21 May 2021).

Kay, K. and Shipman, C. (2014, May) The confidence gap. *The Atlantic*. See https://www.theatlantic.com/magazine/archive/2014/05/the-confidence-gap/359815/ (accessed 21 May 2021).

Kibler, A.K. (2019) *Longitudinal Interactional Histories: Bilingual and Biliterate Journeys of Mexical Immirant-Origin Youth*. Cham: Palgrave Macmillan.

Kibler, A.K., Karam, F.J., Futch Ehrlich, V.A., Bergey, R., Wang, C. and Molloy Elreda, L. (2018) Who are 'long-term English learners'? Using classroom interactions to deconstruct a manufactured learner label. *Applied Linguistics* 39 (5), 741–765.

Kieffer, M.J. and Thompson, K.D. (2018) Hidden progress of multilingual students on NAEP. *Educational Researcher* 47 (6), 391–398.

Kim, W.G. and García, S.B. (2014) Long-term English language learners' perceptions of their language and academic learning experiences. *Remedial and Special Education* 35 (5), 300–312.

Kirst, M.W. (2004) The high school/college disconnect. *Educational Leadership* 62 (3), 51–55.

Krathwohl, D.R. (2002) A revision of Bloom's Taxonomy: An overview. *Theory Into Practice* 41 (4), 212–264.

Labov, W. (1966) *The Social Stratification of English in New York City*. Washington, DC: Center for Applied Linguistics.

Lane, S. and Leventhal, B. (2015) Psychometric challenges in assessing English language learners and students with disabilities. *Review of Research in Education* 39 (1), 165–214.

Lareau, A. (2000) *Home Advantage: Social Class and Parental Intervention in Elementary Education* (2nd edn). Lanham, MD: Rowman & Littlefield.

Lareau, A. and Weininger, E.B. (2008) Class and transition to adulthood. In A. Lareau and D. Conley (eds) *Social Class: How Does it Work?* (pp. 118–151). New York: Russel Sage Foundation.

Lau v. Nichols (1974) 414 U.S. 563.

Lee, S.J. (1996) *Unraveling the 'Model Minority' Stereotype: Listening to Asian American Youth*. New York: Teachers College Press.

Li, K. (2021) A tale of community college transfer pathway: US-ELs' trajectories toward healthcare programs. *Community College Journal of Research and Practice*, 1–22 (Online first publication).

Lillie, K.E., Markos, A., Arias, M.B. and Wiley, T.G. (2012) Separate and not equal: The implementation of Structured English Immersion in Arizona's classrooms. *Teachers College Record* 114 (9), 1–33.

Lincoln, Y.S. and Guba, E.G. (1985) *Naturalistic Inquiry*. Newbury Park, CA: Sage.

Link, B.G. and Phelan, J.C. (2013) Labeling and stigma. In C.S. Aneshensel, J.C. Phelan and A. Beirman (eds) *Handbook of the Sociology of Mental Health* (pp. 525–541). Dordrecht: Springer.

Link, B.G., Cullen, F.T., Struening, E., Shrout, P.E. and Dohrenwend, B.P. (1989) A modified labeling theory approach to mental disorders: An empirical assessment. *American Sociological Review* 54 (3), 400–423.

Lopez, J.D. and Horn, J.M. (2020) Grit and retention among first year Hispanic college students at a Hispanic serving institution. *Hispanic Journal of Behavioral Sciences* 42 (2), 264–270.

Ma, J. and Baum, S. (2016) Trends in community colleges: Enrollment, prices, student debt, and completion. *College Board Research Brief*. See https://research.collegeboard .org/pdf/trends-community-colleges-research-brief.pdf (accessed 21 May 2021).

Ma, J., Pender, M. and Welch, M. (2019) Education pays 2019: The benefits of higher education for individuals and society. *The College Board Trends in Higher Education Series*. See https://research.collegeboard.org/trends/education-pays (accessed 21 May 2021).

Malin, J.R., Bragg, D.D. and Hackmann, D.G. (2017) College and career readiness and the Every Student Succeeds Act. *Educational Administration Quarterly* 53 (5), 809–838.

Martin, D.B. (2009) Researching race in mathematics education. *Teachers College Record* 11 (2), 295–338.

Maxwell, J.A. (2005) *Qualitative Research Design: An Interactive Approach* (2nd edn). Thousand Oaks, CA: Sage.

McCormick, A.C. (2003) Swirling and double-dipping: New patterns of student attendance and their implications for higher education. *New Directions for Higher Education* 121, 13–24.

McDonough, P.M. (1997) *Choosing Colleges: How Social Class and Schools Structure Opportunity*. Albany, NY: State University of New York Press.

McKenzie, K.B. and Scheurich, J.J. (2004) Equity traps: A useful construct for preparing principals to lead schools that are successful with racially diverse students. *Educational Administration Quarterly* 40 (5), 601–632.

Menken, K. and Kleyn, T. (2010) The long-term impact of subtractive schooling in the educational experiences of secondary English language learners. *International Journal of Bilingual Education and Bilingualism* 13 (4), 399–417.

Merriam, S.B. and Tisdell, E.J. (2016) *Qualitative Research: A Guide to Design and Implementation* (4th edn). San Francisco, CA: Jossey-Bass.

Merrow, J. (2007, April 22) The smart transfer. *New York Times*. See http://www.nytimes .com/2007/04/22/education/edlife/22merrow-profile-4.html (accessed 21 May 2021).

Miles, M.B., Huberman, A.M. and Saldaña, J. (2020) *Qualitative Data Analysis: A Methods Sourcebook* (4th edn). Thousand Oaks, CA: Sage.

Mishkind, A. (2014) Overview: State definitions of college and career readiness. *College & Career Readiness & Success Center at American Institute for Research*. See https://ccrscenter.org/sites/default/files/CCRS%20Defintions%20Brief_REV_1.pdf (accessed 21 May 2021).

Moll, L.C., Amanti, C., Neff, D. and González, N. (1992) Funds of knowledge for teaching: Using qualitative approach to connect homes and classrooms. *Theory Into Practice* 31 (2), 49–58.

Morton, J.B. and Harper, S.N. (2007) What did Simon say? Revisiting the bilingual advantage. *Developmental Science* 10 (6), 719–726.

National Center for Education Statistics (2014) The condition of education 2014. US Department of Education. See https://nces.ed.gov/pubs2014/2014083.pdf (accessed 21 May 2021).

National Center for Education Statistics (2019) The condition of education 2019. US Department of Education. See https://nces.ed.gov/pubs2019/2019144.pdf (accessed 21 May 2021).

National Conference of State Legislatures (2020) Undocumented student tuition: Overview. See https://www.ncsl.org/research/education/undocumented-student-tuition-overview.aspx#:~:text=Seventeen%20states%E2%80%94Arkansas%2C%20California %2C,undocumented%20students%20through%20state%20legislation (accessed 21 May 2021).

National Government Association Center for Best Practices & Council of Chief State School Officers (2010) Common Core State Standards for English language arts and literacy in history/social studies, science, and technical subjects. *Common Core State Standards Initiative.* See http://www.corestandards.org/wp-content/uploads/ELA_Standards1.pdf (accessed 21 May 2021).

National Research Council (2002) *Learning and Understanding: Improving Advanced Study of Mathematics and Science in U.S. High Schools.* Washington, DC: The National Academies Press.

National Skills Coalition (2017) Forgotten middle-skill jobs: State by state snapshots. See https://nationalreentryresourcecenter.org/multimedia/forgotten-middle-skill-jobs-state-state-snapshots (accessed 21 May 2021).

National Student Clearinghouse Research Center (2019, September) Tracking transfer. https://nscresearchcenter.org/tracking-transfer/ (accessed 21 May 2021).

Newman, K.S. and Winston, H. (2016) *Reskilling America: Learning to Labor in the Twenty-First Century.* New York: Henry Holt and Company.

Nuñez, A.-M., Rios-Aguilar, C., Kanno, Y. and Flores, S.M. (2016) English learners and their transition to postsecondary education. In M.B. Paulsen (ed.) *Higher Education: Handbook of Theory and Research, Volume 31* (pp. 41–90). New York: Springer.

Oakes, J. (2005) *Keeping Track: How Schools Structure Inequality* (2nd edn). New Haven, CT: Yale University Press.

Oakes, J. and Saunders, M. (2008) Multiple pathways: Promising to prepare all high school students for college, career, and civic participation. In J. Oakes and M. Saunders (eds) *Beyond Tracking: Multiple Pathways to College, Career, and Civic Participation* (pp. 1–16). Cambridge, MA: Harvard Education Press.

Olsen, L. (2010) Reparable Harm: Fulfilling the Unkept Promise of Educational Opportunity for California's Long Term English Learners. Long Beach, CA: Californians Together.

Paap, K.R. and Greenberg, Z.I. (2013) There is no coherent evidence for a bilingual advantage in executive processing. *Cognitive Psychology* 66 (2), 232–258.

Park, E.S. (2019) Examining community college students' progression through the English as a second language sequence. *Community College Review* 47, 406–433.

Pascarella, E.T., Pierson, C.T., Wolniak, G.C. and Terenzini, P.T. (2004) First-generation college students: Additional evidence on college experiences and outcomes. *The Journal of Higher Education* 75 (3), 249–284.

Patton, M.Q. (2015) *Qualitative Research and Evaluation Methods* (4th edn). Newbury Park, CA: Sage.

Perna, L.W. (2006) Studying college access and choice: A proposed conceptual model. In J.C. Smart (ed.) *Higher Education: Handbook of Theory and Research* (vol. 21, pp. 99–157). Dordrecht: Springer.

Porter, A., McMaken, J., Hwang, J. and Yang, R. (2011) Common Core Standards: The new U.S. intended curriculum. *Educational Researcher* 40 (3), 103–116.

Przymus, S.D. (2016) Imagining and moving beyond the ESL bubble: Facilitating communities of practice through the ELL ambassadors program. *Journal of Language, Identity, and Education* 15 (5), 265–279.

Reay, D. (1998) 'Always knowing' and 'never being sure': Familial and institutional habitus and higher education choice. *Journal of Education Policy* 13 (4), 519–529.

Reay, D., David, M.E. and Ball, S. (2005) *Degree of Choice: Class, Race, Gender and Higher Education.* Stoke on Trent: Trentham Books.

Regional Educational Laboratory West at WestEd (2016) Long-term English learner students: Spotlight on an overlooked population. See https://ies.ed.gov/ncee/edlabs/regions/west/relwestFiles/pdf/LTEL-factsheet.pdf (accessed 21 May 2021).

Riegle-Crumb, C. and King, B. (2010) Questioning a White male advantage in STEM: Examining disparities in college major by gender and race/ethnicity. *Educational Researcher* 39 (9), 656–664.

Roderick, M., Nagaoka, J. and Coca, V. (2009) College readiness for all: The challenges for urban high schools. *The Future of Children* 19 (1), 185–210.

Rodriguez, G.M. and Cruz, L. (2009) The transition to college of English learner and undocumented immigrant students: Resource and policy implications. *Teachers College Record* 111 (10), 2385–2418.

Rodriguez, O., Bohn, S., Hill, L. and Brooks, B. (2019) *English as a Second Language in California's Community Colleges*. San Francisco, CA: Public Policy Institute of California.

Rosenbaum, J. (2001) *Beyond College for All: Career Paths for the Forgotten Half*. New York: Russel Sage Foundation.

Rosenbaum, J.E., Miller, S.R. and Krei, M.S. (1996) Gatekeeping in an era of more open gates: High school counselors' views of their influence on students' college plans. *American Journal of Education* 104 (4), 257–279.

Rosenbaum, J.E., Stephen, J.L. and Rosenbaum, J.E. (2010) Beyond one-size-fits-all college dreams: Alternative pathways to desirable careers. *American Educator* 34 (3), 2–13.

Ruecker, T. (2015) *Transiciones: Pathways of Latinas and Latinos Writing in High School and College*. Boulder, CO: Utah State University Press.

Saldaña, J. (2003) *Longitudinal Qualitative Research: Analyzing Change through Time*. Walnut Creek, CA: Altamira Press.

Saldaña, J. (2015) *The Coding Manual for Qualitative Researchers* (3rd edn). Thosand Oaks, CA: Sage.

Salerno, A.S. and Kibler, A.K. (2015) Vocational training for adolescent English language learners in newcomer programs: Opportunities or isolation? *TESOL Journal* 6 (2), 201–224.

Saunders, M. and Serna, I. (2004) Making college happen: The college experiences of first-generation Latino students. *Journal of Hispanic Higher Education* 3 (2), 146–163.

Saunders, W.M. and Marcelletti, D.J. (2013) The gap that can't go away: The Catch-22 of reclassification in monitoring the progress of English learners. *Educational Evaluation and Policy Analysis* 35 (2), 139–156.

Sattin-Bajaj, C. (2014) *Unaccompanied Minors: Immigrant Youth, School Choice, and the Pursuit of Equity*. Cambridge, MA: Harvard University Press.

Selingo, J. (2020) *Who Gets In and Why: A Year Inside College Admissions*. New York: Scribner.

Short, D.J. and Boyson, B.A. (2012) *Helping Newcomer Students Succeed in Secondary Schools and Beyond*. Washington, DC: Center for Applied Linguistics.

Short, D.J. and Fitzsimmons, S. (2007) *Double the Work: Challenges and Solutions to Acquiring Language and Academic Literacy for Adolescent English Language Learners: A Report to Carnegie Corporation of New York*. Washington, DC: Alliance for Excellent Education.

Shuger, L. (2012) Teen pregnancy and high school dropout: What communities can do to address these issues. *The National Campaign to Prevent Teen and Unplanned Pregnancy and America's Promise Alliance*. See https://www.americaspromise.org/sites/

default/files/d8/legacy/bodyfiles/teen-pregnancy-and-hs-dropout-print.pdf (accessed 21 May 2021).

Smyth, E. and Banks, J. (2012) 'There was never really any question of anything else': Young people's agency, institutional habitus and the transition to higher education. *British Journal of Sociology of Education* 33 (2), 263–281.

Solórzano, R.W. (2008) High stakes testing: Issues, implications, and remedies for English language learners. *Review of Educational Research* 78 (2), 260–329.

Stanton-Salazar, R.D. (2001) *Manufacturing Hope and Despair: The School and Kin Support Networks of U.S.-Mexican Youth*. New York: Teachers College Press.

Suárez-Oroco, C., Katsiaficas, D., Birchall, O., Alcantar, C., Hernandez, E., Garcia, Y., Michikyan, M., Cerda, J. and Teranishi, R.T. (2015) Undocumented undergraduates on college campuses: Understanding their challenges and assets and what it takes to make an undocufriendly campus. *Harvard Educational Review* 85 (3), 427–463.

Swartz, D. (1997) *Culture and Power: The Sociology of Pierre Bourdieu*. Chicago, IL: University of Chicago Press.

The Community Café Collaborative. (2020) *Who we are*. See https://thecommunitycafe .org/our-work/ (accessed 21 May 2021).

Thompson, K.D. (2015) Questioning the long-term English learner label: How classification and categorization can blind us to students' abilities. *Teachers College Record* 117 (12), 1–50.

Thompson, K.D. (2017) What blocks the gate?: Exploring current and former English learners' math course-taking in secondary school. *American Educational Research Journal* 54 (4), 757–798.

Umansky, I.M. (2016a) Leveled and exclusionary tracking: English learners' access to academic content in middle school. *American Educational Research Journal* 53 (6), 1792–1833.

Umansky, I.M. (2016b) To be or not to be EL: An examination of the impact of classifying students as English learners. *Educational Evaluation and Policy Analysis* 38 (4), 714–737.

US Department of Education (2016) Non-regulatory guidance: English learners and title III of the Elementary and Secondary Educaiton Act (ESEA), as amended by the Every Student Succeeds Act (ESSA). See https://www2.ed.gov/policy/elsec/leg/essa/essatitleii iguidenglishlearners92016.pdf (accessed 21 May 2021).

US Department of Education (2017) Developmental education: Challenges and strategies for reform. See https://www2.ed.gov/about/offices/list/opepd/education-strategies.pdf (accessed 21 May 2021).

US Department of Education (2018a) Improving basic programs operated by local educational agencies (Title I, Part A). See https://www2.ed.gov/programs/titleiparta/index .html (accessed 21 May 2021).

US Department of Education (2018b) Our nation's English learners. See https://www2.ed .gov/datastory/el-characteristics/index.html (accessed 21 May 2021).

US Department of Education Office of English Language Acquisition (2016) *Newcomer Tool Kit*. See https://www2.ed.gov/about/offices/list/oela/newcomers-toolkit/ncomer-toolkit.pdf (accessed 21 May 2021).

US Department of Justice and US Department of Education (2015) Dear colleague letter: English learner students and limited English proficient parents. See http:// www2.ed.gov/about/offices/list/ocr/letters/colleague-el-201501.pdf (accessed 21 May 2021).

Valencia, R.R. (1997) Conceptualizaing the notion of decifit thinking. In R.R. Valencia (ed.) *The Evolution of Deficit Thinking: Educational Thought and Practice* (pp. 1–12). New York: Routledge Falmer.

Valencia, R.R. (2010) *Dismantling Contemporary Deficit Thinking: Educational Thought and Practice*. New York: Routledge.

Vargas, J.H. (2004) *College Knowledge: Addressing Information Barriers to College*. Boston, MA: The Education Resources Institute.

Varghese, M.M. (2013) A linguistic minority students' discursive framing of agency and structure. In Y. Kanno and L. Harklau (eds) *Linguistic Minority Students go to College: Preparation, Access, and Persistence* (pp. 148–162). New York: Routledge.

Venezia, A., Kirst, M.W. and Antonio, A.L. (2003) *Betraying the College Dream: How Disconnected K-12 and Postsecondary Education Systems Undermine Student Aspirations*. Stanford, CA: The Stanford Institute for Higher Education Research.

Wang, X. (2013) Baccalaureate expectations of community college students: Sociodemographic, motivational, and contextual influences. *Teachers College Record* 115 (4), 1–39.

Yin, R.K. (2017) *Case Study Research: Design and Methods* (6th edn). Los Angeles, CA: Sage.

Yosso, T.J. (2005) Whose culture has capital?: A critical race theory discussion of community cultural wealth. *Race Ethnicity and Education* 8 (1), 69–91.

Author Index

Page numbers for entries that occur in notes are suffixed by an *n*; those for entries in tables, by a *t*; and those for entries in figures, by an *f*.

Subject Index

Page numbers for entries that occur in notes are suffixed by an *n*; those for entries in tables, by a *t*; and those for entries in figures, by an *f*.

CPSIA information can be obtained
at www.ICGtesting.com
Printed in the USA
BVHW092230041121
620859BV00001B/1